PURSU
BY THE SOUL
DESTROYER

By D J Hawkins

First published by Milton Contact Limited

ISBN: 978-1-911526-55-1

Milton Contact Limited
3 Hall End, Milton, Cambridge, UK
CB24 6AQ

Content's page

Acknowledgements and Thanks

To my six amazing children.

I want to thank my children who have been amazing and such a great encouragement to me, I am proud of you all and love you so much my heart is bursting. We have weathered turbulent storms separately and together, no matter what came against us, love will always win the day.

Dr Chris Thomas of Milton Contact Ltd. Cambridge.

Where would I be without your support Chris? You have the patience of a saint! Your professional yet friendly expertise is invaluable, you are worth your weight in gold, every kilogram. I couldn't have done it without you and deeply appreciate all your input. You are my lifeline and calm against my technophobic storm. Without your help, I would have surely sunk in the wide vast sea of technology.

Artist Marie Crowley. St. Ives, Cambridgeshire.

Marie, thank you so much for giving your consent to publish your art piece called 'The Puppeteer'; it is the perfect image that brings a reality to the storyline.

Daniel Jones Illustrator. Manchester.

Dan, thank you for your commitment and thought that has gone into designing the perfect atmospheric front and back cover for my book. I appreciate all the support and time that has gone into your design.

Frank Henshall Photographer. Congleton, Cheshire.

Thank you for your friendly professional service in taking photographs needed for my book particularly the art piece, The Puppeteer.

Blade. Cambridgeshire.

Thank you for giving your consent to publish one of our punk photo's, (a crazy time) as well as all the support you gave me when I finally connected with my children, it will always be appreciated.

The Puppeteer: Artist Marie Crowley

I will fulfil your every desire.

I will tug at your heart strings until you dance to my tune.

Do not be deceived by the puppeteer, don't listen to his lies.

Don't walk down any narrow path just because you can.

Introduction

This is a true story not just anchored in the supernatural; I also share about traumatic experiences, some born out of the evil intention of others. I do not hold back on the depth of cruelty that one human being can bring upon another, or ignore the love and kindness bestowed upon me by strangers. I am aware that many of you will be able to relate to some of the traumas I have been through, rape, confinement, homelessness, mental suffering, self-harm, domestic violence and the occult, to name just a few. I never thought I would survive to share my story; I was left for dead on more than one occasion. As a vulnerable teenager I often found myself on the streets facing many challenges until institutional keys turned in the locks of confinement. Young and deeply troubled I sought solace in all the wrong places, my eyes were opened to a world I should have never seen, exposed to areas that most would not believe existed. Growing up, problems were often swept under the carpet, as if they didn't exist. Secrets multiplied like rabbits. It was time to lift the carpet. I believe passionately in encouraging others to talk about their own experiences, especially through the use of the creative arts as a means of release and expression, only then will the sound of silence shout loudly, emotions freed will shatter the iron bars that once caged them in, and paralysing fear will turn into courage and take flight.

We live in a world of the five senses, sight, touch, taste, smell and hearing, yet there is an invisible world equally as tangible as the first. Have you ever been in a room and felt like something or someone was in the room with you? Seen something strange you cannot explain? Or got the chills as if someone had just walked over your grave? Whether or not you have had these experiences be prepared to have your own perceptions challenged and your own foundations shaken as you come on a journey with me.

3

In life many of us have been scarred by our experiences, but there is an enemy that seeks to annihilate souls, its hunger is never quenched, its purpose relentless. I have met with such an enemy, a diabolical encounter that sought to rip my soul from my flesh.

It has been a difficult, amazing, shocking, painful, liberating, and truly miraculous journey, yes, miracles still happen.

At the young age of eighteen a miraculous life changing event gave me a wakeup call of such magnitude it cracked the very foundations upon which I stood, affecting all that I knew or ever believed.

In part two, I conclude my story showing that survival is possible even under extreme circumstances, my life was turned around in the most amazing ways and love without a doubt conquers all.

I hope you will have a wake-up call!

Part One

Success is not measured by what you accomplish, but by the opposition you have encountered, and the courage with which you have maintained the struggle against overwhelming odds. *Orison Swett Marden*.

Chapter One - The Dark Stranger

I grew up on the outskirts of Brighton about three miles out from the city centre with my brother and two sisters, I remember my surroundings quite clearly, a mixture of houses and tall skyscraper buildings that dominated the expanse of the sky, the sun would shimmer and flicker over the numerous glass windows like a firework display, from my bedroom window the view was quite the opposite, I could see a large green field strewn with bright red poppies and tall grass, numerous bright yellow daises scattered like confetti swayed gently in the wind as if nature was dancing with complete abandonment. Beside the field lay a stony pathway that led up to a stretch of woodland, numerous tall trees splayed out their branches like wrinkled arthritic fingers, they gave shade to the birds and cast eerie shadows on the ground below. My heart would skip a beat at the thought of being able to explore the area.

Like many four-year olds I had the curiosity of a cat with a very large nose for poking it in places where it shouldn't belong. The house we had just moved into wasn't so pleasing to the eye, it was stark with plain discoloured walls and hard wooden floors, our own furniture was still sitting in the removal lorry and mum was on a cleaning mission. My father had gone straight to work and my brother and two sisters were exploring the house, which was quite large with four bedrooms.

As I continued to look out the window, I heard mum shout, "Deborah, come away from the window, you will have plenty of time to daydream, help me decide where you want your new toys to go."

I jumped down off the ledge and quickly ran to help. As soon as my toys were sorted, I asked if I could go into the garden. Mum laughed, "Yes off you go, I can see you are eager to explore just don't pick up anything from the ground that looks sharp or dirty.

You are such a curious child, " mum tweaked my nose causing me to giggle, "if you get any problems just shout."

"Ok mum," I shouted back.

I left mum to it and went downstairs straight into the enclosed garden, at first glance, I could see it was empty of any flowers and plants, as I walked down a narrow-cobbled uneven path, I saw in front of me an old rickety swing, I sat down upon the cracked wooden seat hoping it wouldn't break. As I gazed around the garden, I noticed at the far end a shady area where several trees had a bountiful supply of apples; it was a perfect place for a picnic. But what really caught my attention was the large wooden gate.

I jumped down and walked up to the gate to see if I could reach the black handle, but I was not quite tall enough. I found an old box nearby, clambered onto the box and lifted the handle, the gate slowly creaked opened wide enough for me to gently squeeze through the gap. Once through the gate I could see a long narrow road. I looked both ways, there were no cars in sight, I crossed over the road and squeezed my hands together, I was so excited to begin my very first adventure.

At the start of the path, I noticed it was covered with different shaped stones, so I played a game with my feet trying to miss the largest stones. I became totally engrossed and lost track of time as I playfully walked along the path. When I finally I looked up I turned around to see my house had become very small, I felt a sense of victory that I had come so far. As the path's gradient became more difficult to manage, the slight incline became a little more taxing on my legs making them ache, it was hard work. The incline was much higher than I thought, but I was determined to carry on. I continued to climb uphill feeling the warmth of the sun upon my face and a slight breeze brushed through my hair. As I got closer to the end of the path, I noticed a large black car and next to the car a tall man was waving at me. On his head he wore a black hat, the same colour as his clothes. I stood still for a moment unsure of what to do, until he slowly walked towards me.

"Hello", he said in a faint quiet tone.

"Hello" I answered, my voice slightly quivering. As I stood still my legs felt a little shaky and heavy, I felt very uncomfortable.

"What are you doing out here all on your own?"

It was then that I remembered mum's words telling me not to talk to strangers, I looked at him and failed to give an answer, I felt a lump in my throat and wanted to turn around and run back home but my feet stuck firmly to the ground. My heart began to race, causing me to breathe faster. He smiled at me, but I couldn't smile back, then his large dirty hands reached down to pick me up, his grip was tight, I wriggled and wriggled to try and get him to put me back down. I began to sob, unsure of what was happening, I started kicking and screaming, "I want my mummy; I want my mummy."

There was no response, just a weird twisted smile. He held me firmly against his body, walked briskly to the car and bundled me onto the back seat, I landed hard as the car door slammed shut. The cream leather seat had marks all over it and the interior of the car smelt like rotten cabbages, the floor was covered in paper cups and magazines. As the driver sat down, he bellowed at me to "SHUT UP!"

His voice cut right through me, causing me to shudder. As the car engine started, tears dropped onto the seat, I couldn't shut up or be quiet so I screamed as loudly as I could until my throat hurt. I lay on the seat thrashing out with my arms and legs. As the car went into motion I cried out, "I want to go home, I want to go home." but my cries fell on deaf ears.

After a very short time, the car suddenly came to a halt. In my heart I was hoping that he would turn the car around and take me back, but instead the car door opened and I was dragged out across the seat by my feet, I was thrown down onto the dry dusty ground. As I landed, I curled my knees into my stomach, shut my eyes and lay like a limp rag doll. My head throbbed, I didn't want to look at his face or say anything to him, as I lay still, whimpering, I heard the man mumble to himself; I couldn't make out what he was saying, then he just stopped and walked away. Too afraid to move and feeling exhausted I fell asleep just where he left me.

I had no idea how long I had laid there, but when I awoke my legs were stiff and sore. I stood up and looked around, I could see tall towering trees, and to my right a large field, terrified the man would return, I started to walk, hoping to find the pathway that would take me home. I wanted to run but my body felt too weak and heavy. The sun was no longer bright and I could no longer hear the sound of birds singing. I did not want to be left outside in the dark.

As I ambled along the silence was broken by someone shouting, "Deborah where are you?"

It went quiet for a short period of time, then people would start calling my name again. I tried to shout back but my voice wouldn't work, when the silence came again, I let out a small cry.

"QUIET!" I heard someone shout, I heard the rustling of the grass as a familiar voice tenderly said, "I have found her." I glanced up to see tear-filled eyes, my mum lovingly looked down at me and picked me up in her arms, I clung to her as tightly as I could and laid my head down upon her chest knowing at last that I was safe. As I was being carried, I lifted my head up and noticed many people including several police officers walking back with us, my mum explained to me in a soft gentle voice that all these people had got together to search for me, she told me how much she loved me, I laid my head back down, closed my eyes and fell asleep. I don't know what became of the dark stranger, we didn't talk about it.

Chapter Two - Ghostly Foundations

As a family we had moved into the centre of Brighton, my father had bought a large old three-storey town house. Six years had passed by since the incident of the dark stranger, it was now a hidden memory stored away in the depth of my sub-conscious. I am ten years old, my child blonde hair had darkened over the years and was now a mousy brown, my hair was often put in a pony tail to keep it tidy and out of the way, I was quite shy and introverted most of the time and wasn't as boisterous as my sister Anne who was seven years old and quite often had the giggles for no apparent reason.

Anne looked nothing like me, she had bright red fiery hair and was strong and independent, Anne hated school and didn't do as she was told, stubborn and resistant to change, she was very much a mummy's girl. My other sister Jane was four years old with dark hair and a chubby face. Jane was the youngest but always naughty, she was more than happy to play the blame game, you would often hear Jane say, I didn't do anything! And definitely a daddy's girl.

The oldest was James he was twelve and sometimes a bully, when he got bored, he would go off on his own. We were all very different in our looks and temperaments. James had a serious character and tried to keep out of the way especially if mum and dad were arguing. I am sure growing up with three sisters sometimes became too much for him.

My father was hard working and like all hard-working dads we saw very little of him. He was a roofer by trade, he had his own company which involved large properties and hotels. He was rarely home. When he was home, he was very strong on discipline and quite domineering towards mum who was gentle. Dad's build was stocky and strong, and his word was final.

Mum was quite the opposite, she had a very pretty face and a petite figure with the tiniest waist I had ever seen, she enjoyed cigarettes and chocolates. She always aimed to please. Every week mum would have a shampoo and set at the hairdressers, she always looked lovely.

Financially things were improving all the time and now we finally had a home we could call our own. As we settled in, the house became a hive of activity, we were still in our school holiday time and mum was constantly rearranging furniture and cleaning, being quite house proud. Dad had left early for work and the four of us entertained ourselves with games. Outside we played two-ball against the wall of the house which would drive mum mad with the constant thudding. When the rain came, we were in indoors. We played many different types of board games as well as a game called Five Jacks. I was not one for dolls, as I thought they were silly. I had a collection of troll dolls. They were all different sizes with different hair colours. I loved playing with marbles I had a huge collection of different sized marbles which were often rolled down the long hallway through a self-made tunnel, which had its own point scoring system.

I thought it would be fun to explore our new house and look for any places to hide for future games of hide and seek, so I decided to have a look around by myself. Some areas within the house were quite dark, the hallway and stairs had no windows and only a small chink of light came up from the lower staircase at the basement where the kitchen was. The basement was in a sorry state, the cupboards looked neglected and needed a clean and repaint, the cold slabs on the kitchen floor were worn down and there was an old coal bunker under the stairs. The kitchen door led out to the back garden which was completely overgrown and at the end of the garden there was an outside toilet. As hot as it was outside, inside the kitchen was cool, the basement felt a little disconnected from the rest of the house which made me feel a bit isolated, so I decided to go to the base of the stairs which curved round and up to the next floor and explore the middle area of the house.

I shivered as I climbed the stairs, it was dingy and claustrophobic. I got to the top and wandered along the hallway making my way to the large living room at the front of the house, which was spacious. I immediately went to the window and stood in the sun to warm myself up. As I gazed out of the window, the view was a long row of houses, far too many to count. At the other end of the hallway was a bedroom where my parents would be, it had a lovely wooden floor. I climbed up the next flight of stairs where there were three bedrooms, it had already been decided that my two younger sisters would share the largest bedroom, I would have a room to myself and my brother James would have a room of his own. Arguments were futile once a decision was made as to who had what room. All the rooms were in need of decoration, flowered wallpaper peeled off the walls and the dull green woodwork was drab and depressing. Further down from the bedrooms was a large bathroom, the bath was large with heavy thick taps and a dark tiled floor.

I was a bit disappointed that there was a distinct lack of nook and crannies to hide in. The house was pre-war and very old, at night time before getting into bed we would all check under our beds and look inside the wardrobes, because dad often said in a sinister tone that if we didn't go to sleep straight away and be good, the bogey man would get us, which made us all shriek and dive for the covers.

ℰℭℜ

Although I was happy to play with my two sisters, I wanted to be more adventurous and have a look around outside and get to know the area in which we lived. Convincing mum to allow me to go outside was going to be a bit of a challenge as I knew she always felt uneasy of letting any of her children out of her sight.

"Mum, can I go outside and have a look around? I promise I won't go far."

With half a smile and a sigh, surprisingly her answer was, "Alright, but don't be gone for too long otherwise I will worry."

I stepped outside with a skip in my step. Mum had been for some time a little overprotective with us all, I understood why, but now I was ten years old I think mum could see I needed to be trusted at some point. I walked down the road realizing we were now in a much more built-up area than before. I had no idea where the local park was yet or if we had a local shop, I needed to get my bearings.

I had been walking for a while observing row upon row of houses, but then I came to a new road and a large white building caught my eye. I got closer to see a plaque on the wall that clearly stated it was a convent. A large wooden door in the middle of the building stood out boldly and I was really tempted to knock at the door and run. Postman's knock was fun, but it wasn't much fun on my own. I knew nuns existed but only by the films I had watched on television. I stood there thinking what it would be like to live and work in such a place. I had always wanted to meet a real nun so the urge to knock the door was irresistible. I finally plucked up the courage and lifted the heavy iron ring and gave it a good bang against the door.

As soon as I had done it, I let go and panicked, regretting my actions almost at once, I hesitated in my decision as to whether I should stay or run. Before I made my mind up the door opened and a nun with a kind smile spoke to me in a calm tone, "Hello," she said, "Can I help you?"

"Hello," I blurted out with excitement, "I want to be nun." I had no idea why I said that.

With a gesture of her hand the nun said, "Why don't you come in for a moment and we will discuss it, would you like to do that?"

"Oh yes please", I replied, thinking to myself, what ARE you doing!

I stepped inside a large hallway; the marble floor was as shiny as a new pin and velvet clad chairs were neatly placed against the walls either side of the hallway. Pictures adorned the walls and everything was spotless. As the door shut, the bang echoed around the walls. I sat down on one of the chairs and asked a question, "How old do you have to be, to be a nun?"

"If God calls you to be a nun, you will know, you would have to come back when you are sixteen, and if your parents agreed, you could become a novice."

"Oh" I nodded not really understanding why I was asking the question. Maybe it was just my curiosity.

"I will let you sit here for a moment, so you may have a think, and then you must leave."

I enjoyed the short span of time that I had. I would have loved to have explored the whole building. When the nun returned, I thanked her for her kindness and without another word spoken, I left, realizing we did not even know each other's names.

I returned home, concerned I had been gone far too long and decided to keep my new-found experience to myself. I wasn't sure if I should share it as I didn't want to get into trouble. As soon as I got in, I got strict instructions to sort out my school uniform as school holidays were coming to an end.

೮೦೮౩

The thought of starting at a new school made me a little anxious, I was a little shy when it came to mixing with others, so I needed to find extra courage. I had butterflies doing somersaults in my stomach. As I embarked on my first day of school, I wore a fleshy garment of outward bravado as I felt like I was being thrown into a den of lions, I knew I was lacking in confidence. At first the other children seemed friendly enough but at break times in the playground I found myself standing alone. It wasn't long before the children started taunting me "What's the matter with you, cat got your tongue."

I didn't respond and found myself shrinking inside. I really didn't want any kind of confrontation.

"Hawkeye, Hawkeye is shy", they chanted.

On and off that day the teasing continued. But then it got a little physical. My pony tail was pulled often, even in the classroom. I had no idea why I found it so difficult to interact with the other children, apart from being a bit shy. I wanted to run away, but instead I persevered and decided to join a drama group as a way of helping me to come out of my shell. Maybe I would gain some respect from the other children and gain some new-found confidence, our drama teacher Mr. Hughes seemed fun, although at times when he raised his voice and bellowed, he was quite scary.

I got really excited when I was told I could be angel Gabriel in the Christmas play, but on the night of the play right in the middle of my lines, my mind went blank and I could no longer remember my words. As I stood there, in front of all the parents, my legs went rigid and my mouth stayed open like a goldfish that had a locked jaw. Unable to speak I burst into tears and ran off the stage. At home I felt embarrassed by the whole situation. I was told that I had suffered from stage fright.

Going to school the next day wasn't that bad, nobody seemed to be taking the mick out of me and the day was progressing well. But then an ambulance had turned up at the school and a few teachers were dashing about everywhere, the school bell was ringing loudly and everyone was told to go home. Mr Hughes had suffered a heart attack and died. The news shocked everyone at the school and many of us went home crying.

I felt so sad. Poor Mr. Hughes. I felt guilty that I did not have the opportunity to at least say sorry for running off stage. I went home and after a hug from mum I decided to go to bed early, it had been a difficult emotional time. I grabbed a book and decided to read for a while to take my mind off things.

As I settled into reading, every now and then I peered over the top of my book to look down the hallway, the light was normally left on. I felt a little uneasy and told myself I was being a little silly. I tried hard to concentrate on my reading and could not help but peep one more time over the top of my book. As I did so, I noticed in the dark, a moving white shape that seemed to be growing larger. It looked like swirling mist at first but then it became heavier and heavier. The mist moved around in a figure of eight, I was fascinated and scared at the same time, then the movement stopped, and took the form in the shape of a man. A large stocky shaped figure loomed before me; I couldn't quite make out the face as the swirling white substance kept moving. I cringed and gripped my book tightly, hiding behind the pages, in the hope it would all disappear.

Thoughts rushed through my head, what if it's Mr. Hughes? Mr. Hughes had a large stocky figure, he had just died, what if he has come back from the dead? What if he is angry with me? I finally found the courage to let out a scream. I jumped out of bed and bolted straight into my brothers' room nearby, I ran so fast I almost fell over.

"James, James I shouted, there is something in the hallway."

My brother seemed to ignore me. He was lying motionless on a wet bed; his body was as stiff as an ironing board. I shouted, "James, what's wrong with you? talk to me, I am scared."

There was no answer as his eyes were transfixed to the ceiling and James was unable to move.

The last thing I wanted to do was look up, but I felt compelled to do the same.

I slowly looked up and saw a pair of dark yellow eyes staring right back at me. The eyes looked like the eyes of a menacing animal ready to pounce. My legs gave way from sheer terror and I crumpled onto the floor screaming hysterically. I could see my warm breath gushing out into the room which had turned very cold. I could hear my parents frantically rushing up the stairs but by the time they had arrived, everything had disappeared. For a time, my brother and I were inconsolable, when the time came to go back to bed, we both found it very difficult to sleep and all the lights were left on. Mum and Dad tried to convince us that we both had some sort of night terror, but we both knew that was not true.

The effect of witnessing such ghostly unexplainable apparitions left me physically so frightened to get out of bed that I wet my bed often and a plastic sheet was put on top of my mattress to protect it. The bathroom was down the end of the hallway and in my mind that was an impossible task. James was left agitated and nervous and every now and then we found consolation with each other by getting together and talking about it. As a family we all tried to put it behind us and slowly over a period of weeks everything went back to normal. But the normality soon ended when another strange occurrence took place.

I had just come home from school and the first thing that hit my nose was the smell of freshly baked biscuits. I could hear mum singing in the kitchen, she sang so beautifully, I ran down the stairs to the basement and gave mum a big hug.

"How did your day go at school Deborah." Mum asked.

"Ok mum, I am not having any problems at all."

Mum passed me the plate. "Have a biscuit or three" she said with a smile. They smelt so good. I grabbed three biscuits and leant back against the kitchen wall and watched mum continue to bake. I bit into the moist soft oat biscuit and enjoyed every moment, shutting my eyes as if that would make any difference but then I felt a tingling sensation run through my body. I ignored it at first and carried on with indulging my taste buds. But then, I shivered, I felt cold and a bit uncomfortable. I tensed up and took another bite on my biscuit trying to act normal and opened my eyes. Mum had her back to me as she was at the sink washing up and seemed oblivious to my discomfort or the fact that the temperature in the kitchen had lowered, it seemed much colder than before.

Directly in front of me on the opposite wall I noticed something emerging through the wallpaper, at first, I wasn't sure what it was, but then it took shape, red fiery eyes emerged from within the wall, there were no facial features, just eyes that projected its evil stare right at me, making me feel extremely exposed and vulnerable. I tried to scream but nothing came out, I tried to scream again making a strange noise in my throat which made mum turn around, she looked directly at me and said, "What on earth is the matter Deborah, are you choking on a biscuit."

I took a deep breath and my words rushed out faster than an express train at full speed, "I can see red eyes, over there, in the wall, red eyes, red eyes" I blurted. I covered my face with my hands and began to sob.

"Oh, don't be so silly Deborah, a lot of things have been happening, settling into a new school, the death of your drama teacher, it has affected you, it will be alright, it really will be."

"Mum, please look over there", I said pointing my finger to the opposite wall.

Mum did look and the wall was back to its normal drab self. I ran upstairs to my room, perhaps I was seeing things, perhaps mum was right, I am just upset, but that wouldn't explain why James and I saw things at the same time. My world was growing smaller and smaller, if I couldn't get my mum to believe me, then who?

But I was not going to be alone in my experiences for long because of all people that saw the next ghostly apparition was my down to earth dad who didn't believe in such things. We all gathered together as a family in the front room and dad explained why he was selling the house.

Dad shared that while he was in the kitchen a cupboard door came open, at first, he took no notice after all, cupboards doors can come open especially if they were not shut properly in the first place. But what happened next was something else, a glass glided through the air and made its way to the tap, the tap came on and the glass filled itself with water, then emptied itself and placed itself on the draining board. Dad said, he could see no physical body. Then the back door opened and slammed shut. After telling his story dad said, "That's it, as far as I am concerned, this house is haunted, we are moving."

It was music to my ears.

Dad sold the house and we moved about five miles outside of the city centre to an area where many houses were surrounded by hills and horses. It was also a relief to know that the experiences that James and I went through were now believed.

We settled into our new home with great excitement, the house was modern and let in loads of natural light and was one of eight houses that formed a cul-de-sac. The only scary incident that shocked everyone including me was when after being settled in for quite a few weeks, I ran around the cul-de-sac screaming the devil was after me. I was completely terrified; I believed some unseen force was chasing me at the time and no-one knew what to do with me. I had no idea how traumatized I had been left by earlier incidents, I was quite sure I needed some recovery time. The feeling that something was pursing me was as real as the air I breathed. After that one-off experience it never happened again, but I never forgot it and I had no idea where the word 'devil' had come from.

Our new school was within easy walking distance and there seemed to be no more weird happenings. Everything seemed a lot more stable except for the arguments that we heard between mum and dad. Dad's drinking habits had increased as well as house parties. He built his own bar which went the length of a long wall, with his own drink optics.

Dad seem to become more and more the show off, as money came in from all his hard work, the house had dramatically changed in its appearance, Spanish imported tiles were laid in the bathroom and a sunken bath was put in, all the taps were changed to gold plated, only the best Axminster carpets were laid and he built a swimming pool in our large back garden. His new car, a Jag gleamed in the driveway.

During the heated arguments that mum and dad had, we all felt a sense of sadness, we spent our time together consoling each other. Dad often hit mum when he was angry, and then made it up to her by buying her chocolates and flowers. Some time ago a song was released by Connie Francis, it went something like this, "Lipstick on your collar told a tale on you, lipstick on your collar, said you were untrue, I bet your bottom dollar you and I are through, cos, lipstick on your collar, told a tale on you."

And that's what mum was angry over; she saw lipstick on dad's shirt collar. He was never totally loyal to mum and that was the saddest bit of all, as she did not deserve to be treated that way.

Mum's smoking had increased she was smoking at least 40 cigarettes a day. I didn't understand why she put up with dad's behaviour the way she did, but they never separated. In fact, it was all brushed under the carpet, no-one spoke about it. My dads' character was dominant, flashy, and self-indulgent bordering on greed, when he was with the lads, he was suited and booted, wearing gold jewellery and a greased back hair style with a quiff at the front, he wore velvet suits and looked like a gangster.

When dad had one of his parties, we were all sent off to bed and told firmly not to come downstairs. His bar was filled with every drink possible, dad knew how to throw a party, the alcohol never ran out and while the music thumped through the floor, we would sneak down the stairs, avoiding any stair that squeaked, go into the kitchen and raid the fridge as quickly as we could before we were seen, we just grabbed what goodies we could including those left out, like crisps and peanuts, and we would run upstairs to have our own little party.

At the weekends during the day, we were all packed off to horse riding lessons or the ice-skating rink in the centre of Brighton, followed by the cinema. This was great because it was better than being at home listening to sport on the television and dad wanted us all out the way for some peace and quiet.

His discipline seemed to be a bit much sometimes, and mum said nothing. Doors had to be shut quietly, no running, no elbows on the table, we were told to chew our food properly, don't talk with your mouth full, asked to be excused from the table, sit with your back straight, don't slouch, children should be seen and not heard, he would say and so on. It felt like I couldn't breathe, and I didn't dare answer back because I would almost certainly get a clip around the ear. The worst thing was, we sometimes got locked in our rooms, but even if that was meant to be a deterrent it didn't work, we managed to find a way of poking the key through and letting it fall onto a piece of paper on the other side of the door, so we could drag it back through and let ourselves out.

But it was not all doom and gloom. At Christmas time it was exciting; something we all looked forward to, whether dad was drunk or sober he dressed up as Father Christmas and clambered up the stairs with sacks of toys. We all giggled and pretended to be asleep and none of us opened up our presents until the morning. A huge sack for each of us was placed at the bottom of the bed. We were very much a family of ups and downs, sad moments and happy moments.

Things changed drastically for me when dad started to behave in an inappropriate way towards me. He would often say that I was the 'apple of his eye' I wasn't sure quite what he meant, but I kind of guessed I was his favourite. He then said a rather strange thing, that one day, just me and him would go on a holiday, I didn't get that, and felt confused, what about everyone else?

Dad often came into my room to kiss me goodnight, but one night he came into my room and started calling me by my mum's name, smothering my mouth with his lips and putting his hand down my night dress, he was far too heavy to push off. I tried hard to tell my dad that it was me and to get off, but his lips were pressed hard onto mine, I felt like I was suffocating. I guess mum was looking for him as the next thing that happened mum came into the room and dragged him out, she screamed at him, "What on earth do you think you are playing at Alan."

The next morning it was embarrassing for everyone. As my other sisters and brother were sent to school I was told to stay behind. Mum broke the tension first and said, "Alan what do you have to say to Deborah."

My dad looked at me and put his head down, staring at the floor, he said, "I am sorry Deborah, I was drunk, it will never happen again."

 But it did.

I had no idea what to say, I was always wary of my dad but now I was scared of my dad, scared of his temper and the way he looked at me. I just asked if I could go to school and left. When at home, I avoided dad as much as I could, I took extra care when dressing and undressing and felt concerned for my younger sisters, Jane and Anne. I had no-one to talk to about it and like always things never got dealt with properly. Mum didn't want to talk about it any longer, and I had no idea what to do with all my confused mixed-up feelings. My sisters and brother had no idea what had happened, I couldn't tell them. My home was meant to be a safe place, but I didn't feel safe, I felt very insecure. I often got home late from school and for a while my parents were very upset with me as I constantly played truant.

After my 11 plus exam, I went onto the secondary school of my choice. One thing I could never do well on was maths, so getting into grammar school was a definite no. I found it difficult to concentrate on my school work. I was often kept in detention for my lateness or for not turning up at all, but that didn't deter me from repeating the same behaviour. At school there was always the threat of being punished physically, it was either the cane for the boys and the slipper for the girls. I was not going to let anyone hit me with a slipper, although there was one occasion. I will never forget the time when my music teacher hit me so hard around the side of the head, he perforated my eardrum. I had been late for a lesson. The teacher was suspended and the hole in my ear drum needed a skin graft.

My secondary school was a 2 mile walk from home, and winter months were taxing. When it snowed it came down hard and the snow would be deep, up to my knees in some places. But I had to walk to school regardless of how cold it was or how deep the snow. My legs would be patchy and purple by the time I got home. I would cry with the pain as my body warmed up near the fire. My mum was puzzled by my purple legs and decided to call the doctor who said I had sluggish circulation.

School was a mixture of boredom, being absent and having a crafty fag behind the school gym, I enjoyed art and English, and sometimes cooking. I was quite proud of myself if I managed to successfully complete a dish or take a cake home to mum. I enjoyed country running and hockey, but hockey was extremely physical and aggressive. When I wasn't at lessons, I was with a few other girls messing around in an empty room that was never used much in the school.

We practiced a levitation game where each person present held their fingers lightly under your body, they repeated the line, light as a feather several times, the person who laid in the middle had to visualize themselves floating and feeling light as a feather and the idea was that you would levitate. When it was my turn, I could really visualize myself floating and then next thing I knew I seemed to be somewhere else. I did in fact feel extremely light and as I allowed myself to relax, I heard the other girls gasp, I had actually risen off the ground, I opened my eyes and came back down with a bump, thankfully not too far. The adrenalin rushed through our veins as we were all rather excited and scared at the same time.

Another strange game we played was to make each other faint by over breathing and then holding the breath whilst another person squeezes you tightly around the body from behind; this was done until you passed out.

The most exciting game to us was messing around with the Ouija. We made our own letters and formed them in a circle with a glass in the middle. The other girls really wanted to know if we could communicate with the spirit world. I never spoke about my own past experiences and felt uncomfortable, but after the glass violently smashed itself against a wall, we never did it again.

I wondered at the time if I had inherited something from my Grandma Mable who often made me feel strange. I would go to see her with mum. Grandma's bread pudding was irresistible. But whenever we were there, she would instantly make me feel tense; she had to read the tea leaves, read my palm, and tell me my future. When a pot of tea was made and my teacup was almost empty, she would swirl it around three times and read the leaves.

Grandma Mable would often go to meetings that I found out later had something to do with spiritualism, not that I understood what that was at the time. She would stare at me with her dark brown eyes and say, you are going to meet a tall dark stranger, a wonderful man who will bring you great happiness. Your future will be full of great surprises. It didn't make me feel good at all, I felt scared by the intensity of her words.

 With schizophrenia affecting one member in our extensive family, I was beginning to wonder if there was any normality in any of us. I knew our clan was large, but I didn't know most of them and some of my family I had not even met. Many family members seemed to be drinkers and party goers, and hard workers just like dad. Alcohol played a huge part in our family, including racism and snobbery, and things never got spoken about or a problem worked through, it was just ignored and everybody moved on.

I slowly found myself going more and more astray feeling quite isolated. I had only one friend in the school that I liked enough to bond with, her name was Caz. We often walked home together after school and on one occasion our walk turned into some kind of horror movie. We were both staring out across the fields where the horses ran, the daylight was slowly fading, and it was very cold. We were both chatting and were not in a rush to get home, as we laughed and giggled together something caught our attention, we both noticed a rider on a horse cantering fast across the hills.

"Do you see what I see Caz."

Caz didn't answer at first, but then she laughed and said, "It has got to be some kind of joke, look how white the horse is and its rider, and something doesn't look right to me."

We both continued to stare unable to take our eyes away from what we were watching. I started to feel a little nervous.

"Something don't look right to me either, Caz, I don't think the rider has a head."

Stories about a headless horseman had been mentioned in the area for some time, but I never thought they were true. Staring in utter disbelief, we thought if we waited a little bit longer the headless horseman would turn out to be a joke, that it would be some man, dressed up trying to scare people. But that didn't happen, as the rider got closer and closer, what we saw didn't change.

We both ran as fast as our legs could carry us, screaming at the same time. Neither of us looked back and we ran the last two miles all the way to where Caz lived. By the time we arrived to her parents' home we were exhausted. We both broke out with laughter staring at each other still not believing what we had just encountered as we bundled up the stairs to Caz's bedroom.

I had a sleep over that night which had already been arranged, so to take our minds off the spooky moment we got out the microphones and like two typical teenagers, (well almost teenagers) we started singing loudly pretending we were both pop stars. Once we had finished singing, we settled down for the night. We both had a single bed each, Caz was down the other end of the room. A small dim nightlight had been left on as I explained that I could not sleep in a pitch-black room.

As I drifted off to sleep, I felt a prodding in my back, startled I turned around and looked around the room, I giggled, I thought, I bet it was Caz trying to scare me. I quickly turned back over and pretended to go back to sleep. A few minutes passed when a strong firm finger poked me in the middle of my back again, this time much harder, I turned around and saw no-one. "Caz, you can stop that right now, you win, I'm scared, now let me get to sleep."

I couldn't for the life of me think where she was hiding, perhaps she was under my bed. I quickly looked underneath my bed and saw an empty space. I decided to get out of bed and go down to the other end of the room and to my surprise Caz was fast asleep in her bed. I pulled back her covers and shook her, "Caz, WAKE UP! I shouted, there is someone in the room."

As I blurted out an array of mixed-up words that made absolutely no sense, my breathing became quite erratic. Caz woke up and with eyes still closed mumbled, "Debz, stop it, calm down, there is no one here except you and me."

Frustrated by her lack of concern I shook her again and then calmed down a little to explain what had happened.

"Ok, said Caz, let's bunk together for tonight, but I still can't believe it, you sure it wasn't some kind of nightmare."

"Yes, I am sure, I wasn't even asleep, I thought it was you, trying to freak me out."

"Nope, not me, okay, well you are now freaking me out, so before you jump in with me, put the main light on."

I quickly put the light on and for a while we both peered around the room waiting for something else to happen. As time passed, we both slowly fell asleep and there were no more strange occurrences.

I awoke in the morning and decided to go straight home, I could not see the funny side of last night's experiences even though Caz seem to think it was all a bad dream. I kept the nights events to myself feeling rather stupid. I was surprised at Caz's laid back reaction, she said she wasn't sure what to believe, I couldn't understand that, especially as we both witnessed a headless horseman the day before.

Chapter Three – Rape

Between the ages of 12/13 years many changes had occurred. Because of my constant truancy I had a brief stay in a children's home called Stonepound in Hassocks. I had put my parents under excessive stress and worry. Whenever I returned home, I found it harder to integrate into normal family life because our family was not normal. I started smoking and had to try and hide the nicotine-stained skin on my fingers. I used to sit on the edge of a concrete kerb and rub my skin until the yellow staining came off which left my skin very sore. I couldn't deal with causing my parents anymore upset.

When I was not at school, I wandered around the streets of Brighton unaware of the dangers that it could put me in. One of my truancy days took me to the local park in the centre of Brighton called The Level. I had lost all motivation to do any lessons at school that day so I thought I would be reasonably safe at the park which was a large space with plenty of people about. When I entered the park, I decided to sit on top of the largest slide I had ever seen and to my surprise the park was not inundated with younger children as it normally was. As I sat there thinking about what I would do with my day I heard someone shout, "Hello, do you want to come down off the slide for a moment? I have a present for you, it's from your dad, he is too busy to give it to himself, so he asked me to help out."

'Do you know my dad then." I asked. Feeling a little puzzled and intrigued at the same time.

"Yes, I do know your dad", the man replied, "do you want to come and get your prezzy then? Only I have to go soon."

"How does my dad know I am in the park?"

"Well, that's easy, shouldn't you be at school?"

"Yes, I should, I suppose dad guessed I was here then." Great, I thought I really am in trouble when I get home.

The man smiled and shouted out, "Come on then, I really do have to go."

I slid down the slide with excitement and ran over to the man, it never occurred to me once that if I was playing truant or being naughty why would dad give me a present.

"Just come with me around the back of these bushes, I know it sounds strange but that's where I have hidden your present and we don't want everyone to see, I mean you are supposed to be at school, aren't you?" As I nodded, I thought, the present must be very special to send someone all the way to the park with it, especially as he had to hide it from everyone. As we went behind the tall bushes, I became so excited I found it hard to contain myself. The man took my hand firmly and said, "Close your eyes." I shut my eyes tight and waited. I felt him guide my hand close to his body and then with force he quickly pushed my hand inside his open trousers. "You touch this! this is your prezzy."

I opened my eyes and saw the man had his eyes closed. I pulled my hand away as fast as I could and ran. As I ran, I felt hysterical and my legs felt like lead weights, I screamed out for help as loud as I could. I was so scared and as I looked back, I could see the man running away from me in the opposite direction and a huge sense of relief flooded my body. I broke down and cried and realised how lucky I was. Feeling rather foolish that I believed his story I ran all the way home and went straight to my room. I couldn't speak to anyone as I felt so ashamed and dirty.

In my heart deep down, I suppose I wanted a better relationship with my dad and maybe the offer of a present was just the glimmer of hope I needed. But I was naïve and felt really stupid. Sadly, that experience however did not put me off playing truant at school and instead of going to the park I ended up on the Brighton Sea front. I loved seeing the motor bikes arrive and hear the sound of their engines. The Triumph Bonneville was one of my favourite bikes. Bikers turned up from everywhere, particularly from London with hundreds and hundreds of Hells Angels. The long-tasselled leather jacket was popular and there was a mixture of Mods verses Rockers, as well Skinheads and Teddy boys. Fashion made a loud defying statement within each group.

Every summer the sea front was packed with people, candy floss and the smell of chips, seagulls would often take a dive bomb at you in an attempt to steal a chip, they were often successful, loud rock music blasted out across the beach and the fair ground rides brought in a whole different bunch of people, fights happened often, drinking and beach parties were popular, people brought their own guitars along and the atmosphere encouraged everyone to join in.

I had a change of clothes with me, a suede tasselled waistcoat, long tasselled jeans and jumper, platform boots and a small bag of make-up. What money I had saved up I stole from my dad. Every night like clockwork especially after dad had a drink, he would throw down all his loose change onto his bedside cabinet and fall asleep. I would sneak in and take the odd coin knowing he wouldn't miss it. I loved hanging around the rides watching the teddy boys in their draped jackets, drainpipe jeans and suede shoes, they looked really smart. As I soaked up the atmosphere a biker with long dark hair approached me wearing a heavy looking leather jacket laden in patches on the front and on the back stitched in red was the wording Hells Angels MC England. He came armed with an extra beer and handed it to me.

"Enjoying yourself?" he asked.

"Yeah, love it, you come down from London then?"

"Yeah" was the short reply. "Wanna come for a ride?"

"Yeah ok."

I jumped on the back of his bike and I held on to his jacket. As we rode along the sea front for a few miles he then slowed down and stopped at a house set back off the road.

"I stop here on the odd occasion, it's my mates' pad, but you can come in."

I was more than happy to be with him as I liked him. We entered the house and went into a downstairs room which was quite large, I made myself comfortable. His name was Mick.

"Have another beer" he said, "so you're not at school then?"

I went quiet thinking, surely, I look older.

"Hey don't worry about it, how old are ya, anyway?"

"Nearly fourteen", I lied. I murmured quietly to myself, So, what if I am a year out.

"Come here" Mick said, he put his arms around me and started to kiss me. It was my first proper kiss with anyone and I liked it. We talked some more and drank some more and Mick made it clear to me that he wanted sex. Mick then shared that to be totally grown up my virginity should be broken and that everyone has a first time.

"It will be alright I promise, you have gotta go with someone, right?" "It may as well be me."

I nodded in agreement and decided why not. I liked the attention and I was about to encounter my first ever sexual experience, but my experience with him didn't turn out how I had expected. It was more painful than pleasurable and even with a few beers inside me, I was quite tense. When the deed was done Mick asked me if I was alright.

"No, I'm not alright Mick, it hurt, and I am bleeding."

"Don't worry about it, it sometimes happens, you will be fine. Good to add to my white wings."

"What do you mean your white wings."

"It's when you break in a virgin", Mick said, with a huge grin on his face.

"Well, that's great for you, I am going to get dressed."

I went into the bathroom feeling rather used and had a quiet cry to myself. I was only thirteen what was I thinking. I felt a mixture of liberation and shame at the same time. I cleaned myself up and asked Mick to take me back to the beach or if he didn't mind perhaps closer to where I lived, I was no longer in a party mood.

We both jumped on the bike and Mick sped off fast feeling quite pleased with himself, he dropped me off a few blocks away from my house. I didn't want my mum and dad to see me getting off a motorbike, especially dad, he would have hit the roof. My dad hated long haired greasers as he called them. I said goodbye and sneaked into the house via the back door and went straight up to my room.

Deep down I felt angry with myself, on the outside I portrayed myself as a grown up with a tough exterior, but inside I was quite the opposite. Inside, I just wanted to be loved, but I soon found out that love and sex could be two different things. Allowing myself to be used by a stranger in the end made me feel degraded, I didn't have the courage to talk to my mum about it.

The next morning, I went downstairs to face the music, dad had already left for work, and everyone else was out or at school. Mum smiled and asked me to sit down.

"Deborah, I need to talk to you about something."

"Ok, but first can I say that I am sorry, I have not been attending school much."

"Deborah, I know, I have received a letter from the school and it's no longer in their hands or mine. We have to go to court."

"Why? What do you mean?"

"The powers that be, the authorities say you are out of control, parental control, and it will be the decision of the court as to what will happen next. You simply cannot wander around streets when you feel like it."

I felt so sorry for mum as she really did not deserve the extra worry and stress as she was already coping with dad's behaviour of drinking, bullying and womanizing. We hugged and we both felt as helpless as one another.

When we arrived at the courthouse the only feeling I had was feeling sorry that I had put my mum through the embarrassment of having to answer to the court about my constant bad behaviour regarding truancy. The judge and his words were very clear.

"I am sending your daughter to Middlesex Lodge for reports to be completed. It is an assessment centre. It will then give us a clearer picture of what will happen next. Deborah's behaviour cannot continue like this and she must finish her education."

I remained at Middlesex Lodge for one month then returned home to await the court's decision. As I waited, I decided I was not going to be punished and made the decision to run away rather than be locked up somewhere. I knew this was probably not the best action to take, but to run seemed like the only thing I could do.

With some personal belongings in my bag, I quietly left and as a fair had just arrived on the outskirts of Brighton, I decided to go to it. With very little money I thought it would be better to hitch hike and it wasn't long before I found myself in the area, Hitch-hiking was easy and most people who picked up hitchhikers were friendly and obliging.

I wandered around looking in charity shops and killing time until the fair opened, it felt good to be near the rides, as the daylight hours disappeared, the rides all lit up which lifted my downcast mood. It was near the dodgem cars that I met a young man. He was dark in looks and slender in build but had a very energetic personality. I watched him leap from car to car to collect money and as soon as he noticed me, he shouted out, "Want a ride then?"

"Sure, although I only have enough money for one ride."

As I jumped in the car and got comfortable, I was happy to hear him say, "There is no charge for you, my name is Tony, what's yours?"

I answered giggling, "Deborah or you can call me Debz."

I enjoyed several free rides that evening and had a great deal of fun. When the fair had finished Tony and I got together for a chat. I found out he was sixteen and the fairground had been his life, travelling everywhere with his family. I told him that I was only thirteen and that I had always looked a lot older for my age.

"Don't you have a home to go to then?" Tony said with a big warm smile. "You shouldn't really be out and about on your own, you are too young."

"I don't want to go home, it's complicated, can I stay with you and I will go back tomorrow."

I had no intentions of going home. I felt I could trust Tony and he had already said he had no intentions of getting involved with me.

Tony explained he slept on a large bus that had been converted inside into sleeping areas for men.

"You can come back with me for just a while, the men are all out drinking somewhere, so if you wanna stay with me for a bit you can, but then you must go before the men get back."

As we got closer to the bus which was parked up by a large open field Tony told me to be quiet so that we didn't attract any attention.

Tony and I went onto the bus and went upstairs where we sat together on a bed in the corner of the bus.

"Debz you know that you won't see me after the fair has finished, I travel with the fair, it's how I live, and you cannot come with me."

"Yeah, I understand, you're good company, I just need to chat, and then I will go."

I shared about my home life, the weird experiences, my dad's perverted nature, and how I felt miserable being at home, how guilty I felt upsetting mum. Tony listened very well and seemed really mature for his age.

"Listen Debz, sorry you can't stay here for the night, you are best off going home, things will work out, you need to stop running away and knuckle down at school. I think you should go now, because the men will be back soon and this is no place for a young girl like you, it was a mistake to bring you here."

I nodded in agreement and asked for a hug knowing I would not see him again.

Tony tensed up.

"What's wrong Tony", I asked.

"Shit! I can hear the men coming, it's too late for you to leave, you can't be seen here. Get under the blanket and cover yourself up, don't move, don't speak, be very still and quiet. I will sneak you out later, do you understand?"

I nodded, but not really understanding why he was being so dramatic about it all. I felt scared for him and me. I did what he asked, Tony laid down on the bed shielding his body in front of mine. I heard the boots of men stomping up the stairs, they were loud and rowdy.

"Tony," boomed a voice, "How are ya! Are you alright? Tony me lad, come on have a beer, get that down yer."

"Just one then, looks like you have all had a great night out, I need to crash soon."

All the men cheered as Tony joined in with them.

"You can catch your beauty sleep some other time Tony", it was then that one of the men yanked Tony's arm and said, "Get up off that bed yer lazy git."

As they pulled Tony off the bed another voice said, "What have we got here Tony, looks like we have got ourselves a stowaway."

The blanket that was hiding me was pulled back and I found myself staring at a group of drunken men.

"Whooooah Tony, you know you are not allowed to bring the ladies back here, who is she then?"

I noticed Tony's voice was shaking when he answered, "Just leave her alone will ya, she needs to go back home, and she is hardly a lady as such, she is just a kid, thirteen."

"Yeah, well she looks older to me" said one man.

The men got closer and pulled Tony out the way. For the second time Tony insisted that they leave me alone, but they didn't listen, in fact they got quite angry and one of the men punched Tony hard in the face. "Shut up Tony yer wimp."

34

My heart was pounding in my chest. I knew that I was in deep trouble. I froze, unable to move or speak. I was already in shock that they hurt Tony who was reeling with pain. As they continued to push Tony out the way he stumbled by the top of the stairs and fell down the stairs, I never heard him get up. The men just laughed.

One of the men who stank of alcohol moved onto the bed and got on top of me. "Come on darling, let's have those clothes off, I want some of you", he said laughing.

The man got on top of me, he was so heavy I struggled to move or breathe as his weight slumped down onto my body. I started to cry and a hand came over my mouth pressing down really hard. The man on top of me shifted his weight so another could rip off my trousers. Then the men started shouting, "Come on then, get in her." I went rigid and numb as the man started to penetrate me, violating my body. Tension seared through my muscles and every jolt and thrust was like a piece of hot iron burning my skin creating a deeply embedded pain. No-one was coming to help me. After a few moments I heard him give out a grunt of satisfaction and he slowly got off me leaving me sore. As I tried to move off the bed, another man pushed me back down saying, "It's my turn now my lovely, you love it, don't ya?" Laughter and cheering continued and as soon as I tried to protest demanding they get off me, a hand went back over my mouth.

I no longer felt any emotion as I died inside. Pain seared through my body as my mind went blank. The stench of sweat and drink filled my nostrils and the noise they made with their cheering and laughter made me sick to my stomach. As each man took his turn my soul had entered hell. I had no thoughts, just an eerie stillness as if my mind had broken off from reality and gone to another place.

When it was finally over a voice said," come on, get up, and don't tell anyone, otherwise something bad will happen to you, now get dressed and get off the bus."

At first, I couldn't move, I couldn't respond, I was pulled up from the bed and told again to get off the bus. I slipped on my trousers and was shaking so bad I didn't think I would make it down the stairs. One of the men pushed me, "Come on girly, move, get off the bus and keep your mouth shut."

As I descended down the stairs, I could still hear them laughing, I had to grip the rail to steady myself to get to the bottom of the stairs, I noticed Tony was unconscious. His face was covered in blood, his nose almost certainly broken. I decided to leave him and get off the bus before the men changed their minds and came after me.

I started to slowly walk away from the bus feeling physically sick. The lights from the windows of the bus slowly disappeared into the background, it was now pitch black where I stood. I collapsed onto the ground and felt something was wrong. I could feel blood trickling down my legs. With a sense of urgency, I started to crawl through the grass hoping that the men could no longer see me. Time seemed to slow down and panic set in as I tried to crawl faster. I had got a good distance away from the bus and looked back to see that no-one was coming after me. Ahead of me I could see the headlights of a car. I started to cry, "Please, please, don't go, come this way."

I stood up and felt dizzy, but I needed them to see me, but couldn't stand for long. I fell down again, feeling weak and disorientated. Shutting my eyes, I hoped in my heart that whoever was in that car would be kind.

"Are you alright young lady?" a voice said. I lifted my head up to see two police officers standing in front of me. I breathed out a deep sigh of relief. My body went limp as I croaked out, "I need help." I don't remember anything after that. In the police station a female officer explained that I was to be examined by a doctor. Drained and still in shock I sat motionless not wanting to speak. After the examination I was asked several questions and I did my best to answer them.

In the moments I was left alone my thoughts wandered, those men had no excuse for what they did to me. Their hearts were like granite, stripped of my humanity, they took what dignity I had left, they ravaged my body like a pack of hungry wolves, tearing at my flesh. They were only concerned about satisfying their carnal nature, I could still hear the sound of laughter and smell the stench of their foul breath.

Both of my parents were notified and were told to come to the police station. The doctor explained to them that I had been raped. That I was in need of medical attention, I needed several stitches. I heard my mum weeping. I felt guilty I should never have left home.

The police had already left to go and arrest the men on the bus. The bus had not left to go on to its next location yet. In their arrogance they believed that I wouldn't say a word to anyone, but I did. With enough forensic evidence those responsible were brought before the court and the men concerned went to prison for a very long time.

Back at home there was no pressure from anyone including the school authorities. I remained in my room and slept the hours away. I felt used, degraded, contaminated by men who had no idea of how much damage they had caused me both physically and mentally. I alternated between being extremely moody and depression. Every day I sat in a salted bath to help the healing and every day I could not scrub away the filth I felt upon my body.

Chapter Four – Rebellion

I lacked motivation to get back into a routine and really did not want to attend school. I felt vulnerable and believed the whole world knew about my ordeal. But that wasn't the case. I didn't want to integrate and at the age of fourteen I was very much a loner. The school authorities by this time alongside the judicial system decided the best way forward for me was to attend an approved school which was in Addlestone in Surrey. I was to stay there for at least one year.

When I arrived, I was pleasantly surprised by the surroundings, the grounds were beautiful. As I entered the premises in front of me lay a circular lawn, around its edges were bright colourful flowers of every description. Surrounding the lawn set further back were eight houses all in pristine condition, the windows encased in a brilliant white wood, gleamed. Everything looked fresh and tidy. I went into one of the houses where I was allocated to be and was shown to my room, I was to share with three other girls. We were all the same age and had all failed the system one way or another. I took up touch typing which I really enjoyed and the staff there were disciplined but pleasant.

After just a few weeks I started to feel quite restless. I wanted to go home, then I changed my mind and wanted to run away. My mixed-up feelings churned away inside me like an old washing machine and it went on for days. It was so easy to run, there were no locks on the doors except when we went to bed at night. I felt like a nobody, I had no idea who I was anymore. It wasn't that the place was bad, its purpose was to educate wayward girls, give them discipline, study, and routine. I needed more. I hated being told what to do, how I should feel and how to behave. What was the purpose of all that discipline if they didn't understand how I felt inside? When everyone heard the dinner bell and went to the main hall, I left and didn't look back. I had no idea where I would end up, but it seemed this pattern of running away had become deeply engraved in me and there didn't seem to be an answer on how I could be stopped.

My hitch-hiking took me to Cambridge. I was not afraid to hitch hike, most people did it, but I was very wary of men and if I didn't like the look of someone I didn't get in the car. Cambridge was a young person's city; it was filled with students and the atmosphere was buzzing with energy. It didn't take long before I made friends with a few people who were older than me but still quite young. They were all sitting on a large green in the centre of the city chatting about the next time they were going to have a trip. It never dawned me that they were talking about a drug, known to most as acid, or L.S.D. I was invited to go with them and they asked me if I had ever had a trip before. I lied to them and told them I had taken it just once. I also lied to them about my age as I didn't think they would offer me any acid if they knew I was only fourteen. I wanted to try it, they seemed so excited about it. We strolled across the green and entered a large house. Beautifully decorated, I had never seen a house quite like it. I tried to remain a bit laid back about it all as I wanted to give the impression of maturity.

"Nice pad", I said.

"Yes, my parents are away" the young girl said. "So, we can all have a good time in a safe place."

We all got comfortable and I was expecting some form of a tablet, but to my surprise I was offered liquid to be injected into a vein.

"You look a bit concerned Debz do you still want to go ahead?" We have all done it this way before, it's good."

I agreed, but felt a bit nervous. After a few attempts to get my veins up they decided not to bother and they gave it to me by mouth. I then relaxed and waited to see why acid made everyone so excited.

I was sitting in a large armchair and about twenty minutes had passed when I felt like I was coming up in a fast elevator. I was unable to move but stayed calm. As I looked down at the carpet, I saw faces made up of thousands of small golden cubes. I sat there amazed at the detail. Time was lost and I couldn't control the dribbling from my mouth which felt like a huge waterfall. I finally managed at some point to get up but found myself back on the floor sitting on a long shag pile rug, which had turned into an animal. Lying on top of the animal's stomach were babies and they were being suffocated by their mothers' fur. I started to pull the babies off her, one by one I started to save them. But in reality, I was tearing up a rug. When I had finished, I lifted my head and looked around the room, some of the people were in their own worlds enjoying their trip, but one man looked at me and laughed, he said, "You haven't tripped before have you?"

I admitted to him that I had lied and started to feel a little embarrassed.

"I am so sorry about the rug."

"I am not worried about the rug Debz, the acid you took was really good stuff, once I saw you dribbling and unable to move, I knew you weren't telling me the truth. You have no idea if your trip could have gone the other way. A bad trip I mean. I think you should leave. The effects of the acid will wear off in a few more hours, but I don't like being lied to."

I left the house like a scolded puppy with its tail between its legs and made my way out of Cambridge, which took a while. I still needed to adjust and come down completely. I noticed that sounds, feelings, colours were all exaggerated and seemed more intense. I liked acid but next time I wouldn't want to take it in liquid form.

Staying on the run was hard, I got caught a few times, but I continued to run away again and again. Each time I was on the run I indulged in drug taking. Barbiturates, speed, the occasional smoke with resin, but acid was my favourite indulgence. I liked the way that drug took me out of myself, each micro dot had a different name, Yellow Sunshine, Blue Cheer, White Lightning, Burnt Orange, Black Magic and Strawberry Fields, were just some of the ones I remembered.

Sometimes whilst tripping, coloured rain splashed down onto the pavements spreading the colours everywhere. At the beach seaweed became strange crocodiles, pavements I walked on were spongy and it would take forever to get anywhere because I would become fixated on everything around me. There was no perception of time and I didn't really care how much time passed me by. I survived on the streets by stealing items and pawning them in a pawn shop. Other times lorry drivers would pick me up and buy me a meal. I washed myself down in the lady's toilets and I crashed wherever I could, under the stairs in a block of flats, in a barn, or even in a telephone kiosk.

One lorry driver was not so friendly as most. When I refused him sex, he dropped me off in the middle of nowhere, in the heart of the country and told me to get out and walk. There was no street lighting and I was so afraid. I hated the dark, but it was better than being forced into sex. Inside I just wanted someone to tell me everything would be alright, but that never happened. As a young woman alone, I was very vulnerable, and men wanted to take advantage of that fact.

On one other occasion I was hitch-hiking when a driver picked me up and gave me a card, he said, "Take this card with you and contact Russian Dave, he will give you a job, he runs a night club and restaurant, I am sure he can help you."

I thought naively that I could get a job perhaps washing up, or clearing tables. When I found the place, I knocked on the door and a shutter moved across to reveal a small opening.

"Yeah, how can I help you?" the voice said.

I handed the card through to the man on the other side of the door and said, "I am looking for a job."

The door unbolted and I stepped inside a large room which was busy with people talking and dancing. I was told to wait at the bar. After waiting a few minutes, I entered an office, a man rather rugged looking sat behind the desk.

"How old you?"

As always, I lied and said I was fifteen.

"The driver who gave you this card is a friend mine; do you always travel alone? You're very young."

"Yes" I replied not wanting to mention at all that I was on the run.

"Let me explain how this works. I run this nightclub; we have lots of punters who come here for a service. We give them what they want. The girls who work here encourage the men to buy them drinks and take them to my restaurant for a meal. This brings money into my club, the girls also earn their money by being paid for sex, from that I get my cut. My girls get very well looked after, I can set you up in your own flat, give you clothes, as long as you do all these things that I have mentioned. Before you make a decision, why don't you hang around for a bit and watch how the other girls operate."

I nodded. There was no way I was having sex with anyone.

I was left by the bar and was told I could wander around to get a feel of the place. I saw everyone having fun, the women had really nice clothes and shoes, and jewellery. They certainly made good money. I didn't go upstairs as my intentions were to get out of the building as quickly as I could. I waited for the security guy to go the other way and as soon as I got my chance, I left the building. My eyes had been opened to a different way of life and I wondered how many of those women were truly happy.

Back on my travels I was picked by the police and ended back up at the approved school. This time I was going to be punished.

The head of the school spoke to me and said, "Deborah you have consistently run away from this school with a blatant disregard for anyone's feelings. You refuse to be disciplined, you miss lessons, and do not appreciate what is being done for you. You will now be taken to the Birds Nest. It is a room in a separate building from the school and other houses, and there you will have time to think about why you are so rebellious."

I was quietly escorted away. The Birds Nest was placed at the very top of the building. The door to the room I was going to stay in was made of steel. There was a small opening for a tray of food to be passed through. There were no windows in the room except a small narrow strip of glass that allowed some ventilation and light to come in. In the corner of the room, I was shocked to see a large bucket with a lid. I was told this would be emptied once a day. I had a place to sleep in the corner of the room with a blanket and one pillow. My meals came up on a regular basis, but no-one stopped to talk to me. The room was hot and stuffy even with a small ventilation strip, and the bright light on the ceiling was far too bright. I hated it all and felt utterly despondent. I was allowed magazines, so I read them every day but soon got bored with that. As the days passed, I wondered how long they could keep me up here. I started to suffer with anxiety, I wanted to get out. I started hearing things, breathing, which really freaked me out. There was no bell to ring for help. I'd put my hands over my ears hoping for the sound of breathing to disappear, but it didn't go.

Oh, great I thought, I am going mad. I waited until the next time a staff member brought my lunch, I pleaded with her to let me out explaining I was hearing things. Luckily for me, it was my last day, I had been up in the Birds Nest a whole week and it had dragged by so slowly. I was expected to fit back in with the rest of the girls like nothing had happened. But I was actually traumatized by hearing and sensing that something else had been in the room with me. I had no intention of staying at the school and I had no intention of getting caught. I was going to leave no matter what. I was nearly fifteen and my year was up and the thought of going home was to me equally depressing. The first chance I got I left without a word to anyone.

I had no particular plan about where to travel to, so I just stuck out my thumb and decided wherever the driver was heading, I was heading there too. My first lift took me south to a place called Chichester. When I arrived there, I wandered around getting to know the area. After a while I plucked up the courage to go into a pub hoping that I looked old enough to buy a drink.

As I observed my surroundings, I noticed a man in his twenties, he caught my eye, he was tall, medium build and quite good looking, with the most amazing blue eyes. He had dark blonde hair and looked smartly dressed which made me feel a little shabby. He struck me as a confident person, he was aware I was staring at him.

I decided to get myself a soft drink as I didn't want any questions about my age. Every now and then he stared at me and smiled. I was very mixed up about my feelings on men. On the one hand I wanted to be protected and loved and on the other hand I hated men and thought they were vile creatures. As the time passed, he came over me and introduced himself. "Hi, my name is Paul."

"Hi, I'm Debz."

A short sweet introduction led on to a long lengthy chat. I ended up blurting out my whole life story to him and expected him to get up and walk away. But he didn't. To my surprise he offered to help me but explained he lived with his disabled mother and that I would have to be very quiet as she was not to know I was there.

I was so relieved that I did not have to sleep outside. Paul seemed a kind man and now that he understood what I had been through I felt I was going to be safe and ok.

That night I stayed very quiet in Pauls room, but the time came when I needed to use the toilet. So, I crept down the hallway to use the loo and bumped straight into Pauls mum.

"Who the hell are you and what are you doing in my house?" she literally screamed the words out and was completely outraged at finding me in her home.

Paul quickly came to the rescue.

"How dare you bring this slut into my house Paul, who is she? What is she doing in my house, answer me Paul?"

"Mum, I am sorry, she needs help. I met her down the local pub."

"Really, well you know my rules, I want her to go right now."

Pauls mum was a very large lady who leant on a walking stick, but she seemed quite robust and a little scary.

Paul tried one last time to reason with his mum.

"Mum her name is Debz and I don't want to argue, she needs our support just for tonight."

Sadly, for all Paul's politeness, it didn't work.

"My word is final Paul; she has to leave."

The conversation came to an abrupt end. Paul turned around to face me and said, "I want you to go home, promise me you will, I will give you the train fare, no hitch-hiking. I want you to be safe. I will give you my phone number. I have to respect my mum's wishes; she is not well. We will try to work something out."

I hated to leave but he made sense and for first time in my life I actually listened to someone and acted upon it.

When I got back home my parents were not surprised to see me. They already knew I had been on the run. I shared with Mum about the Birds Nest and how disturbed I was and dad kept his distance from me, he said very little. I told mum all about Paul and how he helped me and that I wanted to keep him as a friend as I felt we had bonded, explaining nothing physical had taken place. Mum was worried about the age gap, I was fifteen, Paul was 23 years old.

My dad had a fit and screamed, "My daughter is not going out or befriending a man of 23 and that's the end of the matter."

Mum came up with the suggestion that maybe I could see Paul every now and then under supervision, but that too, was out of the question.

Dad went ballistic, "NEVER, NEVER, NEVER!" was his answer.

I missed Paul and really struggled, I liked his company, so I told mum that I was leaving, that I didn't want to be any more trouble, but I did want to see Paul again.

This time I didn't sneak out the door, I wanted to be more grown up about it. So, I packed a bag of things that I needed and told mum I would leave when dad had gone to work. I really didn't want to face him and his temper. I was going to miss mum and my brother and sisters, but I had to follow my heart. Before leaving I rang Paul, he said that he would sort something out. I couldn't explain why I felt so strongly about Paul I just did. I knew my dad would be fuming about it. I was searching for happiness and I believed in a very short space of time that I had found it. If love at first sight was true, this must have been it.

When I arrived in Chichester, Paul had secured a place for us to live, but my time with him was short lived, unbeknown to me my dad had reported me missing to one of the local Brighton papers. Alongside my picture the words said, 15-year-old girl missing from home, has anyone seen this girl? I suppose news travels, or I was on some kind of database, because my picture led to my arrest. It happened when I took a trip to the local shop for groceries, I caught the attention of a female police officer. She approached me and said, "Hello my name is PC Barnes, your face looks familiar, I am sure I have seen your picture somewhere. Do you live in Chichester?"

"No", I replied, "I don't."

"I am pretty convinced that you come under our missing person's list. Would you mind coming with me to the local station so we can sort this out?"

"I am not coming with you; you've got the wrong person."

"I think it would be in your best interest if you do what I ask", the young PC stated.

I could see the conversation was going anywhere so I smiled, turned around and started running. I ran as fast as I could hoping that she wasn't as fit as me, I kept running for at least a mile and decided I needed to find a hideout as quickly as possible.

Ahead of me I could see a metal scrap yard with cars piled high on top of each other. I ran into the yard believing I had lost her. I crouched down behind a stack of cars and got my breath back. As I slowly raised my head I peered through a gap and noticed PC Barnes was standing right at the entrance to the yard.

"Come on" she shouted, "I know you are in here."

As the copper started to walk slowly towards me, I thought to myself the whole thing was pointless, I am going to make a stand and fight if I have to. I shouted back, "You have no idea what you are doing, I am not going home, you don't understand."

There was no response. I stood up and found by my feet a metal bumper that had come off one of the cars. I picked it up ready to fight my corner. As she got closer, I jumped out and lunged straight for her. I hit the officer several times and each time I hit her I screamed, "I am NOT going home."

The police officer struggled not only with me but with her radio and started calling for assistance. I felt angry that before I had a chance of happiness somebody was going to take it away from me.

Within a short space of time the yard was filled with police officers that immediately restrained my outburst of violence. I was taken straight to the police station where disapproving looks from many of the police officers were aimed right in my direction. I knew I was not going to win any popularity contests. PC Barnes had many friends and was a popular person, the fact that she had been hurt went down like a ton of bricks. I found out later that the metal bumper that I had used on her body had caused many deep lacerations. As I sat in my cell, I was informed that the police officer I had hurt had gone to the hospital for treatment and would-be off work for the next few weeks.

My heart sank, I had never been violent before and to be honest I no longer recognised who I was. After a night in the cells, I was summoned to court to face a judge, my parents were informed and were invited to be present at the court hearing.

As I stood in the dock the judge looked at me sternly and said, "Deborah, although you are only fifteen, due to your history of absconding you will be placed in Holloway Prison for social reports, you will stay in the hospital wing. Physically assaulting a police officer in the line of duty is not something I take lightly. You will remain there for a period of six to eight weeks until all necessary social reports are concluded, I will then see you back in my court for sentencing, do you understand?"

I was shocked to hear I was being remanded in a prison at my age, but Holloway apparently took young offenders, and there was nothing I could do about it.

Going to Holloway Prison was the most terrifying daunting experience for me to come to terms with. A huge antiquated building that was dismal and soulless. When I was taken into the dormitory, the ward was kept simple, just rows of beds, the plain walls were in desperate need of a new coat of paint and the whole ward needed a deep clean. I realised there would be no privacy or quiet. Girls as young as fourteen were there. The older women were scary, most of them had serious drug problems or were mentally ill. Every day these women would queue up for their daily dose of physeptone to help with their withdrawals or they were in need of other medication. The language of most women was foul and Lesbianism was rife. I was terrified someone would either bully me or approach me for sexual contact. When night-time approached it only went quiet when it got quite late into the early hours. The only reprieve I got was when I was taken off the ward to go for psychiatric reports or see another specialist. On one occasion while waiting to be seen, I thought I would strike up a conversation with an inmate sitting next to me.

"What are you in here for then?" I asked her, trying to sound tough.

"Murder," was the abrupt answer.

I didn't speak after that. As I waited, I noticed two prison officers escorting a woman down a narrow corridor opposite me. As I continued to stare, she reminded me of someone, and then it dawned on me who she was, the moors murderess Myra Hindley, her stark blonde hair stood out against her deep-set jet-black eyes, her face was stern and intense. I shuddered and looked away thinking this is no place for a young teenager to be.

My time inside Holloway dragged by and every moment of it was tense, there was always someone screaming, crying or fighting. I couldn't wait to get out, it was such a dark disturbing place. My time finally came for me to return to the court and with all my heart I was hoping the judge would be lenient. My mum was there waiting to see me we barely had a moment of eye contact. As I stood in the dock for most of the time my eyes focused towards the floor.

The judge wasted no time in addressing me. 'I have made a decision Deborah, having taken everything into account concerning your social reports, I have come to conclusion you will not be going home. You are charged with assault and ABH causing actual bodily harm to a police officer and my order is that you will be detained in a closed borstal called Bullwood Hall for a period of six months to 2 years, dependant on your behaviour'.

My heart sank, I looked over at my mum who was clearly upset and I felt so ashamed. My days of running were over. As I was led away, I could hear my mum crying in the background, I had broken her heart, I was overwhelmed with sadness.

Borstal – Bullwood Hall

HMP Bullwood Hall, as captured on Google Earth 2006, image Landsat/Copernicus

As I arrived into the courtyard of Bullwood Hall, I looked up to see a large old Victorian building, with row upon row of windows. I had no idea what I was entering into, but it had to be better than Holloway prison. I could hear the voices of a few girls shouting out of the window to each other. I noticed a plastic cup was tied to a long piece of string which was swinging between windows. I found out later it was one way to pass a note or tobacco to someone in the next cell. The building was made up of three main wings, a work room, and a psychiatric unit for the very disturbed run by a qualified psychiatrist. There was also a punishment block which housed one padded cell.

I was told by the staff that it was a privilege to bunk up with a friend and share a room and those privileges had to be earned. Bullwood Hall had a reward system which was colour coded. It started with a yellow band, then went up to green and top privileges for a red band. Each time you graded more freedom was given. It was even possible to get released early if your behaviour was good. The layout on each wing was just like a prison, there was a ground floor and an upper floor, both identical, floors that extended in length holding loads of single cells, and just a couple of privileged cells to share with someone. Recreation time was in the evening after you had done your chores or been to work in the factory, or attended school lessons.

As I entered onto the wing as the newbie everyone just stared. Some of the girls were tough looking and quite scary. I was taken to the office where they checked me in and took my details. I was then shown to my cell. I was asked to think about whether I wanted to continue my education as I was only fifteen or work in one of the workshops. If I went to the workshop, I earnt a small amount of money to buy toiletries and tobacco. I chose to work in the workshop. My job was working on a machine that helped secure a top to the main cylinder of a thermos flask. But every area had its temptation. The girls that had been there longer than me invited me into a storeroom that held large containers of glue and I soon realised that glue sniffing was something they all did for a quick high, of course I was completely unaware of the dangers.

As I settled in, I realised so many young women had very difficult lives, one woman in particular had a hard time as she was known for being cruel to her baby. Other women were extremely violent and often bullied the weaker ones, taking their tobacco when they felt like it. At recreation it was meant to be a time of chilling out, playing music and mingling, but fighting and the clashing of personalities always happened, many wanting to be top dog. Nearly all the women were tattooed and several of them had self-harm scars, some quite serious. I had been in borstal only one week

50

and ached to get out. I could see that staying long term in Bullwood Hall was a place that either toughened you up or broke you. I wanted neither.

At break time, I noticed a lorry arrive with deliveries and decided I would be the first person ever to escape a locked borstal, when no-one was looking, I was going to hide in the back of the lorry. As soon as I saw my chance I didn't hesitate, I got in the back and hid behind some boxes. As the lorry driver shut the doors my heart raced, yay! I thought, I've done it, I am out. I would be back on the road in no time and as the lorry went through the main gates, I was feeling quite proud of myself.

I had probably been in the lorry for about an hour when the lorry started to slow down. In the background I could hear the sirens of a police car. My excitement of being free fizzled out as the lorry came to a standstill, I could hear voices. 'Open up, a police officer shouted, you have a stowaway on board'. I felt gutted that I had been caught. I got off the lorry without a fuss, there was no point in fighting. I got into the police car and went straight back to the borstal. On arrival I was taken straight to the governor's office, reprimanded and was immediately put down as an escapee, one who could not be trusted and to be escorted everywhere until further notice. I was punished by having to clean and polish long corridors and sent to solitary confinement for a period of one week.

Time was added onto my sentence, so I knew I would not get out in six months. The only good thing that came out of it was that the inmates had started to respect me. My escape had given everyone something to talk about for a while. After completing my time in solitary confinement, I came back to the main wing and joined the others, most of the girls had nick names and I decided to call myself Toni. I took on a new identity and Deborah as far as I was concerned no longer existed.

Once alone in my cell I tattooed my skin, it was a common practice in borstal. I used a metal ashtray, broke open a pencil to get the lead out, used a bit of my spit and started to mix the spit with the lead which was used to tattoo my skin. Most of my tattoos were done with a fine needle, but one tattoo was cut in with glass, it was a long tattoo going the length of my forearm which said Hells Angels, below that a circle with the number 13 inside, the 13th letter of the alphabet was M for Marijuana. On my left thumb was the 1% per cent mark. The Angels proudly displayed 1% when the American Motorcycle Association started labelling the Hells Angels as outlaws, that 1% of riders that gave the rest a bad reputation. The Angels took this as a compliment. On my right thumb was tattooed an inverted cross, across my fingers I tattooed the word 'acid' across my right wrist the word 'hate' across my left wrist the words 'living death', on my left arm the word 'Hendrix and Freedom', on my left shoulder a large inverted cross with the name Satan above it, on my right shoulder the word 'hell'. The last letter was a P for Polly who became a close friend especially in areas of the occult.

Polly was in borstal for desecrating graves whilst on acid, so acid became our first soul tie. The second tie was in connection with the supernatural. I had shared with Polly about my past with regards to the ghostly happenings I had experienced as a child and Polly shared her deep interest in the occult. So, one afternoon in our free time we decided to get together to pray the lord's prayer backwards just to see what power it would generate. To say the words literally backwards took practice. But we were both determined. Polly had already read books on Witchcraft and black magic and we made a pact to remain united. I knew from my own past that there was more to life than what a person saw with their own eyes.

During this experimental time, I started to self-harm and some of the cuts needed stitches. My arms would often be bandaged from the wrist to the top of my arm. When the doors were unlocked in the morning members of staff would find my cell floor covered in blood. I found self-harming gave me the release I needed of pent-up emotions and afterwards I actually felt better.

My personality had changed a lot in the first six to nine months I had developed a hard exterior just to survive. But the day came when Polly was being released and going home. She said I could visit her anytime and she gave me her address. I suddenly felt very alone.

Time seemed to drag by until a member of staff asked me to step inside the office. I was told to sit down. "I have some bad news for you Deborah." I immediately reacted, "My name from now on is Toni so that's what I want to be called."

"Ok Toni, well arrangements are being made for someone to take you to see your mum, she is gravely ill."

I went quiet, it was not the kind of news I wanted to hear.

"I am sorry to have tell you this, but your mother is dying."

"Dying?" I repeated the word. "Dying?" I felt stunned. My mother had been sick apparently for some time, but not one person in my family let me know.

"I do not know why you weren't informed Toni, but I believe your father said it was cancer of the liver."

I couldn't speak, I just sat there shocked, and the only thought that went through my mind is that my mum who sang like an angel was dying.

The very next day I was taken to the hospital and went straight to her bed. As I looked at her, I noticed how thin and frail she looked and how much discomfort she was still in, regardless of how much medication the medical staff had given her. Her skin and eyes were yellow and yet she managed to smile just a little. I took hold of her hand and at first there was just silence. But mum broke the silence and said, "Deborah, I want you to know that I love you, I hope one day you will settle down and meet a good man who will take care of you, I want you to be happy."

"Thanks mum;" I felt my throat go tight as I held back the tears,

"I am sorry for everything mum."

"It doesn't matter," mum said, "just promise me you will settle down."

I nodded and told my mum I loved her.

I could see mum had very little energy, how weak she was, a nurse tugged at my sleeve, it was time for me to leave. The visit was short and sweet and one I will never forget. At least we shared a precious moment together.

I travelled back in the car to the borstal without speaking one single word and could not really take it all in, the next morning I got the news that my mum had passed away.

I expected to break down and cry, but I couldn't. I sat in my cell looking into space until a staff member shared that I would be going to mum's funeral, but I would have to be handcuffed. I didn't care. I had not seen my family in nine months, and I felt sorry for my two sisters and brother who must have seen the awful decline of mum's health over a period of time. I heard my father was in extreme grief. When the day of the funeral came, I still had not shown much emotion, I had held it all back and like a dam holding back volumes of water I was ready to burst wide open. As I arrived, I got out of the car and was immediately handcuffed with my hands at the front of my body which gave me some movement being less restrictive.

As I made my way to the chapel a huge gathering of family members were there and many faces, I did not recognize. My mother had chosen cremation and the service went well until the coffin in which she lay went behind the curtain, never to be seen again. It was then that tears came pouring out from all around me. I sat rigid on the front row unable to move as I heard the wailing of broken hearts. When I finally got up to leave the only person who would give me any contact was my brother James. My sisters were not there.

James came up to me and gave me a hug. "Hi sis, he said, how are you?"

I nodded unable to answer as I kept my brother tight to my chest. James shared that our dad had not let Jane and Anne attend the funeral as he felt they were too young. As I looked around me, I could see some of my family members were just staring at me which made me feel uncomfortable. I said goodbye to James and left feeling very empty, drained and sad. The dam had not burst yet and I wasn't sure when it would.

Back in my cell I had never felt so alone as I did then, I felt angry that a mum only 37 years old should die so young, where was the justice in that. I felt angry about being kept in the dark about how ill mum had become, and equally angry that no-one in the immediate family had come to visit me or at least pick up the phone. I became overwhelmed with guilt knowing I had caused a great deal of pain to mum with all my constant bad behaviour, but comforted by the fact that I had spent time with mum in the hospital and there was a peace between us. Now death had snatched my mum away I had no chance of making things right with her, sad because we never had much mother and daughter time together, angry that a twisted evil disease had invaded her body.

During the night the staff kept an eye on me by constantly opening my cell door, "Toni, are you alright? Is there anything you need?"

I just shook my head to indicate no.

Morning came and everyone went about their business as usual. I had no appetite for breakfast and chose to remain in my room. The weight of sadness, confusion, anger and grief filled me up to boiling point and I knew the dam was about to break.

Some of the inmates came to my room to ask if they could do anything for me, everyone knew by now.

"Yes, I answered, 'you can do something for me, I want to wreck this shit hole."

A few of the inmates grinned. I continued, "Did you know I was handcuffed at my own mother's funeral?"

"Ok we are with you, let's do it."

A group of about six of us suddenly went on the rampage, we turned over tables and chairs, we destroyed everything we saw, screaming and ranting our way through the wing, others joined in and some ran in fear, shouting that they wanted 'Off the wing' With a small amount of staff on that day, one left to get help, and the other two members of staff were heading for the office presumably for their safety and to call for help, I ran after them grabbing one of them by the neck and said, "Open the office door now, I want to see all the files."

We found all the files and decided to rip them all up, by the time we had finished the office was a wreck. I tried to get an outside line to ring the press to let them know how angry I was that I was hand cuffed at my mum's funeral but I was unsuccessful, so I ripped the line out of the wall in frustration. The two members of staff that let us into the office had legged it and whatever we could destroy on the wing was destroyed. When there was nothing left to wreck, I sat down wanting to cry, but was unable to do so.

I had no idea what time had passed, but suddenly the main doors of the wing opened up and in front of us we saw several men in white coats. I laughed thinking who are they and what are they going to do. Men in white coats, really? But one by one the men took each one of us to solitary confinement and when it came to my turn, I screamed, kicked and punched until every limb was held tight to stop me from thrashing about. I was carried by four men all the way to the punishment block and was confined there for a whole month.

Inside the cell it was cold and bare, during the day I sat on a raised concrete slab until later in the day when I was given a mattress and one blanket. I was not allowed a pillow or books or even a sheet to lay on. In the corner of the room was a bucket with a lid for me to go to the toilet in. It was then that reality kicked in and I burst into tears, the dam had finally cracked. During my month in solitary, I went through many emotions, sadness, anger, depression, hope-lessness and a feeling of great emptiness, nothing made sense any more, I hated the authorities, I hated life, but I knew I didn't want to remain in confinement. I asked to see the governor to see if she would let me back onto the main wing and when she came to see me, instead of being smart and asking if she would let me out, I picked up the bucket full of urine and chucked it straight at her. I ruined my chances of getting back onto the main wing. After a month had gone by, I finally heard footsteps down the corridor. I was mentally and emotionally exhausted. A meeting had taken place with Dr Berry and it was decided amongst the staff to place me on the psychiatric unit. I am now sixteen and served a year in the borstal. I envisaged staying for the full term of 2 years at this rate.

I was escorted to the psychiatric wing and I was pleasantly surprised how nice it looked inside. It wasn't clinical like the rest of the borstal; in fact, it was quite homely. The walls were freshly painted with warm colours, there were comfortable soft chairs, nice beds, and a large lounge area with a television. Doctor Berry had a strong calming influence on all those present and no more than ten girls were allowed on the unit. It was explained to me that I would have psychotherapy every day and we were going to have quality time with Dr Berry and other staff members to address any emotional needs. My first reaction was that I had no feelings either way about addressing my emotions, I had cried them all out down in solitary, mum was dead, my relationship with my father was dead, family ties were all but severed and my best friend had gone home. So, I said to the staff, that I doubted if I had anything, I could share with anyone.

But they didn't listen, on my first day I had to go to the psychotherapy group meeting. We were all encouraged to talk about our problems, the person who shared about themselves talked and everyone else just listened, they were not allowed to interrupt. After the person had shared, they had to stand in the centre of the floor surrounded by the others and then each person had a say. If the other girls wanted to insult the person standing in the centre or be critical that seemed to be fine, Dr Berry did not interfere, but watched from the side-lines with great interest. Sometimes we had to express ourselves through art instead, talking and counselling was on offer most of the time.

I had been on the unit six months and had very little desire to work on how I felt, I didn't see the point, no-one could take away the pain I felt. I had stopped self-harming, which was an improvement, but my personality had become quite introverted. Every now and then drugs got onto the unit and on one occasion I took some Dexedrine (speed). For my blatant lack of respect for the rules I was sent back down to the punishment block. After several days of being alone with my thoughts I was summoned to the governor's office.

"As you like to be called Toni, I will address you as Toni for the last time, I see very little point in detaining you at Bullwood Hall any longer. You have been with us sixteen months and we have seen very little progress, your refusal to participate fully at the unit with Dr Berry indicates to me and to the staff involved that we are wasting our valuable time. I have made the decision to give you a dishonourable discharge and you will be sent home from the punishment block tomorrow. You will be given back any articles that you came here with plus some money to get you home. Your train ticket will be purchased for you to return home to Brighton. I hope in the future Toni, that you find some stability and happiness, I hope it works out for you."

At first the news didn't sink in, what! they are letting me go? They are kicking me out of borstal? This was not what I expected at all. The idea of going home gave me mixed feelings, but maybe going home was just what I needed. The next day I collected my belongings and boarded the train to Brighton.

Scapegoat

I arrived home to a sad and slightly tense atmosphere. The house seemed lifeless and empty without mum. Apparently, dad had not dealt with his grief very well and had ignored his children. It was like he had disowned them. I had been home for about two weeks and my father blurted out something I never ever expected.

Dad pointed his finger at me, with disdain in his voice he said, YOUR behaviour made her ill and caused her to get cancer, 'YOU, are the cause of your mum's death. All the worry and stress you put her through, it's your fault. You are the black sheep of this family, always have been, YOU caused her cancer do you hear me, get out of my sight'. That day other members of my family were present, and not one of them corrected what my dad said.

In total silence I went upstairs knowing I was no longer welcome. I could hear the words reverberating in my head over and over again, the loss of my mum pained me deeply but to blame me for her cancer made me feel wretched, for some reason I believed every word my dad said that day. As my dad watched me walk out, he never spoke another word to me, not even goodbye. I walked for miles until I came to a main road and got in the first car that stopped to pick me up.

Chapter Five – 3am

My existence was lived out between dark country roads and busy cities. During my travels I remembered Polly's invite to come and visit her anytime, so I decided to pay her a visit. As I knocked on her door, I felt excited to see her, our bond inside Bullwood Hall was strong and I was hoping she would be pleased to see me.

As the door opened, a huge grin appeared on her face. "Oh, my goodness, Toni", she said.

I was thrilled that I had met with such a great response. We hugged and then went inside her flat which was really cool. Her walls were covered in lots of her own artwork, which was amazing; abstract and fantasy art were depicted in vibrant colours. I stood there in awe of such amazing talent.

"You like my work, Toni?"

"I love it Polly, how have you been doing?"

"I am doing ok, behaving, but still doing acid, as you can tell by some of my paintings. But I don't want to ever be locked up again. Are you just passing through, sit down, tell me more about what you are up to?"

We spent the night catching up, drinking a glass of wine and talking about the occult. Polly had a large collection of books on the occult which looked fascinating. I stayed the night collecting my thoughts about what to do next, I knew I couldn't stay with Polly as she had a partner, she was serious about, I felt I would be in the way.

The next day I woke up early and decided to quietly leave without a fuss, I took with me a couple of books, one on the black arts and another on witchcraft, I left a note to let Polly know I would look after them well. I felt a little guilty for taking them, but I didn't think she would mind too much. As I left, I looked behind me to see Polly had done well for herself, she was settled and had matured in many ways, I was pleased for her. I quietly closed the front door and began hitch-hiking. I ended up in Sheffield where I spent my first night sitting on a wall outside a night club watching people go in.

A man close by came and sat next to me.

"Hi," he said, "not seen you here before, my name is Kevin, are you going inside the club?"

"No not really," I replied, "I have no money and I am not dressed for the occasion. I have just arrived in Sheffield so don't really know the place; I am just passing through."

"Not dressed for the occasion? I think you look rather nice."

"Thanks." I was wearing my black velvet bell-bottom trousers and a white cheesecloth top.

"Have you got somewhere to sleep tonight?"

"No, are you offering?"

"Yeah, I suppose I am. I live just outside the city about seven miles. I can see how young you are, under 18 right? If you like you can stop at mine, the company would be nice, no strings attached, I promise."

How lucky was I meeting a man who not only wanted to help but was in need of some company? I needed to get my head down somewhere and it was better than sleeping in a doorway.

"Ok, I will take you up on your offer, thanks."

"Sure, tell me your name, I will look after you."

"It's Toni."

"That's a strange name for a lady. Shall we go then? This is no place for you to be hanging around anyway."

I nodded in agreement and observed him for a moment, he looked like he was in his thirties or more, twice my age, his clothes were smart and was definitely dressed up to go into the night club, well, until he met me. My hope was that he was a genuine person who was as caring as he appeared. I was taking a huge chance getting into a car with a stranger, but then I did that all the time when I hitch hiked everywhere. I suppose this was up a level as I was going back to his home. I decided to take a chance, I was feeling tired of all the travelling.

We arrived at his home in a small village. Kevin explained that he was going through a divorce, but the house was his and that he worked full time in computers. We sat and chatted for hours, I explained a bit of my history, he listened well, and didn't react to anything I said, he made me feel quite comfortable. I shared about my interest in the occult and Kevin said he accepted me as I am and had no intentions of wanting to change anything, that I should just relax and not be concerned or worried.

It took me a while to get use to Kevin's home, but I settled in rather quickly. The house itself was rather boring and plain and after a few days had passed, I asked Kevin if I could paint the walls. Kev didn't seem bothered either way and left me to it each day while he was at work. I cleaned and redecorated a couple of rooms, I did a crazy colour in the kitchen which ended up black and silver and on a main end wall Kevin painted a picture of a traveller walking along a winding country road, he said it reminded him of me.

In the main bedroom I painted the floor and the walls purple. Candles were lit all over the house as I much preferred candles to light bulbs, the light hurt my eyes. Around the house I lit incense sticks, patchouli was my favourite. I was quite impressed Kevin allowed me to basically transform his home to suit me. He was pretty laid back, and that was great.

I had no desire to go back on the road for a while, I liked the fact that I had no worries. A few weeks had passed by and I had immersed myself in reading about magic. I wanted to test it out and made a decision to do an invocation to call up Satan, it was something I took seriously. I spent some time thinking about it, after all, what if it goes wrong, what if I can't handle it, what if Satan truly appears, then what? I had little understanding on such matters, I knew some people in the occult believed in a literal figure, others didn't believe at all. I wasn't sure what I believed but I knew there was another dimension because of my experiences as a child, I wanted to find out more. The basics of witchcraft bored me, I always found myself rebelling against too much structure or mainstream belief systems, So, if I was going to do something that involved the black arts then it may as well be with the master himself. If Satan can bless me with his power and help me to be strong then I would never have to fear anyone or anything, even if my deal with him came at a cost, it would be worth it.

Week after week in my private time I concentrated all my energy on connecting with Satan. I shared from my heart stating that my soul would be his. I didn't bother with a circle of protection or particularly stick to what had been advised, Satan would either come or not. I would lay down everything for that exchange to take place, because I had an opportunity to have Satan share his ancient knowledge and power. I had never felt so bold in veering onto a path limited to a few. I had so many questions and very few answers, I needed answers. After lighting some candles, I would sit down and simply invoke in my own words that Satan appear, I felt my own words and energy was purer than a formula written by someone else. It had to come from the depth of who I was.

When I couldn't sleep, I spent my time walking outside in the dark and when the moon was full, I would sit for hours beneath its light, my heart felt call to Satan never left my lips, Satan was often addressed as 'father'. I had no idea if I had completely lost my marbles, but I felt good, I had a deep curiosity and compulsion to delve deeper. A couple of months had passed, and I had not once slackened in my dedication and intensity to invoke the master to connect with me, giving all reverence and honour to my 'father' continually laying down all the areas of my soul.

Not once did I share with Kevin what I was doing, this was my private time, my personal space. One evening I went to bed around 1.30 am and placed my head down on my pillow, I needed to switch off, my mind needed to wind down. I drifted off to sleep in the hope of waking up the next morning refreshed, but for some reason I didn't stay asleep for long, instead I was violently pulled out of my sleep, I sat bolt upright in my bed and looked at the alarm clock. It was exactly 3am. In the pit of my stomach, I knew something was about to happen. I got out of bed and quietly left the bedroom and slowly went down the stairs, my heart began to pound in my chest. With each step I took I could feel a tugging deep in the core of my being, it was so strong it felt like a magnet had latched onto me.

As I stood in the kitchen the atmosphere had drastically changed it had become heavy and thick, and the temperature plummeted so low it was almost too much to bear. I noticed my breath hung in the cold air, my whole body shaking from the cold. Every bit of space filled up with an energy that pulsated around the room, my chest tightened, and my breathing became much more restricted. I felt insignificant and small and within seconds a searing pain cut through my body and mind removing all sense of reason, my soul screamed inside but I made no noise. I wanted to retreat but couldn't move, fixed to the spot, consumed and overwhelmed by a stature so great that its oppressive presence devoured me from the inside out. I concentrated really hard on taking one small step back whilst at the same time trying to take a deep breath in.

A sense of urgency began to grow in me to leave the room and for the first time I felt an indescribable sense of fear and finality. I knew to try and strike a deal with such a formidable power was beyond my control, I had been arrogant. My mind detached from my world around me as if it was no longer of any significance, my whole being was being forced into a realm that was unbearable for any human to endure. I was either going to die or become insane, either way, I wanted neither. With all the strength I had left I slowly stepped back and screamed out aggressively a resounding NO! Making it clear the deal was off.

I made a concerted effort to get to the bottom of the stairs, I had no desire to look behind me. My body felt like it was bound in lead chains. Madness swirled around inside my head like a raging tornado. As I concentrated all my efforts on getting up the stairs, I looked to the top landing which seemed to be so far away. As I started to climb my ears hurt as the sound of pounding hooves struck the floor behind me, fast and frantic, they smashed down into the ground with determination. I understood immediately this dark creature that I had summoned was still partly in his own dimension, its spirit was continually trying to catch up with my own dimension, and as the two worlds merged closer to each other, the power of its presence grew stronger and the noise of its hooves grew louder. As I neared the top of the stairs a succession of thuds came crashing down, time was running out.

As I opened the bedroom door, I saw Kevin, the colour had drained from his face.

"What have you done?" Kevin shouted.

The thunder of hooves continued pounding the stairs, but had picked up speed in a desperate attempt to fully arrive.

Kevin immediately shouted out, "In the name of Jesus, get behind me Satan."

The words cut into the air with force and authority, Kevin stood strong and did not move from his position, in an instant the sound of hooves retreated and went down the stairs at such a phenomenal speed I could scarcely take it all in.

I sat down on the bed violently shaking. Kevin sat down next to me, grabbed my hand, and shook his head in utter disbelief at what just happened. The dense atmosphere in the house slowly started to lift and some of the coldness had dissipated.

After a few minutes Kevin gained back some composure and said, "I should have burnt your books, we have both been foolish. Did you think, Toni, that perhaps, just perhaps, you were out of your depth? Did you think you could invite evil in and not be overpowered by it without Jesus Christ in your life?"

Kevin was angry. He continued, "What on earth possessed you to summon up Satan? Satan is a powerful fallen angel, a creature who tried to defy God himself, cast down, existing between the earth and the heavenly realms, Satan can only be present in one place at any one time, which is why his pursuit for you was so intense and critical."

After a long pause I asked Kevin a question. "What were those words you spoke, get behind me?"

65

"Toni, the words get behind me Satan are in the bible, it was when Jesus was talking to Peter, Satan was using Peter to stop God's plan, Jesus rebuked Satan and corrected Peter at the same time. It's a long story Toni, I am a Christian, but I lost my faith or so I thought. The pain of divorce had taken its toll on me I suppose. I gave up on God and stopped practicing my faith. But it seems from tonight's experience God has certainly not given up on me or you for that matter. There is no other name more powerful than Jesus, it is the name above all names, and that name has saved us both this evening. The power of Jesus has sent Satan back to his realm."

As we both sat on the bed, a deep calming peace filled the room.

"Kevin, can you feel something?"

"Yes, I can, I believe it is the presence of the Holy Spirit." Kevin knelt down and thanked God as I looked on in total bewilderment. All my shaking had stopped and I knew that we had both been protected. I felt safe, the atmosphere was peaceful, peace was all around us. We never got to sleep that night, we talked until the sun came up.

I realised that the name of Jesus held great power, but I didn't really understand, I wasn't a Christian. The longer I stayed in the house the more uncomfortable I felt until it got to a point that I had to leave. I felt sad and torn about this because although I liked Kevin, I didn't like being in the house anymore. I thanked Kevin for all that he had done for me and wished him the best. Still obsessed with keeping my books, I took them with me and very little else. I seemed unable to let my interest in the occult go even after such a traumatic experience and showed no interest in the Christian faith even though it was clearly obvious that the power of Jesus was far greater than anything I could invoke. I needed to be alone and by going back on the road it would help me take my mind off things. So, we said our goodbyes and I went on my way.

God had not forgotten me

I stood in the pouring rain with my bag of books on the occult and shuddered as the rain drenched my clothes. As the downpour continued, I stood there with my thumb stuck out hoping someone would take pity on me and stop. As I waited, I thought to myself that I must have some kind of self-destruct button firmly lodged in my brain to want to hold onto these books, but I seemed very reluctant to let them go.

Whilst deep in thought a car had pulled over into a lay by leaving its hazard lights on, I was so relieved that I ran to the car and couldn't wait to jump in and get dry. My clothes were stuck to my skin and my long hair looked a complete tangled mess. I looked over to the driver and introduced myself.

"Hi, my name is Toni, thanks for stopping."

'You're welcome," the man responded in a cheerful tone, "I am heading for Portsmouth if that's any good for you. My name is David."

"Portsmouth is fine, don't have any particular plans one way or the other." I jumped in the car and the man drove off down the motorway.

As I looked around the car my eyes came back to the dashboard and on it, I noticed a round sticker, which said, I am the way, the truth and the life. I had no idea what those words meant or who said them, so I asked David.

"What do the words mean on the sticker?"

David smiled and answered, "They are the words that Jesus spoke."

Great, I thought, that name again.

David continued, "What do you believe in then?"

I felt myself tense up before answering the question, "I believe in this," and picked my bag up showing him all my books. "I am aware of the name of Jesus, but I don't want to talk about it."

"I see," says David, "well why don't I tell you more about what I believe and who Jesus is, because Jesus is a saviour to everyone who repents, he doesn't want one soul to perish, including yours."

I nodded and realised I was now stuck in the car going down the motorway with a Jesus freak. David carried on talking, about the miracles Jesus did, how Jesus is alive in people's hearts, my ears were totally battered, and I didn't really understand one word he said, but I did know that his name had great power.

As he continued to share with me not one word sank in, it was like he was speaking in a different language. All I could think about was getting to Portsmouth and getting out of the car. I heard the name Jesus so many times I really thought the man was crazier than me. David finally finished with "Jesus died for your sins and wants to rescue you from the power of darkness, Jesus came into the world as a light."

I finally snapped. "Really, well I believe in the power of darkness, in fact I have had a pretty close encounter recently, darkness has followed me in one form or another for most of my life, so that's all I know, I know darkness more than I know the light."

For some reason I held back on the fact that I had encountered the presence of the Holy Spirit and became a witness to the fact that the name of Jesus sent Satan packing.

I started to feel agitated and asked if the conversation could end. David agreed and shared that we were nearly at our destination.

"I have some friends in Portsmouth Toni, I am quite sure that they would be very happy to help you for a few days. I am sure that you would like to have a hot bath and some food, right?"

"Yeah, ok sounds good to me."

When we entered Portsmouth, David drove to a Methodist church called Wesley Central Hall. It was there that I met a lady called Marie, a deaconess, whatever one of those were. David shared that although they were good Christian people they probably wouldn't be as full on as he was in the car, and that I should take advantage of their help.

Marie's build was petite and delicate, her manner warm and friendly. She seemed very relaxed and easy to approach. Her husband however seemed stern and a bit stand offish, I didn't like him much.

As David said goodbye, Marie and I got chatting and after about 30 minutes her husband butted into the conversation and said, "Marie, I believe this lady needs to see a psychiatrist, she is not well."

"I disagree," Marie stated, "Toni needs our prayers, support and love and I shall take full responsibility."

"Fine, I think it best that Toni stays with you in the flat." Marie smiled and explained the flat was additional accommodation to the house they lived in and was used purely to help others.

Marie took me to the flat which was clean and modern, but very basic. As soon as I sat down on the sofa, I fell asleep. Marie must have just left me there and covered me with a blanket, because that's how I found myself when I woke up the next morning. I had a good sleep and felt so much better. Marie explained that at some point if it was alright with me, that she would like to pray with me. I said yes in the hope that if I complied, I could stay around for a bit. The journey down from Sheffield to Portsmouth was a long one and I didn't want to go back on the road for a while. So later that day I had my first experience of someone praying for me. As Marie prayed it was if I had gone deaf to the words, and each day Marie prayed it was the same, except I felt a churning on the inside of my stomach and felt a little mixed up regarding my feelings. I thought the whole thing seemed a bit pointless, but Marie had something else up her sleeve, she wanted to take me to a meeting.

"Toni, I am not going to pray with you today, we are going to a meeting to meet someone who I think will be of help to you. I don't want you to feel nervous in any way, the lady who is speaking tonight is called Doreen Irvine, she was a Witch but is now a Christian."

"Fine Marie, I will go, sounds interesting if nothing else."

As the evening approached, I must admit I did feel curious. When we entered the hall, it was already buzzing with loads of people.

Marie took me down to the front row of seats and told me to make myself comfortable. I sat down and decided not to look behind me as the throngs of people poured in. The meeting began with singing, hundreds of voices sang out praising God, some people were clapping. I couldn't understand what all the excitement was about. When the singing stopped Doreen told her story about how she was once bound by demons, involved in Witchcraft and lived a sinful life, but then Jesus delivered and saved her. Her story did hold my attention and for once I felt able to relate to someone who not only got caught up in areas of the occult but was now set free from them. After Doreen had finished speaking, I was ushered to the front.

"Toni, let Doreen just pray with you, ok'? She may even have a prophetic word for you."

"A prophetic what?"

"Oh, never mind," Marie smiled, "just wait there."

Doreen came up to me and laid her hands upon my head, she spoke quietly to me and said, "One day you will be wonderfully used." I thought ok then, sounds great, but I have no idea what you mean.

I returned to my seat thinking is that it. How does she know I will be wonderfully used; does she have a direct line to God? When the meeting had finished Marie and I made our way back to the flat. Marie told me not to worry about things, whether I understood them or not, but to hang on to those words and one day I would understand.

The next day Marie came round to pray with me as usual but this time Marie's prayer was a little more aggressive which surprised me. Marie commanded that all spirits of darkness to leave me and through the blood of Jesus Satan's power over my life is broken. As Marie continued in her spiritual warfare, I felt my body go rigid and cold. Around my neck I was wearing a pentagram necklace which abruptly pulled itself in an upward motion then dropped back down, immediately it tightened itself around my neck causing me to choke. I lifted my hand up to release the necklace but as I did it snapped off my neck, falling to the floor.

I screamed out to Marie, "What kind of God do you pray to? Look what your God did to me! My pentagram is lying on the floor broken, your God tried to choke me!"

Marie instantly defended herself explaining that God is not the one that is violent and that I was to remain calm and she would be back with extra support. I didn't like the sound of that. Marie left and so did I. I didn't like what was happening and I had no intention of staying around to find out what would happen next. If God was love God has a funny way of showing it. I could no longer trust God than I could trust people. As usual my failure to face up to things seem to repeat itself often. I didn't realise it then but with no genuine repentance in my heart Satan was staying.

Chapter Six – Halloween

I decided to head to my hometown Brighton and, as soon as I arrived, I went straight into a popular pub which often had live bands playing. With what little change I had left in my pocket I bought myself a beer. I sat down and reflected on the last couple of weeks. As I sat in the pub I listened to the music and tried to chill out, but felt a little edgy and paranoid, as if someone or something was following me. The beer slipped easily down my throat helping me to relax. I had no idea what I was going to do for the evening or where I was going to sleep, but for now I was ok.

As I supped my beer, I noticed a couple standing at the bar, every now and then they would glance in my direction. I gave a half smile and continued to enjoy my drink. As my glass emptied, I noticed the couple had moved and were making their way over towards me. As they both got closer the lady asked me if they could join me as they noticed I was sitting on my own, the man offered to buy me another beer.

I wasn't really in the mood for any kind of conversation, but they struck me as interesting people and I definitely wanted another beer.

The man was rather strange to look at, he was tall and thin, with curly dark hair which receded at the front but was long at the back right down to his shoulders. He had a twisted smile and his hands were pale like his face, his fingers were very long. His clothes hung loosely around him as if they didn't fit properly, to me he looked starved.

The woman had rather plain looks and was much shorter than her partner. She wore a long black velvet dress which matched her black thick hair. Her complexion was also pale, but she looked a lot healthier. As the night progressed, I no longer felt inhibited in any way and enjoyed listening to the music and making small talk. I found out that the man's name was Bill and the lady's name was Pauline, which struck me as rather funny, because their names didn't seem to match their quirky dress code and looks. They had a bit of charisma about them.

They both admitted that they were Witches and understood the left-hand path and those that veer off that path into other areas of magic or occult practices would experience many challenges. They told me that they were happy to chat further about things and that I was very welcome to stay with them at their place for a bit. I wasn't sure at first what to do, they seemed sincere enough, even if they did seem a bit gothic in their taste, but in light of recent experiences at Kevin's home I had mixed feelings. In the end I went with them partly because I needed somewhere to get my head down and partly because I was curious about them as people.

When we arrived at their apartment, I could see it was basic and clean.

"Welcome to our humble abode Toni." Pauline said with a huge grin.

"Thanks for letting me stay the night, I appreciate it."

"Well, if you're happy to sleep on the sofa for the night, we can sort things out better tomorrow and you can decide what you want to do, I expect after a few beers you want to crash."

I slept like a log that evening and in the morning, I woke up with a bit of a hangover.

"Morning Toni,"Pauline said, full of energy, "hope you slept ok."

"Yeah, I slept like a log, but a bit hungover."

"Sorry if I woke you up but I was just putting some books together for you, they are on the table for you to look at when you are ready, I thought you might be interested in them."

I nodded, got up and went into their bathroom to freshen up. When I came out, I sat down and had myself a strong coffee hoping it would kick start my day.

I glanced over at the table and noticed the books Pauline had referred to, I also noticed all around the room on many shelves were a large collection of books.

My first remark to Pauline was, "Surely the books on the table are not all for me, are they'?"

Pauline smiled saying, "Toni, to understand yourself you need to take time out to study. Know your strong and weak points. Forget about being homeless for a while and travelling on the road, settle here with us, face your fears, receive knowledge and learn how to channel that energy of yours."

I liked Pauline so I agreed to hang around for a bit. "Where do I begin?" I asked.

"I want you to start with learning the witches' alphabet so that all your written work cannot be easily deciphered if it fell into the wrong hands. As a student you must train and discipline yourself and understand your true value, understand how the laws of nature work."

"Why are you so keen to help me? Will it help me truly to understand and give me answers to my many questions?"

"Of course, it will help you", Bill said, as he stepped into the room, "and once you can control the power and energy that flows through you, you will be in control of yourself so much better, and your insecurities and fears will go."

I thought about Bill's words and agreed that I did want to have better control over myself and my circumstances; in fact it was crucial to my survival.

I was encouraged to choose a goddess I could identify with and to study the attributes of my chosen goddess and to think about a new name for myself that would be used only in occult circles. It was explained to me as Halloween was approaching that I could join in the celebrations with them and, although they were not a full coven yet, I could be blessed into their circle, swearing an oath of loyalty and secrecy that all that went on in their meetings was to remain with the members only.

It all seemed rather intriguing and to finally have something that I could hold on to that might make sense to me had to be given a chance.

Finally, preparations were made for Halloween, I had only been with them a couple of weeks, but it felt so much longer, Bill explained that the people coming would be wearing robes, but later the robes would be removed. Pauline was busy preparing food and baking cakes and getting the main room ready. There was a bustle of energy everywhere.

After a few people had arrived we formed ourselves into a circle, Bill then spoke out a litany of words as those around me started chanting. I was asked to come forward and Bill sprinkled me with water using my chosen goddess's name, he then asked me to promise never to divulge whatever goes on in the group, I made that promise. Bill then presented me with a gift of jewellery, an amulet, which he also blessed.

As I looked into his eyes, I felt uneasy, he seemed different to me. His voice had changed to a much deeper commanding tone and once more he stated I was never to break the vows I had just made. After muttering to himself he said loudly, "So shall it be."

I was bewildered to say the least, but also felt a little special that I had a sense of belonging. When the ritual had finished the party began. Food and drink were plentiful and tarot cards were laid out on a table if someone wanted a reading.

Bill shouted, "If we are going to have a party then we should do it in style!"

The next thing I see is Bill handing out microdots, small little tablets of acid (L.S.D.). Hawkwind was playing in the background and Bill said, "Everyone, this little drug is the portal to the spirit world, let's celebrate that fact, the veil between our world and theirs is now open."

Bill then grabbed my hand, "Come with me, come and lay down with your high priest and priestess."

I had not heard that reference used at all in the days I had been with them.

As I approached the bed, I felt myself getting high on the acid I had taken. Within minutes we were all naked and Pauline had moved away to allow Bill control. As I lay on top of his thin body, I became aware how dark and unclean his soul was, he mumbled some words and told me that a protective force field had now been placed all around us and nothing could enter it or penetrate it. As I felt my soul join to his I found myself entering his body, I travelled through his blood at a tremendous speed, I could taste his blood in my mouth. My thoughts inside my head were screaming that I wanted to get out, but I couldn't, I was heading one way, inside this man's soul, everything became distorted. A vile taste continued to fill my throat and everything became dark. I struggled to breathe and felt trapped within a malevolent place that sought to torment me. I had no idea how to stop what was happening, I just wanted the torture to end.

I was not sure how much time had passed between losing consciousness and waking up, but I found myself lying on the floor with a blanket over my body. As I tried to make sense of what happened Bill was nearby laughing, and said, "Toni, welcome back, you have just been to hell and back, did you enjoy it?"

I stared at him in total disbelief, if only he knew how dark his soul actually was. I wasn't awake for long as a surge of panic rushed through my body and I blacked out for the second time. When I awoke, I realised no-one had called for any medical help, in fact most of the group had left. I felt something was very wrong and I knew I would never be the same again.

I found my clothes and got dressed, then sat down to gather my thoughts. I found it difficult to get myself together enough so I could leave, I was so distracted and remembered I had taken some acid. For some reason I felt compelled to look up when I did, I saw myself trapped inside an invisible box surrounded by pitch black darkness. I could see myself thumping on an invisible wall screaming for help, but no-one could hear me. I quickly shut my eyes thinking, that can't be me, I can't be in two places at the same time.

I wanted to escape, get out, get away from these people. I realised they didn't really care for me at all. I stopped looking up and tried to think how to get away without being seen. I stood up and walked to where the carpet ended and a small patch of lino began which led to the main exit door, as I looked down the flooring became alive. The coloured lines turned into crazy electrical worms that sent sparks out near my feet, thrashing worms that wanted to hurt me. I found I couldn't step on them, so I lifted my head, took a deep breath and focused on the task in hand and went straight for the door.

As I stepped into the hallway, I heard a voice say, "Where ya going Toni?"

"I don't feel right Bill, something's wrong, in fact I am still seeing things."

I knew I wasn't going to get away that night. I felt so afraid.

"You will be alright Toni, you did have a rather trippy experience that caused you to black out, why don't you rest up."

I nodded in agreement and went to the spare room. I was not going to sleep my brain seemed very much awake and all I could think about was leaving.

The next day came and Bill approached me to remind me that I had made some promises to them to stay loyal. He then spoke in a threatening tone and said, "Let me tell you what will happen if you leave. Have you heard of an astral bell?"

Without waiting for a response, he continued, "Well, it can be used to summon back those who break their promises." He smiled, "The bell will keep ringing until you return or go mad."

He smiled again and then left the room. I shivered inside, these people on the outside seemed sincere, interested, even kind, when I first met them, I thought they were really interested in helping me understand my past and present, but I had been a fool, on the inside they were ravenous wolves that wanted to chew up their prey, spit you out, and rearrange you into something they wanted, at whatever the cost. They wanted to groom me. I began to feel panicky, but I knew they both couldn't watch me forever; I knew I would find a time when I could slip quietly away. But something had altered in the way I saw reality, even though I had come down off the acid I was still seeing things. I felt different, sometimes my body felt numb, as if I wasn't actually in it and I often thought I was going to die, it felt just like the 3am experience at Kevin's as if my soul was being dragged out of my body and I would lose it, but not with the same intensity.

When I looked into the bathroom mirror my face looked disfigured. One moment I saw my face normal the next it changed, my skin had all the colours of decaying leaves and I lost the outline of my face, sometimes my face split into two images, one side that was normal the other distorted. I noticed my eyes were different, one minute normal the next minute I would see another set of eyes, black and sinister, that neurotically darted from side to side, as if looking for a way out. As I started to cry, I immediately muffled the sound as I didn't want anyone to hear me. I had to stay strong and go along with whatever they wanted; my moment would come to run.

That moment did come. A few days later when Bill and Pauline were preoccupied preparing further studies for me and talking about their next steps of how to enlighten my mind, I chose to make haste, although I was not quite under false imprisonment the threat and warnings particularly from Bill were genuine, I was convinced that if I had stayed any longer there was the potential to not be able to get away. Luckily for me the front door was not locked and I quietly left. I shook from top to toe as I made my way out, if either of them had caught me leaving I could not have dealt with the confrontation, I felt too broken. I was just thankful that I had narrowly missed not only being groomed to a place where I probably would not have recognized myself, but I had just avoided a long-term entanglement with some dangerous people. Their intentions were dark, and I couldn't bear to think what else could have happened.

Chapter Seven - Torment

I could think of only one person who was able to help me and that was the man I met and loved when I was fifteen, Paul. My borstal days had kept us apart amongst other things, but I felt convinced that he would help me if I was desperate.

I made my way to Chichester and instead of enjoying the travel and meeting people, my reaction to the environment around me this time was different. Most of the time I felt jumpy, I had to concentrate on not going into a full-blown panic attack. Every now and then I got a flashback and tasted blood in my mouth. I wanted to hide away from the world, I was paranoid that Bill and Pauline would find me, I hated people looking at me for any length of time, I didn't want to mix with people or have conversations, I found it hard to smile yet alone laugh. Life for me had become a real challenge as I no longer felt I could function normally.

When I got to my destination, I found Paul in one of the local pubs, 'Well, well, look what the cat dragged in', he said.

I beckoned him over to the door as I couldn't go inside the pub. I was unable to cope with the noise and had definitely lost what social confidence I had left. Paul stepped outside and immediately gave me a hug.

"Toni, it's so good to see you, been a long time, how are you doing?"

Feeling my body go tense, I pulled back from his embrace.

I broke down in tears unable to share with any kind of clarity about what had happened to me recently. I could see the look on Paul's face and it warmed my heart to see that he still felt concerned about me.

"Toni, take a deep breath and try to calm down, I won't leave you, let me take you home, let's go."

Paul took me by the hand and we slowly walked to his mum's house. I waited outside until I knew I was going to be accepted.

"Toni, you can come in now, mum says it's alright."

Once inside, it took me a while before I felt settled and confident to share about what happened. Paul listened intently while his mum was out in the kitchen making dinner. After I had shared Paul came up with a suggestion.

"Toni, I know someone who may be able to help you. I was in prison once on the Isle of Wight and while I was there, I met a priest named Eddy, he would understand your involvement with the occult, I think it would be good to contact him and get some advice, if possible, some help."

I knew I needed help, so I agreed.

The priest not only responded; we were to meet him at Portsmouth Cathedral where he would perform an exorcism. I was willing to try anything as long as the nightmare would end. All I knew was, I was either brain damaged from having some sort of breakdown whilst on acid or my participation in the occult had affected me in ways I still did not comprehend or maybe it was both. When the time came to make our way to meet the Priest, I was nervous and tired. Paul kept close to my side with his arm around me helping me to feel secure. I had no idea what I was letting myself in for, but what other choice did I have?

We waited outside the cathedral until the priest arrived and let us in. He seemed extremely calm and carried with him a black large bag.

"Shall we go inside" he said.

It was early evening and there no-one else present. Once inside Eddy asked me a question, "Toni, I believe from what Paul has shared with me that you recently spent some time with people who introduced you to the occult and that you participated in a

Halloween celebration which also involved some drugs, is that right."

I nodded. Eddy continued, "Do you know what an exorcism is?"

I shook my head and said, "No."

"Let me explain, you have opened yourself up to occult powers, by the sounds of things these people mixed and mingled their beliefs to suit their needs and it's my job to cleanse you from their influence. We need to break the hold that Satan has on you by renouncing your involvement with such practices. You need to repent of everything you have done in order to be set free, do you understand?"

"Yes, I suppose so, 'I just want to feel more normal."

"Let us get started then."

The priest stood before me in all his vestments, around his neck he wore a purple stole, a band of cloth that looked similar to a long scarf, the stole hung loosely down in front of his chest. He then traced the sign of the cross in the air above me and did likewise where Paul was standing and then lastly himself. He then sprinkled holy water over me and whilst holding a crucifix in front of me he started to pray, first it was the Lord's prayer followed by a much longer prayer, saints' names were invoked and we all answered at the end of each name, a united response 'pray for us.

I was asked at some point during the long-winded prayers to renounce Satan and all his works and to repent of my sinful behaviour. I didn't know what 'sinful' meant, but the priest said that any form of idolatry and practice of the occult was forbidden in the Bible.

The priest then shared about how Jesus exorcised some demons out of people in the scriptures. It was then that I felt afraid, is he saying that I have demons?

As the prayers continued and the priest commanded Satan to leave, I felt extremely uncomfortable, my body was ice cold and deep down I felt a strong resistance to his prayers. I waited and waited until the priest had finished his ritual. I felt much worse than

81

before. I had no idea how much time had passed but I was glad it had ended.

"Toni, I have done all I can for you, we must leave it in the hands of God. I am sorry that I cannot do more for you, but the majority of my work is in the prison, I have to go now."

I nodded, not wanting to talk to him. I felt angry because I knew nothing had changed.

Paul shook Eddy's hand and thanked him while I stood there totally unresponsive.

"Toni," Paul asked, "what's the matter with you, you should have thanked the priest, he has come a long way to help you and he did his best."

I couldn't explain to Paul why I felt the way I did but I knew one thing, I was not free and maybe it was case of a damaged mind rather than demons. I couldn't get my head around it all. I was at least willing to accept help, but I was not sure that was the right kind of help. However, I now felt even more confused because my body remained ice cold and rigid and I had sensations flooding through my body that I could not explain.

Paul had arranged to rent an apartment, so we had some privacy but checked on his disabled mum when he could. I felt utterly drained and depressed and I had no idea what my next steps would be. Perhaps I was simply going mad and would end up in some mental institution.

Over the next few weeks, I just got worse, I heard voices screaming at me to die and every now and then I would hear a bell ringing.

"Paul, can you hear a bell ringing?" I would ask.

Paul then shook his head and said, "No Toni, I don't hear anything."

Paul realised I could not be left alone and decided to get a job as a lorry driver so that I could go on trips with him, his expertise was in welding, but that was laid aside. I became totally dependent on Paul. I hated the way I had become. If Paul left me to go to the local shop for a few minutes by the time he had returned I was in an agitated anxious state. Breathing into a paper bag was becoming a common practice.

I found it hard to communicate and sometimes when Paul had to stop to get food and drink, if he managed to encourage me to go with him into the café, it would always turn out to be a negative experience, I was convinced someone had poisoned my food and I wouldn't eat it.

This caused a lot of tension between us and sometimes arguments. I know I frustrated Paul a lot, but I couldn't stop my reactions. Paul even tried eating the food off my plate to show me it was safe, but I didn't want it. I would snack on things that were sealed in a packet, but that was it.

My social skills had taken a nose-dive and my life had become isolated from the rest of society. I found it difficult being receptive even to Paul and my sleep patterns were all over place, I didn't sleep much. I would cat nap and the rest of the time I would be awake filled with anxiety and strange feelings.

At times I felt my soul being wrenched from my body and I would scream, I would totally detach from myself. Paul would do all he could to pacify me. Paul was beginning to suffer himself, he was drained, had to work to earn some money and look after me at the same time. It was tough for him too.

Paul took me to a doctor who gave me a tranquilizer to help with the anxiety, and it saddened me greatly when Paul took some of my tablets to ease his own stress, at one point he had actually overdosed. Physical contact between each other had become impossible, even a hug triggered me off as I would slip into a void.

Neither of us knew what to do, who to go to, and each day was demanding and stressful to us both, it had a huge detrimental effect upon our relationship.

I thought about death on a daily basis and even when I was sitting next to Paul in the cab of his lorry I would scream out, "I am dying, I can't breathe."

Paul most of time had to pull the lorry over when this happened to spend time with me, calming me down. While we were in Port Talbot doing a delivery, I had another freak out and Paul took me to a hospital, they wanted to detain me explaining they were very concerned for my welfare, but I refused to stay. My crying and strange behaviour happened on a daily basis and poor Paul was showing signs of utter exhaustion. On top of all this happening we both had the shock of our lives when a strange paranormal encounter took place.

Paul had been driving through the countryside, the cab inside was nice and warm and we were listening to music playing through the radio when all of a sudden, the temperature dropped dramatically and the music stopped.

"Oh, what now," Paul said, "that's the last thing we need."

"Paul, I am scared, something is not right, look Paul, there is a man in the middle of the road waving us down."

"Bloody hell! Why is he standing in the middle of the road?" Paul slowly applied the brakes and hoped he could stop in time. Paul started shouting, "Get out of the road you stupid man."

"Why won't he move Paul?"

I covered my eyes with my hands not wanting to look anymore. Paul continued to apply the brakes, but it was too late, we both heard a thud against the lorry and the man's body hit the front of the cab. The lorry came to a stop and with the engine still ticking over Paul looked at me with dread in his eyes. Neither of us could believe what we saw, and it made no sense at all.

"Why wouldn't he get out of the way?" Paul got out of the cab and walked to the rear of the lorry, I joined him.

We both looked down the road and couldn't find anyone. Paul went back to the lorry and got a torch. As we continued to search for a body on the road, in the hedges, anywhere, no-one was found.

"I don't believe it," said Paul, "a body can't just disappear, we both saw him, didn't we? Where is he? This is bloody unbelievable."

I could see Paul was shaken and the colour had drained from his face.

"I told you Paul, something wasn't right."

We both looked one more time just to make sure scouting the area thoroughly, but nothing.

We got back into the cab and instantly the music came on and the heater started working.

"Paul, everything's working again. Can we get out of here, that was not a man, but a ghost, please, let's just go."

Paul nodded and we drove off, both shaking, both still in shock. Paul continued lorry driving to earn an income and we had no more repeated episodes. I was convinced that Bill had something to do with it but kept those thoughts to myself. So many feelings were packaged tightly inside me it led me to take the next bit of drastic action. As Paul was driving down the motorway in the early hours of the morning out of the blue, I grabbed the steering wheel and screamed at Paul, "We must all die!"

The lorry veered out of control but not enough to flip us over, Paul managed to correct the swerve and we were fortunate that no one was in the way at the time. Paul was horrified at my actions, now he had the added concern that I wanted to kill myself. I tried to tell him it was the voices in my head and that I didn't want to die.

In my desperation somewhere deep down I started to call upon the name of Jesus. In my head my thoughts went like this "If you are real Jesus like everyone says you are, I need your help, I really need your help."

I repeated this cry inside my head several times a day hoping for some kind of miracle. I had no idea if Jesus could hear me or not, but it made me feel better and bought me some sense of peace.

Chapter Eight –Saved by the Morning Star

After the failed attempt of wanting to end the voices in my head Paul took me to the local doctor's. I managed to share snippets with the doctor and had no idea how much sense I made to him, but I did manage to share something. The doctor said that I had symptoms of paranoid schizophrenia. I had heard that label before from granny Mable, that my uncle had it, the doctor explained that taking L.S.D was a major contributory factor. I was given Largactil tablets that would help me with my symptoms.

I took the tablets for a few days but threw them in the bin as they made me feel even more confused and lethargic. At eighteen I should be enjoying life but instead I was now seen as someone who had a mental illness. I didn't want to be drugged up; I needed a miracle. I couldn't accomplish the smallest of tasks, going to the shops was a nightmare for me. As I walked along the pavement I would cling to a wall and keep my head down. Most of the time I didn't make it to the shop because I hit panic mode and would run back home. If I was left for too long, I couldn't cope, I was afraid of my own shadow and felt constantly overwhelmed by life. Social interaction was non-existent. I felt paranoid about people especially if they looked at me, because I was afraid, they could see my madness.

Paul decided to take a bit of time off work. It was our first day together, I was sitting on my bed trying to relax to music and Paul was at the other end of the room reading a newspaper.

All of a sudden, a strong surge of fear coursed through my body, it wasn't the first time I had felt such fear, at first, I tried to ignore it. Then it happened again, like a gigantic wave it washed over me drowning out what little peace I had. I quickly looked over at Paul desperate for his attention but couldn't speak. Things started to happen fast; it took all my strength to contain myself to keep some form of control. I was going completely mad as all normality went out the window. I became engulfed in the hellish experience of my mind separating from my body. With my hands on my head, I started to rock backwards and forwards on the bed.

At first, I thought I was going to faint as the room began to darken and any audible sounds in the room became a distant murmur. As I pushed down on my head my hands went straight through, shocked, I screamed out in utter horror, before I had a chance to work out what was happening, it just got worse, my hands then touched my brain, which had turned to plastic. I had no idea if this was some sort of horror flashback from my acid days or sheer madness had filled my mind, but I was crushed by the sheer enormity of my own anguish. From the very deepest part of my soul and in utter desperation I burst out in a loud scream, "JESUS CHRIST HELP ME!"

With deep conviction I screamed out the name of Jesus again and again, as my soul became exposed with all its ugly scars and pain, voices surged through my mind one upon the other competing to see who would be the loudest, my sense of self no longer existed, hell had cracked wide open, its grip squeezing every drop of sanity and life out of me. No priest, or doctor, or medication could help me now, I felt damned as my mind began sinking into an abysmal dark hole, I cried out one more time, "JESUS CHRIST HELP ME!"

This time I was heard. In the midst of all the terrifying screams, love penetrated my soul as quick as lightening striking the earth, a graceful gentle presence removed all desperation, compassion and mercy knew no bounds. Every tension was eased, every tormenting voice hushed into silence, as strong hands reached down to a hopeless soul, hands that lifted me out from the bowels of hell and carried me to the mercy seat of heaven. The raging storm of madness that filled my mind had become still. Within seconds a deep peace gave me back for the first time in a long time a form of stability and normality I had not known since my childhood. I knew in an instant that what had occurred was life changing. I felt whole and complete wanting nothing more than the presence of Jesus, his love encased itself around me like an armour fit for a thousand gladiators. Oblivious to my surroundings I sat like a small child in complete trust to a wondrous love that had filled me up and locked me in. As I soaked up this tangible love that had put my life back together, I knew I was freed from the chains of doom and hopelessness, death and madness, torment and pain, I remained in peace not wanting it to end.

Paul approached me and asked me if I was alright. I had no idea how to explain such a wonderful moment, but I did say this, "Paul, when I screamed out the name of Jesus, when I called his name, he answered me, Jesus is real, did you feel anything?"

"Yes, Paul responded, I did feel something, I can see you are at peace, but I don't understand."

"Nor do I, all I know is, that when I called Jesus from the depth of my heart, he heard me and he came."

For the rest of the day, I enjoyed a blissful peace. Feeling normal was just amazing, if the doctor's diagnosis of me was correct that I had paranoid schizophrenia I don't believe I had it anymore. If it was demonic, whatever was hounding me had gone. I could look into a mirror without any distortions. I stopped smoking as I had no desire to smoke. I had no desire to drink. Later that evening I heard a knock on the door, it was a nun collecting jumble for the local convent to raise funds, I don't believe this was a coincidence. I invited the nun in so that I could share with her what had happened. I thought if anyone could answer my questions, she could.

The nun introduced herself as Sister Lelia. She explained and quoted from the Bible from Acts 4 verse 12 that there is salvation in no-one else. God has given no other name under heaven by which we must be saved. And that everyone who calls upon the name of the Lord will be saved, (Romans 10 verse 13) and that is what has happened to me. I was saved. I was so thankful that it had been explained to me, understanding the depth of God's love for me while in such a state left me in awe. Everything had changed. I was loved back to wholeness, I had a future, and I knew that nothing in this world or beyond this world could separate me from my Saviour Jesus Christ. To this day I cannot grasp how merciful God is, it cannot be measured.

2 Peter 1 verse 19, 'until the day dawns, and Christ the Morning Star shines (or rises) in your hearts.'

Jeremiah 10 verse 6, 'Lord, there is no-one like you! For you are great, and your name is full of power.'

Colossians 1 verse 13, 'for he has rescued us from the kingdom of darkness and transferred us into the kingdom of his dear Son, who purchased our freedom and forgave our sins.'

Part Two

Chapter Nine - Domestic violence and persecution

After my rather dramatic conversion to Christianity Paul and I rented a private house in Portslade in Sussex. Paul had found new employment as a manager for an American company selling electrical equipment. Sadly, a rift had opened up in our relationship. Paul reacted with disdain to my becoming a Christian and this saddened me immensely. I tried to not show my enthusiasm quite as openly, knowing that the change that had occurred in me would have impacted Paul in ways I needed to understand. On returning from a visit to the convent with Sister Lelia I was met with a very grumpy reaction.

"What's happened to you? Are you turning into some kind of religious nut?"

"No, of course not, I was just visiting Sister Lelia, she has become a good friend."

"You spend a lot of time at that convent." Paul snapped, "Has that become more important than me?"

I found it childish that a fully grown man had become jealous and competitive of me spending time with nuns or God. I tried to reassure him that he had not been forgotten at all.

"Paul, you know that I love you, but my Christian faith is part of who I am now, you were there when it happened and you can see how different I have become, how much I have changed."

"You have changed too much. I want my old Toni back."

"Paul, the old Toni has gone, I don't ever want to go back."

Paul went quiet. In my heart I had hopes of Paul arriving at a place where he would accept my new-found faith instead of fighting me on it. I had already confided in Sister Lelia who had advised me to pray and be patient.

As time passed, I continued my visits to the convent and eventually came under instruction to become a Catholic. I was given a small yellow book called 'The Thoughts of Jesus Christ' and was told to read it. I was buzzing with excitement but felt I had to hide that excitement so that I did not upset Paul. From my biblical studies I could see that a couple of things were not right, firstly, I was living with a partner but not married and secondly, I had fallen in love with someone who still did not believe and as the scriptures put it, I was unevenly yoked to a non-believer. Both these areas bothered me. In order to put one of them right I plucked up the courage and suggested to Paul that we should get married because I loved him and that in God's eyes it would be better to marry than stay as we were. Paul's reaction was unexpected; he not only agreed to marry me, he said that as long as we compromised and we married in a church of his choice, then that would be fine. I had the distinct impression he was not keen on the Catholic church.

I agreed and arrangements were made for us to be married in a Methodist church in Hove and we busied ourselves with our wedding arrangements. I found, in the centre of Brighton, a shop that sold a beautiful hooded dress with Mari bone feather. The feathers went all around the hood, around the cuffs and the hem of the dress. It was a perfect winter wedding dress. I was informed that my dress would be ready in six weeks. A surprise was waiting for me when I got home. Paul told me to look out the window and said, 'See that gold Jag, that's ours, it's for our honeymoon'. I was so excited that everything was coming together and that the tensions between us were no longer there. As a young Christian woman of 19 years, I had everything I wanted. When the day of our wedding arrived, we had a small number of friends which included Sister Lelia. I invited my dad to come to the wedding to give me away, but he refused, my attempts to bridge the gap and be forgiving didn't work. A man I knew who was a journalist gave me away instead.

The Methodist minister Rev Peters on the day did a great service for us all. After the ceremony we had a small reception back at our house with food and drink and a few wedding gifts displayed on a table for us to open. When we said our goodbyes and thanked everyone for coming, we stepped outside to see the ground laden with thick snow, the Jag gleamed in the cold frost. We both jumped in the car and couldn't wait to get away for our honeymoon. I tried to hide the sadness about my dad not coming but Paul had picked up on it. "What's wrong Toni?" Paul asked.

"I am just thinking about my dad, I thought on such an important day he would have made the effort to come and give me away."

"Toni, your relationship with your dad or lack of it has been damaged for a long time and to top it all you know that your dad never really liked me, did he?"

I nodded in agreement. "I want to take him some wedding cake."

"Why? just because we have got married it doesn't mean his attitude will change."

"Maybe your right Paul, but I need to try, I know what my dad is like, but I just want to find some kind of peace between us."

"Ok Toni lets go if that's what you really want."

As we arrived at my dad's house, I asked Paul to remain in the car. I knocked loudly on the front door.

As the door opened, I noticed my dad looked a little embarrassed.

"Dad, I am sorry you felt you couldn't attend the wedding, I just came to give you some wedding cake." I looked at my dad and waited for a response or even some kind of apology. Instead, he just ushered me in to the hallway.

"Well, you know how life is Deborah, I am just too busy."

I hadn't heard the name Deborah for a very long time. I thought quietly to myself, 'too busy' what type of excuse was that?

I felt uncomfortable as a thick silence centred itself between us.

"Well dad, I will be going now, enjoy your cake." I had no more words left to say. I placed the cake gently into my dad's hands and walked slowly away. In my heart I wanted to hear my dad say something, anything, but nothing.

A tear came to my eye as I opened the door and shouted back, "goodbye." As I got into the car I burst into tears as waves of pain and confusion robbed me for a moment of any joy I had been feeling.

"Come on Toni," Paul said, "let's go, we can talk later."

After a week away in a secluded hotel, life went back to normal. Paul returned to work and I became the proud housewife taking great care of our home and wanting to please Paul. Each day I would have a quiet time of prayer and study, and sometimes I would write out the scriptures onto pieces of paper made to look like a scroll and place them on the wall. The scriptures had only been up a few days and Paul decided to voice his opinion.

"What is this?" pointing to the scrolls.

"It's just a few lines of scripture Paul, I thought they would look nice on the walls and it gives me encouragement to read them."

Without another word Paul walked over to the wall and ripped all of them down. I sat there stunned. But his next step went too far, he picked up my Bible and started ripping the pages out.

"What are you doing?" I shouted. Paul's face looked angry, page after page was ripped out and thrown down onto the floor.

"That's what I think of your God." shouted Paul. Just over a week ago Paul was completely different, how could Paul change so quickly.

Paul then walked over to the silver cross that was given to me from the convent, he pulled it off the wall and let it crash to the ground. This display of rage was incomprehensible, and I had no idea what to do about it. He walked out of the room and seemed satisfied with himself.

After I had allowed the dust to settle, I tried to talk with Paul.

"Paul, is there anything troubling you? do you want to talk?"

"No Toni I am just tired."

"TIRED?" I shouted back, "I tell you what Paul, I am tired of trying to please you, I am tired of tip-toeing around you, I am tired of your

95

anger, since we have come back off our honeymoon you have been distant and less loving. I don't want sex with you, it's banned." My remarks to Paul had surprised even me.

A huge fist hit me straight on my face breaking my nose. I reeled back as I heard the bone break and blood shot out gushing everywhere. Pain spread through my face and within a short space of time I had two black eyes and a swollen cut top lip as well.

Paul grabbed my arm and dragged me to the car and took me straight up to our local hospital. The x-ray confirmed I had a broken nose and I was given some pain killers and sent home. When we got home, Paul cradled me in his arms and apologized several times.

Later, Paul made it very clear to me that the topic of Christianity was banned, he became more dominant as I became more passive, sinking into my own shell. I didn't have it in me to fight back. The only reprieve I got was when he was at work. I felt such loyalty to Paul who had been so faithful to me, now it was my turn to be faithful to him. I was not sure how much I could take of his moods or his anger and from that day of him breaking my nose things had changed drastically. It was like living with Jekyll and Hyde. As I healed, I had my doubts as to whether I should have married Paul, I had no idea he would be violent. There were no signs of violence before. Since getting married it seemed I was now his possession to do what he liked with.

On one occasion Paul came home from work and as soon as he entered the kitchen he stood there and stared at me with such intensity it unnerved me. I had just turned off the gas after boiling the kettle when he came at me in such a threatening way I reacted in fear and picked up the kettle and threw it at him. As the kettle flew towards him Paul managed to send it flying through the air with one kick.

"I am going to kill you!" he screamed.

I knew he meant it as I looked into his eyes they were filled with coldness. Within seconds both his hands were around my neck. As his grip got tighter, I prayed quietly inside my mind asking Jesus to spare my life. Paul was shouting at me, "You and your bloody Christianity." The pressure inside my head was unbearable, I could no longer breath and my temples were bulging. It was then I sank into darkness and my body went limp. I had no idea how long I had remained unconscious on the floor for, but I realised much to my relief that I was still alive. I burst into tears and slowly got to my feet.

Shaking and weak I glanced around, but Paul was nowhere to be seen. I was afraid he would finish the job and decided not to hang around, I went straight to my neighbour who was elderly but very kind. I explained what had happened and my neighbour wanted to call the police.

"No, it's ok, don't call the police", I croaked.

We both sat in the kitchen on stools looking out across the back yard into my kitchen. As I continued to stare, I noticed Paul returning with the Methodist minister, they both stood in the kitchen having a discussion, so I quietly opened a window and listened to the conversation.

"I don't understand Rev Peters I honestly thought I had killed my wife, she stopped breathing, where is she?"

"I am sure Toni will return Paul; you are going to have to be patient."

My elderly neighbour squeezed my hand and asked me what I was going to do. I thanked my neighbour for all her help and decided to be brave and go back.

As I made my way through the back gardens, I opened up my kitchen door and stood there trembling. Rev Peters came up to me and gave me a huge hug and ushered me upstairs.

"Come with me Toni, I am sure you are still in a state of shock. Let us all sit down and see what we can do to sort this out."

Rev Peters then asked Paul a question. "Why did you do it Paul?"

At first Paul didn't answer, he just stared at me, and then he looked over to the vicar whilst pointing his finger at me and said, "I hate God, SHE, has become a stench in my nostrils!"

97

I couldn't believe my ears; I was a stench in his nostrils. Paul was actually quoting from the scriptures and he didn't even know it. (Isaiah 65: v5)

"Listen Paul," said Rev Peters, "You cannot kill your wife's faith, why are you so jealous?"

Paul went quiet, I knew this was just the tip of the iceberg. Something didn't feel right. There was a lot more going on and I really didn't know Paul as well as I thought I did. Trust between us had now eroded to a much lower level.

Rev Peters continued, "How can you hate God when you say you don't believe in him? Why attack the woman you love?"

"Don't know." answered Paul.

"Look I am here for you both, I married you, and you must both work on your marriage, and Paul, you cannot be violent to your wife, this must stop."

Paul looked over at me and apologised again, "Toni, I am so sorry, I really don't know what came over me, it will never happen again, I promise."

Rev Peters got up and told us we could ring him any time and left us to sort things out. When he left, I felt uncomfortable, how could I fight off a man who was six foot three and weighed fifteen stone.

For a while, things were calm, but I found I could not relax, it was like I was waiting for another thing to happen. We had gone out for a couple of evening meals and we both worked a little on our relationship. I noticed though it didn't take much to rattle Paul's cage as he seemed to want to be in control all the time. A minor argument developed when I said I wanted to visit Sister Lelia at the convent. As soon as I mentioned the convent his cold angry stare had returned. I didn't go in the end just to keep the peace. I tried to show an interest in his hobbies; he liked playing cricket which I thought was so boring, but I went to his cricket matches and watched him play. I went to the super league darts matches and watched him enter competitions, Paul was extremely good at darts. I tried to give him what support I could. I started to doubt myself.

Maybe I was a bit of a religious nut, maybe my passion for Jesus needed to calm down a bit.

As the evening drew in, I decided to go to bed early and relax, hoping for some me time, but Paul followed me to the bedroom. As soon as I got into bed Paul decided to get on top of me and pinned both my arms down. Out of the blue he said, "I don't want to hear about religion and the convent."

Just above the bed hanging on the wall was a small crucifix that Paul had not taken down. As I lay there Paul released my arms and with his right hand, he took the crucifix off the wall, holding it tightly over my chest like a knife, with knuckles turning white, he said through gritted teeth, "You know that I love you don't you?"

I nodded. I had to remain calm. His behaviour was like something out of psycho.

"Yes Paul, I love you too." hoping my answer would pacify him.

"Yet," Paul continued, "I am angry with you right now, so angry that I just want to stab you with YOUR Jesus, right through your heart, I do love you, you know that I love you. It's good for YOU that I love you, although, sometimes I hate you. I don't want to argue with you Toni, it's all got to stop."

Wow, none of what Paul had just said made any sense at all. His behaviour was erratic, how could he threaten me and tell me he loved me at the same time?

I realised that to disagree with Paul now would not be wise.

"I agree Paul, we don't have to argue, just put the crucifix down," I pleaded, "PLEASE."

Paul stared back at me for a few minutes, it felt like hours, and then he slowly put the crucifix back on the wall. Confused but extremely relieved I turned over in my bed and shut my eyes.

That night Paul hugged me and said, "You know as a Christian you are to forgive me" and then turned over and went to sleep.

On top of everything that was happening I found out Paul had recently lost his job, due to fraud. It's not that we needed extra money, but it seemed Paul had not been honest at work or with me, finally his crime came before the court. I found out not only was he being dishonest at work, he was gambling on the horses and greyhounds. We had been married a year and it had been a tough year, but it was about to get tougher, Paul was being sent to prison.

I can honestly say that with Paul in prison I was able to relax. I had my own space to think for a while, but I also felt very sad indeed. I felt as always that I owed it to Paul to try and work things out. I decided to go chat with my friend Sister Lelia. We all agreed rather than me being left alone in the house feeling sorry for myself I was to go and live and work with the nuns in a nursing convent home in Littlehampton. The mother superior would train me in auxiliary nursing and give me bed and board. I thought this was a good idea. When I arrived, I noticed the building was very large, with three floors. Inside it was beautiful, highly polished wood flooring enhanced the entrance and the standard of cleanliness was excellent. I settled in with ease and couldn't wait to get to work.

My day started at 6am followed by benedictions at 7am, breakfast and then work. I attended mass daily and in between my nursing training I cleaned the rooms and corridors, it was hard work. I was advised that I could leave the convent after work but had to be in at 9pm. I found out that nuns were human too, they had tempers, worked hard, had a sense of humour, and were dedicated to their elderly people who they cared for, and it goes without saying they were dedicated to their religious beliefs.

All the nuns had different personalities, we had the flying nun who would jump on a moped and with her habit flapping in the wind, she would take off like a bat out of hell. She made me laugh, there was nothing sedentary about her. I also remember the nuns who worked hard in the kitchen and sometimes when things didn't go right, the pans also went flying. And then of course there were the patients all of whom had their own large private room. They all had beautiful rooms with many of them bringing their precious treasures with them. I would often sit with them and listen to their stories of how they grew up and the challenges they faced.

Mr. Hayden was one of my favourites who kept wanting to go to the seaside. In his pyjamas he would often take himself to the lift and leave the building and several members of staff would be out looking for him. Caring for the most vulnerable in society helped me appreciate life and I was truly thankful for the opportunity to work in a nursing convent. In my quiet times I often thought about Paul and if he was learning any lessons in life. I had a decision to make as to whether I should save our marriage.

As a Christian I had taken my vows seriously, as a person who had lived with a complex bully, I had become a little broken. Divorce was not an option to take lightly. My faith in Jesus Christ had not wavered in fact I believed he kept the grim reaper from my door, I had no idea what Paul would be like on release or if he had changed for the better, but a year had passed very quickly and it was now time to meet with Paul.

Paul actually came to the convent on his release and I waited with mixed feelings. I had known Paul since I was fifteen and now in my early twenties it was not so easy to just walk away. When Paul arrived, we went into a room to discuss our situation.

"Hi Toni, you look great," Paul said, 'I have missed you so much. I am not sure how you still feel about me, but I would really like to try again, if you will have me back."

I felt moved by his words. "To be honest Paul, I am not sure how I feel, but one thing I do know is that when I married you, I meant every word."

"Me too Toni, let's give our marriage another go, we could have kids and be a family, have a new beginning."

"Paul, I would love to have children, I suppose my greatest concern is your temper. I don't know what you are like anymore, we have been apart for a year."

Paul nodded, "I understand Toni, but I have calmed down loads, let's do this, start again somewhere else, give me a chance to prove myself."

"And what about me going to church, being a Christian, is it going to be a problem?"

"Honestly Toni, I just want to be with you, you can go to church, whatever you want."

"Ok well, where are we going to live'?

"Don't know," answered Paul, "why don't we stick a pin in a map and see where it lands and wherever it lands, we will live there."

Paul smiled at me and gave me a huge hug. I felt a warm bond develop between us and decided to have some courage and try again.

"That sounds like a crazy thing to do Paul, but let's do it."

The pin landed in Norfolk.

I said my goodbyes to the Mother Superior and all the sisters, it was hard leaving them all, I was given a work reference and the rest of my pay and savings, I felt a big chunk of my heart was in that nursing home. It was a great experience and one I would not forget. As I waved goodbye, I felt tearful, I really would miss everyone. With my savings and pay and Paul's savings we had enough money to find a house to live in which was in a country village not far from the town of Swaffham.

I got a job working for Thetford social services as a home help. I cycled everywhere to keep fit and loved my new job. Paul did some welding and driving jobs and for a while everything was perfect. On my 21st birthday I was expecting our first baby. As my belly grew, I loved the fact that new life was growing inside me and feeling the baby's first kick was great. I found myself talking and singing to my belly most days. I was happy. I worked all through my pregnancy until I could no longer ride my bike because my bump had got so large. So, I happily stopped working and put my feet up, resting my swollen ankles.

When I went into labour Paul had just got in from the pub after going out with his mates and was pretty drunk. When my waters broke, I had to convince him that I hadn't wet myself I was in labour. We got to the hospital and to everyone's surprise Paul fell asleep in the corridor on a long seat and started snoring. The nursing staff tried to wake him up, but it was no good, he was out cold. So, labour happened without the support of my husband.

Sarah was born five weeks early and had lost a little weight due to be jaundiced. Sarah was placed in the special baby unit at King's Lynn hospital until her feeding improved and the jaundice was dealt with. She was beautiful, with thick dark hair and I felt confident all would be well.

As Paul continued to work, I became the busy mum, my only concern was Paul had begun drinking and stayed in the pubs a lot, playing darts and meeting with his friends. I decided to go with the flow and concentrate on raising Sarah and grow vegetables, I kept myself very busy. In the village there was only one bus a week, because transport was non-existent at the weekends the priest would come out to see me bringing communion.

Our home was old, in the kitchen was a Rayburn oven where I boiled the nappies in a huge pan. In every room in the house there was a fireplace and I was more than happy to keep the fires burning in the winter months. I quite liked using a chain saw to cut my own logs. I had heaps of energy and was used to hard work after living with the nuns for a year. I even polished all the copper pipes in the house.

Eight weeks had passed and to my delight I had fallen pregnant again. With any pregnancy, I planned things well in advance due to the fact the hospital was 25 miles away. I wanted a large family and my second child this time was a boy called James. It was a difficult birth with the umbilical cord wrapped around my son's neck twice. On delivery, James was badly bruised and had breathing difficulties from the start, in fact for a while he stopped breathing. He was rushed straight off to the special care unit and I was told later that he was an asthmatic. Everything was going well and Paul on the odd occasion got a little controlling over small things. About eighteen months had passed when I fell pregnant with my third baby – wanted just as much as my other two. I loved having babies, but I knew in time I would have to give my body a rest. I was six months into my pregnancy when Paul gave me some unexpected news and my happiness bubble burst.

"I am leaving you," he said, "I have met someone else and I think I love her."

I was devastated. I screamed back at him. "You mean to tell me that while I was carrying our baby you have slept with another woman? You have committed adultery?" I burst into tears feeling physically sick, how could he betray me like this.

Paul went upstairs and started packing and with a quick sorry, he left. Paul's fling lasted two months and he came back begging for me to forgive him.

"Come on Toni, you are the Christian in the family, you have to forgive me."

Even though he broke my heart I felt powerless, I did forgive him and thought how much the children would need a father. I hated myself for being so weak and asked him was it because I had lost some of my figure that he wasn't so attracted to me anymore. He simply said, "I am still attracted to you, I have no excuse for my behaviour, it won't happen again."

I simply resigned myself to trying again, I didn't want any arguments or debates, I just wanted things back to normal. Our third baby was born a little girl named Jenna and it was the quickest labour I had, just four hours. I held her in my arms thanking God for this precious bundle of life.

A year later I had my fourth child Catherine who was the heaviest, almost 10lbs and just as beautiful. I felt so blessed to have such beautiful children. I had never practiced birth control and felt no desire to start, but four children were enough. Paul decided that the best way forward was for him to have a vasectomy, that way everyone was happy.

With four children under the age of five I was a pretty busy mum, in the summer the kids loved making mud pies out in our large garden. One of the funniest memories was when I left Sarah for two seconds and she ended up in the coal bucket licking coal. Yuk! It didn't seem to affect her.

As we had outgrown the house, we decided to buy a property which was based in Thetford. Being less isolated I had the chance of meeting more people. Paul over the last couple of years had remained the family man and seemed to be doing well, we still had the odd argument which was mainly over how the children should be raised. I felt Paul was too bullyish with regards to discipline, and he often picked on James who was a sensitive young boy with a gentle nature. Most of Paul's comments were negative instead of positive and Paul seemed to ignore my concerns. Over time Pauls control escalated and he would often say to the kids "Do this or else." or "Do you want to be smacked?"

We were all becoming more aware of his dominant moods and a little fearful.

Paul enjoyed being the lord of his manor and I was beginning to dislike him. He would often shout instead of talking at a normal level and I couldn't do anything right. I was told "You are the woman, it's your job, you are the weaker sex so that makes you less intelligent, only good for being in the kitchen and so on."

 At times he would pin me up against the wall by my neck and say, 'Get things right you stupid bitch'. It didn't take much to upset him, I was too soft with the kids, the dinner was crap, there was always something to criticise me for.

I found great comfort in my faith at this time and in being a mum to my kids. When Paul was working away, I loved being with my kids. We even got a puppy and named him Rambo, a black Labrador. We all loved him. At the back of our house was a small park and a section of woods where the dog could go, and the children could play. It was perfect. Having been isolated for some time I hadn't met many people at all, so I decided I would step out and join a local church. I really liked Father Patrick and it made all the difference meeting up with others and socializing. The kids were also much happier when dad wasn't at home being the dictator.

Chapter Ten - Demons

As the days passed, I became increasingly anxious about how strange I felt. It all began one Sunday when I was attending mass. I sat at the back of the church during the service and all I could feel was anger. I was so angry I found it hard to control my thoughts as my mind began to fill with abusive words aimed directly at Father Patrick. I wanted to walk straight down the aisle and slam the Bible into his head. I knew I was tense about things at home, but this was not me and totally out of character. I wanted to destroy everything inside the church until there was nothing left. One Sunday I plucked up the courage to tell Father Patrick.

"Toni, this may be repressed anger with all the difficulties you have had with Paul, maybe you also blame God?"

"No Father, I don't think so, I don't feel right. I made my choices; I don't blame God."

"I will pray for you Toni. If how you feel continues to be a problem, come back to me and we will continue to talk some more."

I went back home unconvinced.

Little by little things began to happen. I started to hear for the very first time the odd voice. It didn't feel like it was coming from inside my head, it was outside, a loud voice that shouted my name. It was so loud it made me jump. At night-time my dreams became disturbing. I would see strange creatures that would either attack me by biting my flesh or by cutting my skin with their claws, sometimes they would assault my body sexually. I would cry out and try and fight these hideous creatures off, but I felt paralysed and couldn't do anything about it. I couldn't move, I couldn't wake up properly, and there was this heavy crushing weight upon my

106

chest making it unbearable. Every now and then I would feel a presence in the room but not see anything.

Why was this happening now? Since the day of my salvation in over ten years I had not touched any drugs or drink so what was the cause? I was not alone in my strange experiences either, my daughter Catherine saw something in our house. She saw something in the hallway and screamed out, "It's touching me mummy."

When I asked Catherine, what was touching her she said that it was green, large, with hair all over its body. She cried hysterically and it took quite a while for her to calm down.

I gathered my other children together and asked them if they had seen anything strange, the answer I got was, "No mummy, apart from your face, sometimes your face changes."

My heart sank, my children didn't see me as normal anymore. I knew I felt different but had no idea my face seemed different to my children.

That night I didn't sleep at all and went to see Father Patrick the next day. I shared everything with him and mentioned more of my history so that Father Patrick could have a clear picture of the whole situation.

"What shall we do Father Patrick?"

"Toni," he replied, "I think what is needed is an exorcism, but to do that I will need permission from my bishop, this type of thing takes time because I need to get a special dispensation order."

Memories quickly returned from the past when a priest attempted to do an exorcism or deliverance in Portsmouth Cathedral and nothing happened and in fact, I got worse.

"Why can't you pray with me now Father Patrick, I need help now, I am scared, my children are scared. I want you to come to the house and cleanse it and then pray for me."

"I am sorry Toni; I need to get permission first."

"How long will that take?"

His reply shocked me, "Six months."

"I cannot wait six months!" I shouted, "do you or do you not believe in the power of Jesus? Have you no faith?"

Father Patrick shook his head and looked sad. "I must work within the rules of the Catholic Church, I am sorry. I want you to go to the doctors, get a check-up, maybe some of what is happening to you is down to stress or a hormone imbalance."

"That doesn't explain everything Father Patrick, especially what my kids have seen. I am desperate for help, I will go and see the doctor, but I can no longer stay with the Catholic Church, I can't agree with your rules."

I said goodbye to Father Patrick and asked him to continue to pray for me but shared I would not be coming back. I saw the doctor and was given a mild tranquilizer and a short-term treatment plan of hormone therapy, but I soon discovered the treatment made no difference at all, but at least I tried.

My eyes had been opened to so many areas of deception within the Catholic church that I had felt convicted for some time that much of the church's teaching was not biblical and this was the final straw.

In order to resolve what was happening I decide to meet with other Christians in a nearby church and get some support. This wasn't Catholic so hopefully I wouldn't hit upon the same issues. It was called the Church of the Nazarene. I knew nothing about their background, but I needed to make friends and as Paul was never at home, taking my problems to Paul was not an option. I arranged for a babysitter to come round and went to my first Bible study group. I was excited. I was finally stepping out in faith and being bold. I entered the church building and went into a large carpeted room where the Bible study was taking place. Chairs were put out in a circle and there was already a good turnout of around ten people. I sat down in one of the empty chairs and waited with the others for the Pastor to arrive. I had already spoken with the Pastor on the telephone and he knew I wanted some time alone with him after the meeting to discuss my issues.

Once the Pastor had arrived, the meeting started with prayer and the atmosphere was calm and peaceful. Introductions were made so that we all knew a bit about each other and then the Bible study began.

We were half way through the study when I felt my body go cold and rigid. Inside my head a voice then bellowed, "LET ME OUT OF HERE."

I tried to ignore it at first, I didn't want to leave but as I remained, the same commanding voice repeated the same words. "LET ME OUT OF HERE!"

I quickly picked up my things and ran out of the room shouting back, "I am sorry I have to go."

I got home to a quiet household with all the children soundly asleep. I paid the babysitter and sat down on the sofa feeling distressed. Great, I thought, I am hearing voices now.

Only a few minutes had passed when a knock on the door made me jump, to my surprise it was the Pastor.

"Come in Pastor, thank you for stopping by."

With a concerned tone the Pastor said, "What's troubling you?"

I shared about all the disturbances in the house, about how the children said my face changed and looked different, about my moods changing, and how I heard voices, I didn't miss one thing out. The Pastor listened patiently and then offered to pray with me.

"Let's put this all in the hands of Jesus, Toni, do you agree?"

I agreed knowing that being in the hands of Jesus was the best place to be. The Pastor prayed quietly at first asking for the holy spirit's presence and as he continued to pray, I started to feel uneasy. When the Pastor prayed, "In the name of Jesus I command you Satan to leave this child alone and oppress her no more." No sooner had the words been said, a rush of cold air went through the room and left.

"Did you feel that?" I asked.

'Yes, I did Toni, it's okay, don't be concerned."

I felt deeply peaceful and was ready to ask a question.

"What do you think is happening to me Pastor?"

"I believe you must still have some ties linked to your past that have not been severed. You have been exposed to much trauma and been involved in the occult; you have gone into areas of darkness you should have kept away from. There are warnings in the scriptures about this. When you got saved maybe God did not deal with everything all on the same day because God knows our human limitations of what we can handle and what we cannot, and maybe you needed to be grounded in the word of God and have your foundations secured in Jesus Christ strongly before God took the next step with you. Sometimes we just don't see all of the picture, just part of it. God has a bit more work to do in you before you know complete freedom."

"I thought that when I got saved it was all dealt with Pastor."

"Yes, it was Toni, all your sins have been forgiven and you were saved as soon as you called out to Jesus. On that day grace and mercy flowed down to you and the angels in heaven rejoiced. But our souls need time to heal, and as a person steps out in faith, just as you have done, further healing and deliverance takes place. You see there is a distinction between soul and spirit, and the Holy Spirit now resides in your spirit, but the enemy is attacking your soul or is hanging onto you in areas that need deliverance."

I knew nothing about deliverance and even though I had studied the Bible it had not occurred to me that I would need further help. I had very little understanding on how a young Christian could be affected by supernatural activity and that I was in a spiritual battle. I had lived a very sheltered Christian life and moved in areas of the Catholic faith which I soon discovered did not relate to some of the scriptures correctly. Since leaving the Catholic Church I felt I would know true spiritual freedom although at the moment it certainly did not feel it was going that way.

"Toni, some people need a bit more help, you have after all exposed yourself to the powers of darkness. It may be that someone more experienced than myself will be able to help you in this matter. God in the meantime will look after you, what God has begun God will finish."

The Pastor then left and I felt a lot lighter in myself and more together.

A few days had passed and nothing else had happened. The children were happy, and Paul had still not been home. To be honest it was quite nice that he wasn't around. As I busied myself at home getting it tidy, I heard a clunk of the letter box, a leaflet fell to the floor, I picked it up and saw that it was inviting people in the area to attend a Pentecostal meeting. I decided to brave it and go along.

I loved meeting other Christians and I wanted to understand what a Pentecostal meeting was all about. I wasted no time and booked in my babysitter.

As I entered the building the first thing that struck me was the amazing singing. I was a bit late and they had already started. I sat down in the back row and listened to a multitude of voices praising God and singing. Some people were clapping and some were dancing. I had never seen anything like it. They sang with strong conviction that lifted me onto my feet, I wanted to join in.

As I stood up my excitement plummeted as I felt my whole body go cold, I went rigid, my teeth clenched together and my muscles in my body tighten. Frustrated by my response I tried to sing out in defiance, but it just became more and more difficult. I sat back down feeling trapped within my own body. I listened to the singing and was determined to listen to the sermon and see it through to the end. When the service had finished, I got up to leave and the minister handed me a card.

"Hi, I believe you need this." he said with a smile. "The name upon the card is a Baptist minister, he is gifted in a special way. I believe you need his help."

I had no idea anyone had noticed my struggles, but this minister did. I took the card and thanked him, I was now convinced God had the situation under control and I was to continue trusting God even if I didn't understand everything, even if I was scared. When I got back home, I went to my room and prayed and thanked God for looking after me. As I prayed the Holy Spirit came upon me heavily and I felt a tremendous strength pour in, for a few moments it was wonderful. Then a strange collection of sounds and words burst out, I had no idea what was happening, so I phoned the minister at the Pentecostal Church. "Sorry to trouble you," I said "but I am talking in a strange language, LISTEN!"

I then started talking and when I had finished, I said, "What is it?"

"Oh, that's fine, nothing to be concerned about, God has given you the spiritual gift of talking in tongues, surely you have read about it in the scriptures?"

"But I didn't ask for that gift." I responded.

"No, you may not have asked for it, but it is the Holy Spirit that decides what spiritual gifts you have, so read up on it., this gift will edify you, build you up amongst other things."

I thanked the minister and decided to read up all about the gift of tongues. After writing to the Baptist pastor sharing as much as I could about my past and present situation, I then patiently waited for a reply. It wasn't long before I was invited down to Kent to have our first meeting. I had no idea what I was letting myself in for, but I had to learn to trust God in the situation and not listen to my feelings that went up and down every day.

I felt nervous and tense all the way down to Kent and almost talked myself out of going there. As I arrived at his home, I knocked gingerly upon the door and told myself I am in God's hands no matter what happens. The front door opened, and I was greeted with a warm smile.

"Hi, you must be Toni. Welcome, come on in, I am Mike."

I was shown around part of his home, some areas were private for his family only and other areas were for ministry work. Outside the house in the garden was a caravan which was for my own use and where I would be sleeping. For my first night there I was left alone to settle in and pray. As I picked up my Bible, I felt led to go to Psalm 46, it began, 'God is our refuge and strength, an ever-present help in trouble, therefore, we will not fear, though the earth gives way and the mountains fall into the heart of the sea.' These words gave me great comfort as I felt like my world was crumbling. Further on in verse 10 it said, 'Be still and know that I am God.' As I read those words again and again, I felt my anxiety slip away and a deep peace came to rest in my heart. The next day Mike arranged for me to meet the rest of his team explaining he would see me later.

I went into a room and sat down and before I could ask any questions a team member asked me question.

"Hi Toni, you have an interesting name, is it short for something else like Antonia?"

"No', I replied, 'it's just Toni."

"Is that the name on your birth certificate?"

I sat there in silence thinking, why on earth are they getting so interested in my name, I started to feel edgy and thought they were all being rude anyway as no-one had said who they were. In an agitated tone I answered, "My name is just Toni."

"Really, well, I feel it would be good Toni if we could start by being truthful. What does the rest of team feel?"

The other two members nodded in agreement. "I just sense that something is not quite right, that the first lie about your life is to do with your name."

I sighed, feeling a little puzzled and frustrated. I hated the name Deborah.

"OK, I came to you for help, so I will be honest, my real name is Deborah, but I changed it by deed poll to Toni. I never use the name Deborah it would be illegal to do so."

"Well now, Deborah is a fine biblical name, isn't it?"

"Yes, I suppose it is, but I just want you to call me Toni, I don't see what all the fuss is about, that is not why I am here, to have a debate with you, over my name."

I was getting weary.

"Ok Toni, I think we will go and see Mike now, and Mike will probably come and chat with you next. Can you just wait here? Thanks."

Thirty minutes had passed when Mike walked into the room, pulled a chair over and sat down directly in front of me. He smiled and just looked into my eyes, all was silent, and it seemed like an eternity until Mike eventually said something. "Deborah, sorry to have kept you waiting, how are you feeling? Deborah is such a good name, isn't it?"

It was like a red flag to a bull. Through gritted teeth words poured out of my mouth in ways that I was not even ready for. "DEBORAH, I laboured loudly, is just a BABY! Pronouncing the name as if it was a filthy word, DEBORAH, I shouted, no longer exists, DEBORAH I screamed is DEAD!"

I clenched my jaws so tightly it hurt. I sat back in the chair and folded my arms tightly staring down at the floor. For a moment there was a heavy silence that was broken by Mike's soft voice.

"Deborah, I want you to understand something before I continue. In the Bible, Jesus dealt with many people who needed some form of deliverance and that ministry and work still continues today. Satan wants to block you going forward, causing you confusion. When you gave yourself the name Toni maybe it was more of an unconscious decision to be close to your twin brother, as you explained in your letter, your dad told you at some point when you were growing up that you were a twin? And that twin was a boy, and if you were a twin, I am quite sure deep down you miss him. Maybe you called yourself Toni to fit in with the borstal girls and you hid behind the name feeling it gave you a different identity that would help you during your sentence. Satan has used this area against you, your own deep needs allowed the enemy to come in especially at a time when you were messing around with the occult and you were vulnerable, it was the foothold he needed, once the door was open, the rest was easy. Satan wants to mess with your identity. His work is to deceive you, Toni your twin brother is with the Lord, he is not here, but you are."

"But I feel like I am the one is who dying Mike."

Mike calmly responded, "YOU are not the one dying Deborah, Toni, a false spirit that has had its hold on you is the one dying, it knows it has to leave. Toni is the lie here not you. Before you came to me God gave you Psalm 46 for a reason, let's look at those words together right now. 'God is our refuge and strength always ready to help in times of trouble.' This is a time of trouble.

And as we see in this Psalm, times of trouble come upon the world, upon nations which are in chaos. But God wants you to know that he can be your protector just as he protects his home Israel, the Bible often uses dual references. Even though you feel there is chaos all around you, God wants you to see he will protect you, just be still and know that he is God. God does not want you to fear. As I pray you will feel resistance, it will pass."

With authority in his voice Mike continued, "In the name of Jesus, I command Toni, a spirit of falsehood, to leave, now! I break every stronghold on this child of God whose God given name is Deborah, Come out liar, deceiver in the name of Jesus!"

Mike then prayed in tongues and as he did, I felt impending doom surround me as if I was about to die. I too started to pray remembering the words of Psalm 46. As our prayers were lifted up to the heavenly realms the hold on me was broken. I no longer felt as if my identity as a woman was dominated by Toni, in fact Toni no longer existed and I felt free. I knew something had happened and Mike sat there smiling.

Mike and I spent more time together that day in prayer and over a period of six months I continued to see Mike. Lots of different areas were covered in prayer, the area of death, all the different trauma's I had been through, all the bad dreams that had invaded my nights, how my children had been affected, my history to the present day, not one stone was left unturned.

This led to me being who I was meant to be, a woman wanting to serve God's heart, a woman at last in peace. Everyone could see the difference. I went to my local church and shared my testimony how God revealed certain areas of my damaged soul and put them right. I no longer suffered any form of oppression. I shared that everyone was to call me Deborah because that's who I truly was, for the first time in years I wore a dress and felt feminine, like a butterfly wanting to spread its delicate wings I wanted to fly. My home became filled with songs of praise to God as I enjoyed my new-found liberty and identity.

Chapter Eleven – The Final Blow

Throughout the next two years I was happy. All the children were doing well and there were no more bad dreams or weird experiences. I didn't share any details with Paul about my visits to Mike except to say I was receiving prayer. Paul hated the new me and the fact I was insistent on being called Deborah or Debz annoyed him. Although our marriage was difficult from time to time it did not take away the joy I felt. My children were happy because they could see mum was happy, but a knock on the front door soon dented what happiness we had. It was a loud hard knock that made me jump.

As I opened the door a man was standing there, he was wearing a suit and tie, quite smart in his appearance. "Can I help you?" I asked.

Pointing his finger across the street he asked me, "Is that your husband?"

"Yes, it is. What's he doing waiting over there? What's this all about?"

"I am sorry, but I have to inform you that your husband has not been completely honest with you or us. I am one of the administrators from London, my name is Mr. Wicks. For a long time, we have not received any mortgage money regarding this property. Your husband unfortunately has been spending his money on other things, well, gambling in fact. He informed us it's not your fault, but he has been keeping the mail that came in the morning post and I believe you have not seen a notice concerning possession on the property."

I stood there shocked. "What do you mean? You can't take my house from me; this can't be true."

I stared at Paul across the road in disbelief.

I invited Mr. Wicks in and closed the front door. I sat down and burst into tears.

"I am so sorry." the man said, "You have three days to vacate the property and take what possessions you can."

I had no idea what I was going to do or where the children and I would end up. I was handed some papers and as the man got up to leave, I said, "Will you let my husband know that I don't want to see him right now and he will have to find somewhere to stay. I need some time to think."

"Yes, of course I will tell him. Again, I am so sorry."

As the front door shut, I had never felt so alone. What would this major disruption do to my children? Losing my home was too much to bear. But I had no choice but to leave. We were given a temporary welfare house to live in on an estate known for bad debtors and residents in similar situations. I moved into the new property and took as much furniture as I could. Thankfully, I had the help of my church. The minister encouraged me and said, "Don't worry Debz, I will find a way to help you, we will find a way forward."

A week or two passed and I was invited to a meeting. Present was the church minister and Mr. Wicks. I was intrigued.

Mr. Wicks kick started the conversation off. "I can see Mrs Crawley that you are nothing like your husband. The good minister here has explained a great deal to me about your situation and problems. The church has offered to pay off the arrears on your mortgage. I cannot give you an answer today, but I will let you know what the decision is on this later."

I couldn't believe my ears that the church wanted to help in this way. I thanked everyone and went back home and waited.

Two weeks had passed, and I received a letter stating I could move back into my home. What a miracle this was! I was told in the letter that if at any time I ever wanted to sell the property any money owing would be taken out of the sale price. I didn't ask if the administrators had taken the money offered by the church, but I was so relieved that my children and I had our home back. Since all this commotion and upheaval had happened Paul had sent me a few letters, letters of deep apologies, asking me to allow him back home.

Paul had indeed punched a huge hole in our happiness bubble and for a while I ignored his letters, but I was weak. I forgave him, which was the right thing to do, because hanging onto bitterness or ill feeling was not beneficial to my own health, but I was weak because in the end I allowed Paul to come back home. I didn't feel strong enough to cope on my own, I didn't know how to stand up to him, there was a mixture of feelings, I felt sorry for Paul, I wanted things to work, doing the right thing for everyone, wanting to overcome my own fears and insecurities, the well of emotions just went deeper and deeper.

Manipulated over the years by a dominant man had made its mark, he knew just which buttons to press, I felt trapped. When I sought advice from the church, I got mixed responses. Some people said, enough was enough the marriage was over and failed a long time ago, others just said, that God does not like divorce, and others said, God would not expect the children and I to continue to suffer in such a destructive relationship, that marrying an unbeliever was unwise and I was now living with the consequences. Others felt I should live alone with my children.

Some were quite theological about it saying that because my husband was a non-believer, I was no longer bound to him if he leaves, and that as he had committed adultery against me, I was definitely no longer bound to him.

After a great deal of prayer and discussion I talked things through with Paul and decided I would give him one more chance. We sold the house and made a brand-new start, I knew deep down this would be the last time, I had no strength left, this was my last attempt at saving our marriage. I have often found it interesting that people will say, it takes two in a partnership to cause a break-up, both are to blame, but that is not always the case.

In 1986, we moved to Cambridge. Paul had already secured employment and we rented a four-bed house in a village called

119

Cottenham. I hoped with all my heart this new beginning was going to be good for everyone. The children started new schools and during the first few months it was stressful. The kids were adjusting to a new environment, making new friends, Paul was adjusting to a new job, and I was busy being home maker but feeling a little lost. I had no support of any kind around me. I had left all the church support and friends behind me. Things were OK for a while, but I had noticed that Paul's drinking had become more frequent. He was often down the local pubs in the village playing darts and drinking. When he came home drunk, he still expected his meals on table, the kids out the way, and sex when he wanted it. There was no respect in our relationship anymore and my heart sank. I hated myself for not being stronger. I was always trying to avoid confrontation of any kind with Paul, but the day was coming when I could no longer run from my fears.

It began one morning when the telephone rang.

"Good morning," said a voice, "can I speak to Mr. Crawley?"

"Sorry," I said, "Mr. Crawley is at work, can I help?"

"Well, he is not at work, I can vouch for that. Is this Mrs Crawley?"

'Yes, it is. What do you mean he is not at work'?

"Has he not told you, I fired your husband about a month ago, his attitude at work was unacceptable."

I couldn't believe it Paul had been leaving the house every day as if he was going to work. Now, it seems he has no work. I didn't want to talk in depth to his employer so just said, "Thanks for letting me know. I am glad you phoned up otherwise this could have gone on for so much longer, goodbye."

I quickly put the phone down and felt angry and disappointed, it seemed we were back to square one.

I decided before the kids came back from school to nip to the bank to check on our account, Paul had not been earning any money so how much had he spent. The news wasn't good, there was just enough money left to cover the rent for a short period of time, I was devastated. It was obvious to me that he had been gambling as well as drinking.

I asked the bank to freeze the account and explained the situation to them. I needed to be brave and confront Paul. I had made the decision to ask Paul for a divorce.

As I waited for Paul to come home, I kept myself busy, my nerves were bad as I knew he might get angry. But to my surprise Paul got home before the children got home from school. Paul stormed in and slammed the front door. He didn't ask me how my day was, he just shouted, "Why have you frozen the account? I couldn't get any money."

"I froze the account, Paul, because you haven't been honest with me, you lost your job, your employer rang. I regret selling our house and moving to Cambridge. At least the children and I would have had some security. I have had enough Paul, I don't want you in my life anymore, I want a divorce."

Paul stared at me hard and long, I had seen that look before. He didn't show one bit of emotion, just cold hard anger that had set in his face like granite. My heart raced so fast I thought I was going to faint. In the background through an open window, I heard the sound of shoes crunching on the gravel driveway, it was James my son coming back from school.

As James was entering the front door, Paul had already grabbed me by my hair and had dragged me from the front room to an adjacent side room. I shouted out to James to get some help. I heard my son disappear and my head came crashing down onto a radiator with full force. I prayed that James would find safety. Paul then pulled me up and slammed me into a wall.

"You bitch," he shouted, "you will never have a divorce, if I can't have you, then no-one else can, no-one, do you hear me."

My head was reeling with pain and I had no idea what would come next. As I looked into his eyes, I could see they were filled with contempt. I tried with all my strength to push him off, but he grabbed me around my throat and started to strangle me. My ears started ringing and my head felt a tremendous pressure. I started praying underneath my breath, "God help me!" I couldn't breathe in or out, and as blackness came, my life was in the hands of God.

I had no idea how long I had been unconscious for, but when I came to, I was surprised. I noticed in the corner of the room Paul was sitting in a chair just staring at me. He looked cold and distant, not himself at all, his eyes were filled with a sadistic madness that made me look away. I slowly stood up and, barely able to speak, I croaked out the words, "Where is James?"

Silence hung in the air like a deadly invisible poison. I knew Paul had not finished with me yet, there was more violence to come. I had to get away from him. With no response to my question, I slowly started walking out of the confined space I found myself in. Paul seemed to ignore me. I croaked out another few words. "Paul, I am going to put the kettle on I won't be a minute."

I prayed, please, please, don't get up or follow me.

As I made my way to the kitchen Paul hadn't moved. I put the kettle on so Paul heard it and went towards the back door which was open. I slowly slipped out and ran across the back garden to the wall and climbed over. As soon as my feet touched the ground on the other side of the wall, I ran as fast as I could. My legs were heavy and I could barely breathe. My throat was so sore and blood poured from the wound and trickled down onto my face from my head. My anxiety levels were through the roof. I got to my neighbour's and, without a thought, barged through their front door which wasn't locked. My neighbour, shocked by my appearance, immediately called the police. As I waited for the police to come, my neighbour kept me calm and gave me sips of water. I peered through the window and I could just make out the face of a madman. Paul was pacing up and down the pavement shouting at the top of his voice, "Where are you, you fucking bitch? I'm going to kill you."

I quickly came away from the window in case he saw me. I was terrified for the safety of my children who, by this time, would have all been home from school. I had no idea what to do.

The police arrived quite quickly and with them a doctor who examined me as soon as he arrived. I refused to go to the hospital and just wanted to see my children.

"We have your husband already." said a police officer. "He is sitting in one of our cars. Your son James is safe, and your other children are also safe."

I burst into tears asking them to take Paul away.

"Paul will be locked up tonight, so you can go back home if you want, we need you to make a statement, and we will put an injunction order on your husband to stop him from coming anywhere near you."

Once I had made my statement, the children and I were left to pick up the pieces. We hugged and cried together and spent all evening in each other's company.

As morning came, I thought it was best to send the children to school to keep them occupied. I was fearful Paul would be released and return. The days dragged by for me and I sunk into a deep depression. I kept the television on all day for company and lost any heart in myself to pray. I was empty and drained of all emotion and absolutely clueless about what to do next.

Later the police informed me that Paul had been taken to court and was given a two-year suspended prison sentence, probation and an injunction order had been served.

A few difficult weeks had passed, I had not spoken to anyone, I couldn't face people and my depression had not lifted, but a knock on the door soon jolted me back into reality. I heard a familiar voice.

"Debz, open the door, I want to talk to you."

I stood holding the children as my body began to shake.

"Go away," I shouted back, "you are not meant to be anywhere near the house, I will call the police."

"Ok fine, at least meet me in a public place, I just want to speak to you."

"Go away Paul, leave me alone."

Paul left, but the next day, the phone rang, it was Paul.

"Look, just listen, I will be two minutes. I just want to meet with you, just once. I will never trouble you again after that, just meet me in a café in town, I can't hurt you in front of loads of people, can I? any way I would go to prison if I step out of line."

To get Paul off my back I went to meet him. I felt safer meeting him in town as I knew he didn't want to go to prison. The fact that he had a suspended sentence hanging over his head gave me some comfort. As we sat in the café his eyes avoided mine.

"What do you want Paul?" I asked, dreading the answer.

"I want to look after the kids, I mean look at you, you are not fit to look after them. The kids are my life, I can't live without them."

Paul then took his grandfather's ring which I knew meant a lot to him and placed it down on the table.

"I will never hurt them, he continued, but if I can't have the kids, I will kill myself and you can have my grandfather's ring."

'You won't take your life Paul'. But then I thought of two occasions when Paul overdosed on my tablets.

Paul was silent for a while and during this tense silent moment my body started to shake.

"I am going now Paul, I am not sure who is in the better position to look after the children, leave me alone, I need to think."

I got home and burst into tears, I knew how shabby I looked, how thin I had become, the meeting with Paul took all my strength. I needed to get some advice, some help, from somewhere, so I decided to go to a nearby church for help.

I approached a local church and a lady minister welcomed me. We went into a small room for privacy for a chat.

As I sat down, I noticed a couple of other people present.

"Oh, don't worry about them, they are part of my ministry team, how can I help?"

"I am not sure if you can help me, I have just been through hell, my husband recently tried to kill me, not for the first time, we are separated and he is not allowed near me, but wants to see the children, in fact he wants to look after them."

I couldn't keep myself together and the tears kept coming

"Is your husband a Christian?"

I shook my head indicating no, what kind of question was that. I could only assume she thought I was a Christian because I had come to the church for help.

"What do you want God to do for you?" She asked.

"I don't know." I wearily replied.

I was becoming agitated. I folded my arms and looked at the floor feeling rather hopeless.

"Why don't we all pray." the minister said. So, we prayed, I never heard the prayers as my head was filled with sorrow and confusion.

When the prayers had finished the minister said something quite unexpected. "Debz, we are a Church of England church and we do not believe in divorce, maybe you should go back to your husband."

I was disgusted with this suggestion and replied, "I could never ever, go back to that monster, you have no idea what I have been through. Have you not heard what I said, he tried to kill me and there is so much more, you haven't got a clue what I have been through?"

"I am sorry you feel that way, you are free to leave."

I felt gutted, I stared at her and wondered what kind of Christian would want to send a distraught woman back to a man who was violent.

"I am appalled that you think I should let that man back into my life."

A cold reply came back from the minister, "I think you should return to your husband."

I walked away as if hit by a lead weight. By the time I got home I was in a worse state than when I left. My faith had taken a huge knock. At home I functioned on auto-pilot and just went through the motions every day, but I had never felt so dead inside. I became more and more introverted and less able to do things. Basic tasks became heavy burdens, I was angry at God and could not believe Christians could be so heartless and ignorant. I felt so rejected.

I lost track of time and was completely blind to any other form of help, it never once crossed my mind to seek help from a counsellor or social services, the depression I was under was more than enough and I was thankful Paul had kept away.

But it was too much to believe he would stay away for good, because he turned up to the house banging on the door. I thought here we go again this man is going to drive me into a nut house.

"Debz, I want to see the kids."

"Why can't you leave me alone."

"Please Debz just open the door, just for two minutes, I promise I won't stay long, I just want to see the kids, I miss them."

"If I allow you to see the kids Paul, will you promise me, that you will go when I ask, and that you will stop coming to the house."

"Yes, I promise."

I slowly opened the door and Paul calmly walked in smiling, 'Thank you' he said.

For a while Paul seemed sincere. He had been with the children for about 30 minutes and the atmosphere was good. Paul then asked the children to go upstairs as he wanted a private word with me, the children left, and that calm feeling I had soon left.

Paul sat next to me and said in a quiet aggressive tone, "I want you to listen to me, YOU are not going to be looking after the kids anymore, I want you to get a few things together and put them in a suitcase and just quietly leave."

I looked at him with utter fear and disgust. "I am not going anywhere Paul, you can leave. You promised me after seeing the kids you would leave."

"YOU!" Paul screamed in my face, "are a joke. Someone needs to look after them, right? And it's not going to be you. If you don't do what I have asked then the kids won't have a mother, NOW, do you understand."

I knew what he meant that he would finish what he started. It was a miracle I was still alive.

Paul grinned and grabbed my arm tightly. The children must have heard Paul scream at me and came back downstairs. I put on a brave face and smiled. I didn't want Paul to erupt any further, so I asked the kids to watch television while me and their Dad was going to do some chatting upstairs.

I shut the door to the front room hoping the children would stay put as I knew that this was not going to end well.

Upstairs in the bedroom Paul picked up a suitcase and threw it onto the bed. Coldly and firmly, he said, "Fill it and f..k off."

The air turned blue with his foul language, reminding me again that if I didn't leave, the kids would have no mother. I gradually felt my resolve diminish and knew that I had a choice, leave or be killed. As I stood there, dithering, tears flowed down my face, my body was violently shaking, but not an ounce of mercy came from Paul. My children meant everything to me. I had raised them mostly on my own, nurtured them and loved them from birth, we had all survived together.

Paul," I barely got my words out, "you don't mean this, let us sit down and try and work something out."

"It's either this," Paul said pointing at the suitcase, "OR, do I have to spell it out for you again, you know what will happen."

I was unresponsive.

"I can end it for you if you like, put you out of your misery, then the kids won't have a mum, but they have me, and this time I WILL finish it properly."

I could see by now that Paul was getting very impatient, in fact he was gritting his teeth. Paul grabbed some of my clothing and threw them into the suitcase.

"Get your suitcase, stupid bitch and say goodbye to the kids. Remember what I said, NO MUMMY!"

A deep satisfied smile came across his face.

I slowly picked up the suitcase and went downstairs like an automated robot. All the children could see something was wrong and started crying.

I looked at their faces and felt so broken inside. I spoke up and said, "Mummy has to go away for a little while, so don't worry."

"Yeah, said Paul, Mummy is not well, she needs to have a rest, Dad is going to look after you."

Paul ushered the children back into the front room and shut the front room door. He then opened the front door and pushed me with some force outside saying, "Bye then." With that the front door slammed shut.

I could hear my babies crying as I stood fixed to the ground. I slowly walked away numb to the core, my mind went completely blank as I put one foot in front of the other, with each step pain and darkness swallowed me up.

Chapter Twelve – Breakdown

1987 had become a year of devastating change. I had lost my home, marriage, children and my Christian faith. I blamed God for everything and was completely devoid of any emotion other than anger. I focused my anger towards God with utter blasphemy, my soul fragmented into a thousand pieces and my mind had finally snapped. The rage and pain were so great I told God to take his Holy Spirit from me. I hated God. Everything I had left behind had been pushed deeply into the recesses of my mind, as a new darkened identity emerged. I no longer had any memories at all of my children or Paul. Dissociation can happen particularly when a person has gone through trauma, for me, my brain had switched off completely except for anger directed straight at God.

With what little money I had I managed to secure a bed sit in a shared house in the city. The landlord was a Christian who owned several properties, I met him whilst in a pub. I had started drinking and smoking for the first time in years. I didn't care that he was a Christian it meant nothing to me anymore, what I did care about was the fact he allowed me to have a room without putting down a deposit, with money limited I took up his offer of help, it was better than being homeless. At the time I met him I was scruffy and looking desperate. Most days I stayed cocooned in my room, smoking weed and drinking. Who I really was had died?

My focus became entrenched in the Satanic bible and within my room I dedicated an altar to Satan. Within the nine Satanic statements I found solace. I connected with an old friend from the past, a male witch, who sent me a cut-throat razor which had the words engraved on the steel, 'I cut my way.' It lay on top of the altar with pride. I ordered books on the occult through the internet and tattooed the image of Baphomet on my arm.

Having denounced Christianity, I found a new way to express myself, through the punk scene and gothic clothing. Punk music and the lyrics gave vent to all my strong emotions and meeting up with others who were the same only fuelled the fire in me. I had changed beyond all recognition. I took up karate and twice a week I would attend the dojo for training. I was determined to get physically stronger and pushed my body hard. I lost weight fast but neglected to look after myself properly. A fat hardened shell developed on the outside hiding all the brokenness of a woman who deep down had crumbled into nothing. Years of abuse, neglect and suffering had finally merged into defiance and rebellion aimed straight at God and anyone who got in my way.

After a while I ventured out to mix and mingle mostly in the evenings, going to pubs watching live bands. It was during a punk gig that I became attracted to a man who intrigued me. His persona was quiet apart from when he got into the mosh pit, quite happy slamming his body against others, he was tall and confident and dressed all in black. He seemed to get my attention. It wasn't long before we became soul mates and a relationship developed. His nickname was Blade. He never asked about my past and accepted me for who I was. A lot of our time was spent watching live bands and as I got to know Blade, it was evident that he had a problem with taking speed. On one occasion when he had disappeared, I went looking for him. Blade would cut himself on a come down from speed and it was in one of those times I followed a trail of blood straight to our front door. When I got inside written in blood on the walls were the words, I LOVE DEBZ.

Our soul tie to each other was dark and destructive. On two occasions I cut Blade with my razor which often started off as a joke, the first cut went the length of his forearm which we pieced firmly together ourselves with butterfly stitches but the last cut ended up in the hospital with his hand being stitched inside and out which was a step too far, and not really very helpful, especially as he needed his hands for his work. Blade ended up with a satanic cross tattooed into his arm and my long hair was cut off and replaced by a flat Mohican.

…and my long hair was cut off and replaced by a flat Mohican

As my anarchistic non-conformity grew, I became confrontational with any kind of authority or system, quite the opposite in character to who I was before, I continued under the disillusioned belief that I was free to express myself in whatever way I wanted with little regard for others. Sometimes I drank far too much and got banned from pubs, if a man even looked at me the wrong way, I was rude, angry and threatening. Sometimes I got banned just from the way I looked. When I was unhappy under the influence of drink, I was a nightmare, I would walk off on my own and cause disruption, picking up bottles left outside, smashing them against moving cars.

After one evening out on the town I hailed a taxi to take me home. I got into the taxi and gave my directions and settled back in the seat. It wasn't long before the driver asked me if I had a good night.

"What's it to you." I answered back with attitude.

"Oh, nothing, just asking, I do taxi work part time to meet people, as people interest me. I am a Pentecostal minister and run a church here in the city, if you need to talk to me anytime, don't hesitate to ring, you look like you need some help, if you don't mind me saying."

"I don't need your help Vicar." I responded with contempt.

"Fine, so you don't need my help, just take my card, if you ever need me just give me a call."

I snatched his card off him and put it in my handbag. Smiling I said, "Great, now that I have your details I can go home and curse you and your church."

The taxi arrived at my destination and the driver had to say one more thing to me.

"I will pray for you."

I was repulsed by his suggestion and answered back, "Fine, you do that, you pray for me, your prayers won't make any difference."

With foul language filling the air I made it abundantly clear that while he was praying for me, I would be cursing him. I gave him my taxi fare and slammed the cab door. That night I cursed him and his church, I thought, how dare he speak to me, the bloody low life. Unbeknown to me God was working on my case.

The next thing to happen was even more provoking. A few days had passed when a woman approached me in the street. I was out taking a walk.

"Hello," she said, "I know you don't know me, but I have a message for you."

"What do you mean, you have a message for me?"

"The message is that Jesus loves you, and you are his child and you do not belong to anyone else."

"WHAT!" I screamed back.

This bold lady then repeated her message and then just looked at me and walked away.

I stood in the street fuming, clenching my hand into a fist I raised it up towards the sky and shouted, "There is no way you can get me out of this situation, it's too late"

In Psalm 75 verses 4 & 5 it says, 'I warned the proud, stop your boasting, I told the wicked, don't raise your fists! Don't raise your fists in defiance at the heavens or speak with such arrogance.'

Twice in a matter of days, God had used two people to reach out to me and I couldn't see past my anger and pride.

But then a third thing happened. The landlord of the property had decided to sell the house and we were told we had to leave. Blade said the only place we could live temporarily was at his mother's and step-father's home. I wasn't keen on that arrangement, but we had no choice we had nowhere else to live. I quickly found out that his parents were Christians; it seemed whatever way I turned Christians were there. While I was living with his parents, I found myself developing a conscience about my relapse, turning my back on God was a foolish decision. I still had the card with the telephone number of the taxi driver, so I gave him a ring. The minister came to the house and every single item connected to the occult was wrapped in the altar cloth and burned. As the minister walked away it was only then that deep repentance came, and I sobbed for days. I felt so ashamed and my grief was beyond words, I prayed to God to cleanse me from every vile word and act I had ever said or done.

Blade not only began to see changes in me, he decided to probe into my background and started asking questions about my past.

"So Debz, I don't know much about your past, do you want to enlighten me?"

"Like what? You know what I'm about, we both like the same things, what else is there to know."

"Well, where is your family? Do you have kids? Have you been married?"

"Blimey Blade, where is this all coming from? Do I have kids? Is that what you asked me. Do I have kids?"

I kept repeating the question as if I hadn't heard it. The word 'kids' got stuck in my head like a needle stuck on a vinyl record, and then it hit me, that lightbulb moment that people sometimes experience, except this time it happened to me.

"Oh my God," I cried out, "My kids, yes, I have four beautiful children."

I sat down shaken to the core and Blade came over and put his arm round me. Almost a whole year had gone by and in that moment, my harden shell cracked wide open, I burst into uncontrollable tears. As the flood gates opened, I shared with Blade everything including the fact that I was once a Christian mum. He sat there listening until I could no longer speak. The first thing we organised was for me to go back to the house in the village to see if the kids were ok. I knew I had to do this alone. Blade was supportive in every way.

I went back to Cottenham and approached the house where my children were. I had no idea what type of reception I would get, especially if Paul was there, but I no longer cared about that, I just had to see my children. I knocked on the door and waited.

As the door opened, I saw the most beautiful thing a mother could see, my babies. But I was also horrified. The condition and appearance of my kids had gone downhill drastically, they looked neglected. Their appearance was scruffy and dirty, and they were all constantly scratching their heads. The house had a strange odour and I could see mushrooms growing in between the wood flooring.

"MUM!" They shouted; it was the best moment ever as we all hugged each other.

"Where is Dad?" I quietly asked.

"He has gone down the shop." they quickly responded.

"Ok, well I can't stop long, but I am going to try and find you some help."

"Mum, are you ok? Why haven't we seen you?"

"I will explain everything soon, but not now, I need to go before your dad gets back." I suddenly felt an urgency to leave, choked up inside I started to leave saying, "I love you all, you will hear from me soon, I promise."

Suddenly all those beaming smiles disappeared, they nodded quietly and shut the door.

As I talked things through with Blade, it was decided to contact social services and I was glad I did, because when I went to see my children again, their Dad was not with them, they were alone.

Attached to the front door was a note telling me that he knew I had been over to see the children and that he had found a new partner. Now the children were my responsibility.

As social services stepped in to help, a friend of mine named Sandra became an emergency foster carer and took all of my four children in. I was so grateful; the thought of my children being split up or being taken further away from me would have been too much to bear. We all needed time to adjust, I had no accommodation to offer them, and on top of everything else I was physically not very well. I had an array of symptoms the hospital was looking into. When they finally found out what was wrong with me, they told me I had a life-threatening condition, called Systemic Lupus, an auto-immune illness where the body attacks itself. As the children stayed with Sandra, I was receiving home help three times a week so that I didn't become too drained.

Bit by bit I met up with the children and found out how their dad had treated them, it was utterly shocking to hear, in their own words they told me how controlling he had become.

Sometimes he left them sitting around the table for hours. He would often go down the pub and then arrive home extremely drunk, his drinking and gambling had become much worse and was still a huge problem. Any birthday money that was sent to the children from their Nan he took for himself. The house itself was not cleaned very much but when it was cleaned it was done by the children, my eldest child Sarah was often left in charge of the others. If the others were sick Sarah had to clean up the mess. It didn't take much for him to lose his temper, and they often got smacked, something we never did as a couple. He became quite abusive, probably as a result of more and more drinking.

My children continued to tell me that at times they were not fed for days and so they often stole food from the local shop. Sometimes the gas ran out and when food what short in supply they had a bit of powdered mash and tinned tomatoes. All of the children were malnourished. They told me on one occasion the house caught on fire after he decided to do some cooking, but he passed out through drink. Another vivid memory they had was when one of the local neighbours came across the road to see if they were alright, the neighbour had kindly cooked them some dinner. It was deeply painful to hear how damaged and neglected my children had become through being left with their dad. Gradually, over time, all of my children gained strength, confidence and health.

Two years had passed, and the children were doing well, they had all settled into their new schools. In April 1990, Blade and I had a baby girl called Rose. We were offered a two-bed property which was a vast improvement to our living conditions. But in August that same year I was devastated to hear that my children were being discharged back into the care of their father. Paul had been in touch with social services and wanted the children back. I begged social services not to allow the children to go back to his care. Social services told me that Sandra could no longer foster all four of them, and as I did not have a large enough house and was still struggling with ill health, they had no choice but to hand the children back to their dad, he was after all their father.

After all the children had been through, I was heartbroken for them and for me and I felt very angry. Worse still their dad was not going to remain in Cambridge, he had plans to take them to Chichester where he grew up. This was absolutely heart-breaking news. The action taken was beyond my understanding in every way.

But social services were soon to discover that my children were no longer in Chichester and worse still, they had no idea where Paul and my children had gone. I was frantic with worry. I felt incensed by the way the system had let me and my children down, so I contacted a family barrister who decided to take my case on and help me track my children down. After all we had been through as a family, I couldn't believe I was now in a situation where I had no idea where my children were, and the barrister concerned was as equally shocked as I was.

We found out that Paul had become ill and had two heart attacks as well as suffering with a stomach ulcer. Because of this the children had ended up in a children's home in Bognor Regis in 1991. Later that year in the month of July, Paul was arrested and remanded in custody, his violence had escalated to other women. The woman he bound and gagged to a chair and terrorized was the woman he ran away to be with when he left a note on the door and left his children. Not soon after that he stabbed his disabled mother in the head with a kitchen knife and beat her up so badly that her face was unrecognizable, she barely survived the attack. In 1992 Paul was sentenced to six years in prison and was diagnosed in prison as a psychopath, he showed no remorse for his actions.

With the support of my barrister, I went immediately to Sussex to visit my children. I made arrangements through the courts to have them come straight back to Cambridge. Finally, in 1993, that action was granted. Three years had passed, the separation from each other and the turmoil and pain that it had caused had scarred everyone. It had been the worst roller coaster ride of emotional pain for us all. If Paul had a plan to keep me from my children that plan was short lived. Love between a mother and her children can never be destroyed, no matter what evil comes against it.

Once my children were back in Cambridge, I managed to see them often, I knew it was going to take some time for us all to mend, we had so many emotional bridges to build and heal. As I was still not in a large enough property all of my children were placed in temporary foster homes, some of those foster carers were friends of mine; everyone was being so kind.

When my children and I first met, we all looked at each other and didn't know where to begin, my children had been through several ordeals with traumatic experiences of separation, loss and abuse. It was difficult at first for everyone, but slowly over time our bond of love to each other grew stronger. During this time of settling down in 1994 Blade and I had divorced. Just one week before Christmas he walked out, he said, "Don't love you anymore, we have nothing in common, bye."

I found out he had been having an affair with my so-called best friend. I was now to bring up Rose our daughter by myself, and that was ok, I loved all my kids. Blade retained his punk identity and to this day he has remained in that mindset.

I found it very difficult being on my own and so I ended up on the rebound from Blade and met someone else. It all looked ok to start with, this man came from a Christian family and we even prayed together. A small hint of excitement raced through my bones hoping that Steve might be my long-term potential Christian partner. On one occasion while out walking, we passed a jeweller's and I stopped to gaze at all the beautiful rings in the window. 'Let's go in,' Steve said. We had a look around and as I was looking; I was drawn towards a ring with emeralds and diamonds. 'That's nice, wow, love that ring'.

'Why don't we have one made up for you? Let's call it an engagement ring. What do you say? said Steve.

'Oh! Really Steve, are we getting engaged? I laughed.

Steve laughed, 'Looks like it'. That day my finger was measured and the jewellers allowed Steve to come in each week to put money down on my hand-made ring until it was paid for.

When Steve wasn't working, we spent as much time with each other as we could, this involved him meeting the rest of my children and me meeting with Steve's parents. Things were moving at a fast pace. Steve also shared with me that he wanted a child of his own, this led to some deep discussions, especially in view of the fact I had a serious risk of losing the baby. I had already had four miscarriages in the past and been told by doctors not to have any more children. With a life-threatening illness, Lupus, it could attack the developing foetus.

I had a chat with my doctor and listened to his advice, if I were to have another baby, I would have to give myself heparin injections every day which was meant to help in the initial stages of pregnancy. The final decision was that I would have one more baby, allowing Steve to become a Dad. During my pregnancy, Steve worked hard and I was happy. I carried full term, but when the time came to give birth, I was rushed off as an emergency to theatre for a C-section. When our baby was born, she was named Lauren. Later, my health issues were discussed. My body had been through enough, and Steve and I decided it would be a good idea for him to have a vasectomy.

Everything was fine although my recovery was slow and for the first time in a long time, I felt everyone was getting to a place of being happy and stable. My other children all continued to come over and see me and sometimes there were sleep over's which was great fun. I was on the waiting list for a larger property so that we could all be together under one roof. But our happy bubble was about to burst.

I noticed Steve had been having mood changes and at first, I thought he was getting cold feet about getting married or maybe between work and being a new father, he was just stressed. When I asked him if he was ok, he said he was just feeling a bit under the weather. Sometimes Steve would actually be physically sick. He seemed to be spending more and more time away from me and the baby. I knew he doted on Lauren and yet he wasn't around much. This concerned me greatly. As I shared my concerns he just smiled and told me not to be so silly, "Come on Debz, let's go out, I will introduce you to some friends of mine'. So, I went along with it, and met up with what appeared to be a nice outgoing couple, Dean and Tina. As Steve was chatting in the front room, I went to the kitchen to get a cold drink and Tina followed in after me. "Are you ok?" She asked.

'Yes, I am ok, just a bit worried about Steve, he seems to be a bit unwell every now and then, and I am not seeing much of him'.

Tina looked a bit on edge then came closer to me and in a quiet tone she said, "Look Debz, I can see you are a very nice person, normally I don't let people know my business, but for some reason I think you should know, you having a baby and all."

"What do I need to know Tina?"

139

"Well, this may come as a bit of a shock to you, but Steve is using heroin, and that is why he is being sick. When you first use it, it can affect you that way."

I was stunned by the news; I had no idea. I knew absolutely nothing about heroin.

"How do you know this, Tina? Are you sure about this?"

"I know Debz because Dean and I also use."

My heart sank to my stomach, I just wanted to run. How could I have been so foolish to trust another man. What was I thinking? I walked out of the kitchen, back into the front room and squared up to Steve.

Staring directly at Steve I said, "I know everything Steve, Tina has told me, you're taking heroin. That explains so much."

Steve looked directly at Tina, "Why did you tell her Tina?"

Tina shrugged her shoulders and went quiet.

Steve then looked at me, "Debz, it's no big deal, I just have it now and then."

"Listen Steve, I don't know much about heroin, but I do know it's highly addictive, I can't believe you are doing this, I want to go home, now."

When we got home, I gave Steve a challenge.

"Steve, you have a choice to make, much as I love you, I am not living with a heroin addict, you either choose me and the baby, or you choose heroin and you leave, I am going to go shopping, when I get back, I want your answer."

For some reason I couldn't feel any anger I was just shocked and sad. I no longer wanted to be in his company and shopping seemed like a good distraction to get away and give Steve some time to think.

I had been gone about an hour and when I returned, I got my answer. Steve was no longer there, all the furniture in the house was smashed, the T.V. had furniture put through the screen, and the whole house from top to bottom was wrecked. I sat down and cradled Lauren in my arms, who was only a few months old. I felt so numb. I had no idea how to begin to put my life right, but one thing I did know I had to stop the cycle of choosing to be in relationships with men who were no good for me or my children. Enough was enough. Finally, it felt like the train that was hurtling down hill had slowed down and grinded to a halt.

Now more than ever I needed God's strength to do the right thing for everyone. In 1996, I was offered a large four bed property, the first bit of good news for us all.

Moving into our new home was exciting, it was a town house, it had a large front room, a large kitchen, four bedrooms, two toilets on two different floors giving plenty of space for everyone. James my son was such a great help, he was now the man of the house and anything that needed doing was done. I was so proud of my kids and now they were all growing up facing life head on.

I needed to grow up a little myself and stop self-medicating on alcohol, drinking alcohol was causing more harm than good and over a few years it had developed into a habit that made me selfish, at times I am sure my children had no idea what to do. When drinking collided with P.M.T I was hard to live with.

 On one of my difficult days, I took one pain killing tablet and mixed that with one drink. I ended up blacking out at the wheel of my car and crashed it into a lamp post. The car was a write off. I didn't have a seat belt on at the time and my leg got caught under the steering wheel as my body came up and forward with the impact, I hit my face on the windscreen. When I came out of the hospital, I was walking with crutches with one severely bruised and battered black left leg and nine stitches in my face. That night I went to bed and had a vivid dream. In the dream I heard a voice, a voice filled with love and authority, which brought me under a deep conviction, the voice said, "Stop drinking or worse shall befall you."

 I instantly woke up and felt God warning me to stop. I wasn't going to argue with God. I stopped drinking completely. I wasn't interested in drink anymore. All I wanted was for me and my children to be happy and for me as a Christian to start being obedient in all areas of my life.

Part Three

Tying up loose ends

Steve found out where we were all living and often came to see Lauren. I spent a couple of years supporting Steve. Sometimes he needed food, other times sex, other times, he just wanted to move back in and try again. Steve attended two detox centres and failed. I tried to help him at my home supporting him doing cold turkey. I went to a G.P and explained that by going through the system i.e., the drug dependant unit it was not helping, Steve was bumping into drug dealers, people offered him Methadone on top of what he was already using or getting off the system. Some people he owed money to, the whole thing was counterproductive, so I asked the G.P. for just one week's supply of Diazepam because Steve was going to detox at mine, and I wanted to help. At first this request was refused, but after a lot of explaining I got the tablets. Steve was desperate to try and kick his habit. I didn't recognize him; he was so thin.

Heroin, the big deceiver, the soul eater, which slowly clamps its deathly claws inside a weakened mind, creating a soulless individual, its parasitical nature shows no mercy as it cocoons the life it enters and paralyses what is left of the heart. What was once a man who loved to give became lost in a self-absorbed delusional nightmare, yet in his mind he is in a dream, bathed in self-denial as lie and lie poured out like a silky-smooth liquid. Ribs protrude through the skin and what was once a healthy body is now malnourished, skeletal, almost non-human. Nothing mattered except the next fix.

The Junkie's Psalm based on Psalm 23

> King Heroin is my shepherd, I shall always want.
> He maketh me lie down in the gutter.
> The streets are my pastures where he leadeth me,
> And the quiet waters in my works go straight to my soul.

Steve tried, I tried. I saw him groaning and moaning, cramping, sweating, and getting desperate. It wasn't easy for him or me. After a few days he left. During all the times I supported Steve I found out he had been stealing from the house, my jewellery, drugs in the medicine cabinet, money, and on one occasion unbelievably we saw him walking down the middle of the street with our T.V in his arms. In the end it all became too much, I stopped helping.

He also stole from his parents. This was a man who could have had everything, he came from a good family who were financially comfortable, when he was young, he was sent to boarding school, he had very good support, when he wanted money, they gave it to him which in the end was detrimental to his wellbeing. He could have started up any business for himself and he would have been helped. His family were there for him, but sadly in the end it made no impact on him stopping he just abused his family kindness.

When Steve was allowed to see Lauren even that turned out to be a mistake. On one occasion I found out he had taken her to an address where she witnessed her dad preparing heroin ready to inject into his vein. I was so distressed I banned him from taking Lauren out anywhere and a letter was sent to him from my solicitor to warn him that supervised visits to Lauren would be arranged if this ever happened again. Deep down I struggled to come to terms with the fact that our relationship had finished, I still cared deeply for Steve and I wanted to help him to be free from his addiction, but no matter how much I wanted him to be free, ultimately it was his choice to make and I needed to learn to let go. Sometimes a deep desire to help someone can get in the way and cause more problems.

All the time Steve had all this help and support it stopped him from taking full responsibility for his actions, he needed to hit rock bottom. Don't take me the wrong way, I am not saying we shouldn't help those who are fighting an addiction, but we need to be wise about how we support them for their own good, not for our own good. Sometimes our best intentions just delay the inevitable and letting go of those we love and care about is no easy task, but it has to be done.

Steve now resides in Vietnam with another woman and we have not seen him since and, although his daughter Lauren tried to communicate with her father via the internet, to see if their relationship could be saved, it turned out to be a dismal depressing affair. Steve had no intentions of facing up to any responsibilities regarding the damage he had caused to those he had affected, and it was evident that alcohol was now the dependant substance he relied upon. In the end, the conversations between Lauren and her dad were so negative and hostile Lauren decided after several attempts to stop all communication so that she could move forward with her own life. This was a heart-breaking decision for her to make but a necessary one.

Alcohol - A Deadly Toxin

Looking back into my history alcohol was a very strong influence.It was easy to get hold of. I grew up surrounded by parties and drink, in fact the whole family was drink orientated.

I have a cousin who was attending numerous AA meetings. One of my sisters died from alcohol; she weighed only 6 stone towards the end, she didn't eat. I drove down to Brighton when I heard she was in hospital very ill, but I was too late. By the time I got there she had gone into a coma, her whole system shut down and she died, in March 2012. My other sister is the only relative left alive that I see is doing great. She has been dry at least nine years and we speak every day. I am not opposed to someone having the occasional drink, but when drink becomes more important than your family, life, God, yourself, or the one you love, interferes with your functioning, changes your personality and other detrimental effects, it's time to stop.

Church v Recovery

My recovery from having a severe breakdown happened over a period of five years, sadly this was mostly outside of the church. I tried to integrate back into church life by attending small house group meetings as well as attending church on a Sunday. I was glad to be placed under a Christian G.P which at least gave me some comfort. There were times when I had the opportunity to meet with my G.P out of hours where we both had time to chat and pray together.

From the church perspective it was obvious that those within the church had no idea how to support someone who had not only suffered a severe mental breakdown at one stage but had exposed themselves to the occult, these were subject matters that for those inside the church were too much for them to deal with. I was told by some Christians they had no experience in counselling others who had gone through such an ordeal, that they were not professionally trained so they couldn't help me, or they didn't have the time to give me the support I needed.

I made some Christians feel uncomfortable. When I spoke freely, I could never quite be myself, some of my tattoo's made people feel uneasy, especially the tattoo of Baphomet. Even though I have tattooed around that image the words, False Light, Defeated, Father of Lies, and above the image a crown of thorns with the words Jesus Saved Me. My brief message to those who felt uncomfortable was not to judge a book by its cover, my advice was to not allow yourself to be affected by fear but act in love, to stop getting on a soap box about tattoos and reminded them that it is written in the Bible, don't judge by outward appearance but look at the heart. 1 Samuel 16 verse 7.

I noticed over time that in many churches there was very little practical help regarding how to support someone in my position. There were no printed leaflets on occult related issues or other modern-day issues, it was lonely experience, and as far as I can see most churches do not have in place today any printed literature or those within their congregations willing to pray with those who come from a difficult walk of life.

I remember approaching a very large church with a great reputation to see if anyone could support me, it was an impressive building, ushers in the car park and doorway, great music, loads of people, yet, I was told they don't believe in deliverance, they are unable to help, but I was very welcome to join their church. Some Christians that I met were completely devoid of any wisdom and discernment and saw demons in every problem and others were saying that they had no experience and didn't know what to do. Demonic activity was a subject they rather not discuss. This saddened me because it is through the power of the love of Jesus souls are healed; we just need to be willing to use our faith and step out for him. Love is what heals damaged souls, we just need to be willing vessels to allow ourselves to be used.

I never once witnessed a pastor or vicar in a church setting give any guidance or teaching on the areas of the occult or speak about how to love the broken. I certainly never heard any preaching on it either and to me that was part of the message of the gospel to love the unlovable and deal with the demonic. As my recovery continued with bouts of disruption, I was temporarily given Diazepam by my doctor to ease some of my anxiety. Nightmares were frequent and I realised that there are consequences to an action a person takes and some of those consequences can be healed and others I may have to live with.

I decided to use creative forms of expression as well as prayer to help me in my recovery process. I wrote poems and songs and kept a diary.

Here is one poem that shows one of my depressive moments

Midnight Blues

Curling odours of darkest poison entangles a wounded mind, a darkened time, a heart so blackened by death itself, I cry, to die.

No flaming arrow or burning light can prevent my soul from screaming, cold spiked weapons of steel plunge deep, to destroy my dreaming.

Reality yet colder still, of battle scars and warfare, of little peace only some release, like a razored knife to dissect my life, to cut so deep, I bleed no more, and there will be no open door, but tunnels and pits and caverns deep, and so I weep.

I choke, suppressed in a powerful force, that seeks to squeeze the life it smothers, no soothing care comes from others.

Damn the devil, his claw has struck, this cord of life in tatters, I moan and groan in agony, a mirror so clear shatters, and what I see, is no longer me, if it really matters.

I knew deep down even after being counselled that I needed spiritual help, I often cried out to Jesus, at times God's peace would come upon me but then I was back in torment particularly in my dreams.

Death, violence and mutilation were dominant areas in my dreams, I saw glass rain down from heaven, a glass man spat glass into my temple, different demonic creatures attacked my body, spirits tried to choke me, a witch wanted me dead. Flies plagued my dreams and spirits of the dead were in the air. I often felt that my soul was being tugged out of my body, that I couldn't breathe.

I went forward for prayer as often as I could and got anointed in oil.

I even saw the head of Psychiatry who felt I wasn't mentally ill but I did have personality difficulties that would get better over time and that I had hysterical dissociative states. I later found out that Lupus can attack any organ in the body and that included the brain which may have added to the problem. I never went back to the hospital and felt praying was the best course of action to take against all my disturbing nightmares. I was confused about the fact I was apparently not mentally ill but was told that I had dissociation issues and personality difficulties.

I was deeply saddened by the fact that a Christian woman down the street from me had committed suicide, she obviously felt she had no way out of her situation either. This all felt so wrong to me.

I love this:

> An objective person says, 'it's logical that someone fell into the pit'.

> A Pharisee says, 'only bad people fall into the pit'.

> A fundamentalist says, 'you deserve your pit'.

> A self-pitying person says, 'let me tell you about my pit'.

> An optimist says, 'things could be worse'.

> A pessimist says, 'things will get worse'.

> Jesus sees the person, takes him by the hand, and lifts him out of the pit.

Back on Track

Counselling was offered to my children and I went to college and attended courses on counselling for a period of three years. Some of the training I received was local at Parkside College in Cambridge and two years was spent training in Chelmsford. A Christian couple who lived nearby offered to pay for all my fees; not only the course fees and material but the fuel costs as well, it was an amazing answer to prayer.

When I attended a residential, I learnt so much about how pain can be released through the creative arts, it was a great experience. Again, the fees were impossible for me to find but another Christian on the course offered to pay for me to go. I spent a whole year being counselled by a qualified counsellor; I used that year to dump every painful emotion I had.

The process was certainly eye opening. I understood how my past actually did affect my present situation, and how many other different factors come into play, my childhood, environment, transference from others, the list was endless. Every week I drove from Cambridge to Chelmsford I would notice something new or different that I needed to tackle, I often went down the M11 having panic attacks, and drove back home from the course, crying my eyes out. It took a lot of courage on my part to stay with the counsellor for a year without walking out, most of my life I had either run away from a situation, or was forced out of a situation, or wanted to avoid confrontation. But not this time.

In 1999 I achieved my advanced counselling certificate validated by a university. Saying goodbye to all those I had made friends with on the course was hard, but we all had signed personal messages from each other to take home with us, many thanked me for my courage and honesty. When I got home, I placed my first certificates on the wall and thanked God for such an achievement. Having worked through many issues I prayed that God would one day, if at all possible, use me to help others.

Here are just a few of the messages that I have kept from those I was on the course with to remind myself that anything is possible and anyone can change.

It's been uplifting to find a new sister. You're the FIRESTARTER, but you're quite cuddly as well.

I've discovered someone really warm and loving who gives out so much. Thank you for letting me see you.

You gave me so much to think about at dinner- please don't ever stop being you.

A Christian with some life!!!

I've enjoyed the puzzle of wondering what you are all about and I still don't know.

Thank you for being willing to share of yourself and to look at areas of your life that you want to change.

Your faith is obviously very practical and real, God grants our hearts desires. Thanks for being frank.

A Vision is Born

All my past experiences coupled with a new perspective of myself and my situation helped a new passion grow within my heart. God had showed me a never ending well of mercy, compassion and patience. I had the deepest gratitude to God. As stability and normality took hold, I had a longing in my heart to share the hope and peace that had developed in my own heart with others, more than that, I realised that many on the outside of church life were needing love, support and salvation. There were Christians who had lost faith for a multitude of reasons and those who had slipped backwards or relapsed.

As I prayed a deep conviction in my heart remained, how could I help others? The church had become predominately a middle-class church system with little understanding on how to help those from a different background. Integration was available to some, but it was on their own terms of how church was already established, conformity and sometimes unnecessary control caused more problems than helping. If I rocked the boat inside the church as it was, I would probably be seen as a dissenter. All I knew was I needed to show mercy as God had shown mercy to me.

In December 1999 I made the decision to walk by faith, to trust God and be mature. Surely this was part of picking up my cross and denying self. As a single unemployed person with no spare money, with health issues, I wasn't sure if I was being foolish or not, but I needed to put my faith into action. I decided the only way to find out was to act upon my faith.

I put together some flyers and encouraged others to come to my home once a week. I placed flyers in hostels and handed them out to whoever would take them either on the street or in shop windows or pubs. Those who found it difficult to come to my home were picked up. In Jeremiah 22 v 16 it says, 'he defended the cause of the poor and needy, and all went well for him. Isn't that what it means to know me?' Says the Lord.

Every Friday evening my home was open to those with broken lives, some who were still using alcohol or drugs, some were depressed, others had minds that were struggling for some degree of normality and were still under the care of mental health teams. They were all seeking for acceptance, love, attention, or even a miracle. I had created a space for everyone who were able to be themselves. As trust with each other developed, pain was released, sometimes with brutal honesty. I called these meetings 'Focus Groups' Focus stood for fellowship of compassion uniting souls. The importance of being able to share in a safe and loving environment gave them all the release they needed.

A meeting would last roughly 3-4 hours and people left when they were ready rather than being rushed out the door, our meetings were never rushed. This was not a church meeting even though Christian content was present, our meetings did not have to be done to a set time or agenda, because that agenda could change in the blink of an eye. It had to be flexible. This was a time when hearts were exposed, where fears were released, courage shown. It was a place where hope and love were offered.

I discovered amongst the pain of each individual talents that were not being used or encouraged, including those who had degrees in art and education, those who had the ability to write poetry or do drama, it was just amazing. Gradually over the weeks I understood how difficult it was for most of them to integrate back into normal society. Many more Focus groups were needed. You see, it was not about me being professionally trained that was the key, although that training helped me to open others up to speak about their pain, it was more about having the right attitude in my heart and moving in faith, imitating Christ, being compassionate, after all healing, deliverance and salvation comes from Jesus Christ. It is the love of God through his Son Jesus that peace of mind can be given, that a soul in torment can be saved and freed.

At the start of our meetings, we sang worship songs of all different varieties, all of them tailored to the occasion, songs that were down to earth with lyrics that were meaningful, some lyrics that could even relate to where they were at in life. For example, a song we sang called Saved by Big & Rich. Let's check out some of the lyrics and you will understand what I mean.

Verse one

There was a time I tried to kill a man, just for looking at me wrong, anger so strong, I couldn't stop myself.

I was killing myself one shot at a time, going insane from the pain, the women and the wine.

But I finally hit bottom in an alleyway, hell wasn't but a breath away, so I hit my knees in the street and begged God for mercy.

Chorus:

Last night I told the devil where to go, you know heaven's got my soul, ain't gonna listen to his lies no more, last night I told the devil where to go.

We also had worship songs. And all of them were enjoyed by all.

As the meeting continued God's word was shared, we would go at a pace that was good for everyone. Questions were encouraged. Sharing with patience and love was really important. It wasn't a time of preaching but more of teaching and discussion. This was a time of healthy debate as well as understanding how God's word could be applied to our lives. Prayer ministry was offered at the end, with the opportunity to repent and be saved, or simply be prayed with.

Refreshments and snacks were offered at the start of a meeting, in the middle of a meeting and at the end of a meeting.

Meetings were sometimes temporarily stopped if someone had an issue they wanted to raise or if someone was upset, we didn't ignore that person and carry on with the meeting or say to them that we would deal with the issue or problem later, later was no good. When pain comes up and out, as Christians we need to meet that pain head on and be willing to give up our time constraints or set agenda's because the state of a person's heart and what they are going through is more important. It is a time when if that soul is willing that Jesus can meet with them and help. A meeting should never override a person's desperate need for help. Focus was a haven for many where the suffering of humanity was touched by the divinity of God. God said that faith unless expressed through love counts as nothing.

After a while Focus meetings met inside a room inside a church in Mill Road, Cambridge and to my surprise the work expanded in ways I had never ever thought about. Every Saturday in this particular church the homeless were invited to have soup, bread and other food inside the foyer of the church. I was informed that although this was a good thing to do, souls were not getting saved, people were just coming along, eating their food and going. So, the first thing I did was put flyers on the tables stating that every Friday in an adjoining room a meeting was taking place and that they were welcome. I erected a stand-up board that said each week what topic we were discussing which could have been anything, Fear, Anger, Loss, etc. This made people curious and some people came along.

Some of those that came along who had addiction problems were happy for me to take them to a Christian rehab centre, and although these centres were strict some people wanted to give it a try. Some people stayed, worked it through and others came back finding the rules too much for them, but the choice was there.

Focus groups ran for about five years in total and during that time I had developed a drama with some humour to show in churches about those in society who were sometimes ignored how they could be integrated into a low-key Christian group or be saved.

I set up a training questionnaire for those who showed an interest in being part of a Focus team and shared my testimony whenever I was asked including sharing in Highpoint Prison and on T.V. as well as articles in local newspapers and magazines. I felt that I was putting my faith into action. I needed more support in the running of the project which sadly was lacking, so I decided to close the project down. I wasn't superhuman and burn out was almost certainly on the cards if I continued, I had my limitations. But it is good to know in my heart that some people were saved and supported.

Number 3

When I had my encounter at 3am it was much later on that I wondered if there was any other significance to that particular time other than the fact the appearance of Satan happened in the 'witching hour' when the veil between our world and the spirit world is known to be at its thinnest. Others say that it is the inverted time of Satan's victory and dark hour to when Jesus died on the cross at 3pm. In Luke 22 verse 53 it says, this is your moment when the power of darkness reigns, this statement was made to the priests, elders and guards when they arrested Jesus and that reign of darkness continues right through to the crucifixion and darkness covered the earth for three hours. It is interesting that some practitioners of the occult mock Christianity and reverse objects or mimic gifts to distort the truth, a cross will be turned upside down, the Lord's prayer will be recited backwards, for example Amen would be Nema and 3pm becomes 3am. And let us be in no doubt Satan only has limited power. Whatever the reason for the 3am encounter, I am no longer bound by occult beliefs. I always pray before sleeping and ask God to look after my mind, body and soul. If you are waking up use that time to pray to God for peace and rest as your mind and body needs it. Find all the scriptures on peace and sleep and pray them out often.

Psalm 4: verse 8 'In peace I will lie down and sleep, for you alone oh Lord will keep me safe.'

Remember every time you draw near to God, God will draw near to you.

Some people say that numbers in the Bible are symbolic ways of conveying God's truth. I found in the Bible some interesting things concerning the number 3 but it is just an interest. I will start with the crucifixion.

Jesus hung on a cross from the sixth hour (2 x 3) midday to the ninth hour (3 x3) 3pm

As Jesus cried out 'My God, My God, why have you forsaken me' Jesus experienced full separation from his heavenly Father as he took the sin of the world into himself. Everyone's sin for all time.

3 in the division of time denotes past, present, future.

3 is the number of divine completeness and perfection.

Jesus rose on the third day. Because of the resurrection we can come out of the kingdom of darkness and be transferred into the kingdom of his dear Son, who purchased our freedom and forgave our sin. Colossians 1 verse 13.

Three bears witness, Spirit – Water – Blood.

Trinity, Father – Son – Holy Ghost.

Jesus was denied by Peter 3 times.

The disciple Paul pleaded three times for his thorn to be removed. Paul was blind for three days and was on the Isle of Malta for 3 months. Paul was shipwrecked 3 times. Paul visited the third heaven.

Judas sold out for 30 pieces of silver (3 + 0 = 3)

Jesus asked Simon Peter 3 times 'Do you love me'?

Jesus did not start his ministry until the age of 30 (3 + 0 = 3), which lasted 3 years.

Jesus died at the age of 33 (3 + 3 = 6) the number of Man. Jesus was known as the Son of Man, as well as the Son of God.

Christ is the three shepherds: The Good Shepherd, The Great Shepherd, The Chief Shepherd.

In Acts 10 verse 30, Cornelius was praying in his house when he was visited by Jesus, a man in dazzling clothes, at 3 o'clock in the afternoon.

In Matthew 14 verse 25, Jesus was walking on the water at around 3am in the morning.

Jonah was in the belly of the fish for three days and three nights.

The placard on the cross was written in 3 different languages: Hebrew, Greek and Latin.

We are made up of body, soul, spirit.

Jesus answered Satan's three temptations by citing three scriptures.

Israelite men were required to celebrate 3 festivals each year. Deuteronomy 16: v16.

Jesus went missing for three days, Luke 2 when he was 12 years old (1 + 2 = 3).

Elijah stretched over a child three times, 1 Kings 17.

Daniel prayed 3 times a day.

In Genesis 15, animals had to be 3 years old for special sacrifice.

Acts 10 verse 16, a vision Peter had repeated 3 times.

There are a lot more references to the number 3 in the Bible, but I have covered some for you. I will let you enjoy finding some for yourself.

What's wrong with the occult?

Those who go beyond the veil are known as occultists, there are many paths to explore from Spiritualism, Witchcraft, Wicca, Satanism, Paganism, Spiritualism, Magic, New Age, Freemasonry and Astrology to name but a few. There are too many areas of the occult to be listed here but most have practices and rituals, which sometimes involve gods and goddesses, altered states of conscience and angel guides.

Those involved in the occult seek to empower themselves by tapping into universal energies/elements or by connecting/invoking a powerful spirit or angel. Those who want to delve into the occult do so to deepen their knowledge about the universe and its forces, additionally to have more influence or control over events, to be able to predict the future, summon a spirit, communicate with the dead, have power to heal or attract, curse or inflict, to bring about a result, to find answers, to belong, to protect, to learn spells for good or for harm, have blessing/love or prosperity, or simply self-empowerment.

Some in frustration have turned away from the established church into the occult for a variety of reasons. Others have grown up and passed on their traditions within their family. There are those who practice alone and those who practice within a coven or group. The occult covers a vast sea of beliefs and everyone can develop their own style and indulge in their chosen practices to suit themselves. The occult is one large cauldron pot of beliefs that can be individualised or kept traditional and there are so many strands of the occult that it is hard to keep up with it all.

I want to break down some of the differences between basic occult beliefs verses Christianity, but I would like to add before I begin that I am talking about Christianity, one who is a Christ follower, who believes in the teachings of Jesus and the way that Jesus encouraged a Christian to live, not religion or religious beliefs that mix biblical teaching and their own doctrines and traditions, with man-made rules. There are many today that have a mixture of beliefs this is called syncretism; that is NOT Christianity. Some believe that you can be a Christian Witch, in fact today it seems anything goes. There is a huge difference between established religion and Christianity, even Jesus had to deal with and rebuke the religious people of his day for their pride and hypocrisy.

Here are some, but not all of the differences between Christian teaching and the occult.

	Occult	Christian
1	Enthronement of self	Self-denial
2	Dualism	God's power is supreme
3	Esoteric Knowledge	Fear of the Lord is the foundation of true knowledge Proverbs 1: verse 7
4	No such thing as Sin	'He who says he has no sin deceives himself.' 1 John 1: verse 8
5	Gods and goddesses	Idolatry is the worship of false idols which are demons
6	Divine goddess within	Holy Spirit within
7	No such thing as Satan	Jesus said, in Luke 10 verse 18 that he saw Satan (the adversary) fall like lightening
8	No such as thing as Hell	Matthew 10: verse 28 fear not them which kill the body, but are not able to kill the soul: but rather fear him which is

		able to destroy both soul and body in hell
9	Astrology	God says it is futile and foolish Jeremiah 10 verses 1-3
10	Veneration of divine nature	Romans 1: verse 25 'They traded the truth about God for a lie. So, they worshiped and served the things God created instead of the Creator himself, who is worthy of eternal praise!'
11	Prayer seen as an energy	Prayer is not an energy. Prayer is your heart talking to God, pouring out one's soul, thankfulness, worship, intercession, and much more.
12	Self-empowerment	Christians allow the Holy Spirit to work through them developing the fruits of the Holy Spirit and spiritual gifts.
13	Different aspects of truth	Only one ultimate truth. Jesus said I am the way, the Truth, and the life.
14	Do what you will	Obeying God's will

Satan's deception and character can be seen throughout the Bible showing itself in different ways and prior to the Lords second coming the man of lawlessness will come and sit in the temple of God, claiming himself to be God this is in 2 Thessalonians 2: in verse 9 it shows this man will come to do the work of Satan with counterfeit power, signs and miracles. He will use evil deception to fool those who refuse to love and accept the truth that would save them.

The character of Satan

Isaiah 14 and Ezekiel 28 are scriptures referring to earthly Kings as well as Lucifer (Light-bringer). The Bible often uses a dual reference. In Hebrew hermeneutics (study of the Bible) it is called remez, a hidden message or deeper meaning. For example, in Ezekiel 28 verse 13 it says, 'you were in Eden' the garden of God, The King could have never been in Eden because this was at the beginning of creation, also see in verse 13, the King of Tyre was born, not created, and in verse 14, King Tyre could not have been a mighty angelic guardian.

In Ezekiel 28 let us see the description of Gods ordained angelic guardian before the fall.

'You were the model of perfection, full of wisdom and exquisite in beauty.

You were in Eden, the garden of God.

Your clothing was adorned with every precious stone, red carnelian, pale-green peridot, white moonstone, blue-green beryl, onyx, green jasper, blue lapis lazuli, turquoise, and emerald— all beautifully crafted for you and set in the finest gold.

They were given to you on the day you were created.

I ordained and anointed you as the mighty angelic guardian.

You had access to the holy mountain of God and walked among the stones of fire.

You were blameless in all you did from the day you were created until the day evil was found in you.'

Then in Isaiah 14 Lucifer is described again, another dual reference, in verse 12 it says, 'How you are fallen from heaven, O shining star, son of the morning.' Lucifer has been thrown down to the earth because he wanted to ascend and set his throne above God's, this was pride in all its fullness.

164

In Luke 10 verse 18, Jesus said, 'I saw Satan fall heaven like lightening.'

Lucifer has now become the adversary of God, adversary taken from the Hebrew means opponent. Satan no longer has his position; he has been cast down.

In Revelation 12 it says that there was a war in heaven and the dragon lost the battle and he and his angels were forced out of heaven. This ancient serpent, dragon, Satan, Devil, the one deceiving the whole world was thrown down to the earth with all his angels who rebelled with him. Satan is known by many names or descriptions, let's look at a few.

Anti-Christ

The Beast

Lawless One

Little Horn

Son of Perdition

Dragon

Serpent

Abaddon/Apollyon – Destroyer

Angel of Light

Accuser

Murderer

Angel of the bottomless pit/or Abyss

Fallen Star

Devil

Wicked One

Enemy

Father of Lies

God of this age

Deceiver of the whole world.

Lucifer (before his fall)

Ruler of this world

Prince of the power of the air

Roaring Lion.

Belial

The first use of Satan is in 1 Chronicles 21: verse 1.

Satan in Hebrew means 'accuser', in Revelation 12 verse 10 it says, 'for the accuser of our brothers and sisters has been thrown down to earth, the one who accuses them, before God, day and night.'

Jesus taught that Satan or the devil is a murderer from the beginning, that he hates the truth and that he is the Father of lies. John 8 v 44

What lies do you believe? Here is just a small example of the lies and deceit you may be under. I have heard many people believe or say these lies. How many can you relate to in this small list?

LIES: I can never be deceived, I'm no good, I am stupid, my family often told me that I am the black sheep of the family, that I will never change. What future do I have?

There is no God, there is no devil it's all fantasy. There is no such thing as ultimate truth, I am my own God, I am worthless and helpless, I can walk on any path they all lead to the same God, I can acquire knowledge from any source it won't harm me, if it makes me feel good do it, indulge in whatever I like, life is for living in the here and now, there is no such thing as sin, there is no hell. There are no miracles, I have plenty of time on earth, humility is a waste of time. Revenge is sweet, if there is a God it will be all rules and regulations with little freedom, I will never be forgiven I am too great a sinner. Jesus was just another prophet. God no longer cares; God is cruel and distant. Love yourself that's all that matters. I can believe what I like, practice what I like, it's my life and I am harming no-one. I am a good person, so I don't need God. Christians use God as a crutch because they are weak. Christians hate sinners and anyone who wants to live their life differently. God did not create me.

What soul? There is no such thing as a soul, I don't believe I have one. When I am dead that's it. I don't need others or be in fellowship with others. It's my body so I can do what I like with it. The Bible is flawed. God is not in control. God doesn't care. Everyone should all be united together into one big spiritual pot that is true unity. There is no such thing as demons. There is no such thing as evil. Satan doesn't exist. I can never have children. I can never be healed. I will never be free of this depression. I can never be free from addiction. There is no hope for me I am a lost cause. I believe in reincarnation so I will continue to exist. We are all part of one cosmic conscience, experience is more important than belief. You can transform yourself. There is no such place as hell or heaven.

This is just the tip of iceberg in the world of lies, but thank fully God has given us all a way out.

Satan is able to transform into an angel of light. In 2 Corinthians 11 verse 14, it says, 'but I am not surprised even Satan disguises himself as an angel of light.' In the Kings James version, it uses the word 'transformed'.

In 1 Peter 5: v 8 it says, 'Stay alert! Watch out for your great enemy, the devil, he prowls around like a roaring lion, looking for someone to devour.'

In John 10 v10 Satan came to steal, kill and destroy.

In Revelation 12 verses from verse 9 it says, 'Satan is the one who deceives not just one or two people or hundreds of people but the whole world.' It also states that the devil has come down in great anger because he knows his time is short.

Satan is a thief, a destroyer, he steals, deceives, transforms, accuses, mimics, he is the author of confusion, a tempter, seducer, one who sows doubt, a devourer, he is your opponent and Gods, blasphemous, a slanderer, disloyal and a dissenter, full of pride and rebellion.

Satan is a created being inferior to God, powerful but not ALL powerful. Satan is not a mythical figure. Satan and his cohorts inhabit a different dimension to you and me. Satan disguises his true nature to lure you in. Satan can do false miracles, bring false healing, a false light, a false peace, and a false truth.

Satanism

Satanists are their own construct of flesh clothed in pride, a self-made idol. 'Those who are consumed by such self-love are enslaved to themselves, for you are a slave to whatever controls you.' 2 Peter 2: verse 19

I want to briefly touch upon the mind set of Satanism, I will not be covering all the different areas or branches of Satanism, but encourage you to do your own research. When I walked on this path for a period time, it gave freedom to my anger and rebellion in every way, but in reality, I was not free at all. I gave the devil a foothold. Once a foothold or stronghold had taken root, all other vile spiritual areas swoop in fast to encase the soul into a prison of darkness and a downward spiral begins.

Satan is seen by some as a symbol of independence and individuality, a concrete belief in being your 'own god', under the banner of freedom, power and strength. Within the empowerment of self, an ego centric lifestyle refuses to be dictated to by others and Satanists become in their eyes their own masters. Theistic Satanists believe in Satan as an entity or personal dark force, as well as other entities, other Satanists don't believe in a deity or entity, most Satanists are atheists who do not believe in the existence of the Devil, hell, God or sin.

Whatever umbrella term a person wants to use to describe themselves or their beliefs, if it is outside the Holy Spirit and what God has taught, it is on Satan's territory or of the flesh. Those who profess that Satanism has nothing to do with devil worship have failed to see that the devil can be worshipped in ways that are less obvious and more subtle. Whatever takes you away from God's truth takes you into deception and lies.

Self-indulgence is the very opposite to one who picks up their cross and follows Christ, denying self, the cross is a symbol of death to our sinful nature and sensual desires as well as a symbol of resurrection. It is through the cross that Jesus died to give us all true freedom. Christianity far from being a control mechanism that oppresses the soul is quite the opposite. True knowledge and wisdom will not come from Lucifer. Isaiah 14: v 12, 'How art thou fallen from heaven, O Lucifer son of the morning.' (KJV) for Satan masquerades as an angel of light. 2 Corinthians 11: verse 14 'He is not light, but masquerades as light. (To pretend to be something different)

The adolescent Satanist uses Satanism as an avenue to shock many, their failure to grow up and stop their selfish behaviour is reaping what they sow, spiritual death. Their unresolved issues connect to music, symbolic accessories and clothing, defiant and destructive behaviour, tantrums, and a blatant disregard for others and property.

Shock tactics and using Satanism as a screen is very damaging to themselves and to their families. Their ego, pride, rebellion and self-indulgence remind me of a hungry creature that demands constant feeding or else.

Some adults (but not all) use Satanism as a screen for all sorts of practices including sex, drugs and any other form of carnal behaviour that they want to indulge in. Self-glorification is a dead end and those who nurture their 'god' within thrives off sensuality, as it feels good, its self-gratifying, appeasing, but the end result is destruction of your own soul.

If a Satanist ever met with the real Satan their gatherings would disperse and souls would flee, for a soul to be in the presence of such an ancient, powerful corrupt creature whose heart is filled with murder and lies would be too much for the mind to bear.

Proverbs 3: verse 7 says, 'Don't be impressed with your own wisdom, instead fear the Lord and turn away from evil.'

In 2 Corinthians 4: v 4 it says, 'Satan, who is god of this world, has blinded the minds of those who don't believe. They cannot see the light or understand the message about the gospel or glory of Christ.'

Whatever title a person wants to give themselves is really not that important, the state of a person's heart is because the heart deceives even itself. Unless a person is coming from a basis of ultimate truth from the creator (God and what God has taught) the mind and what it formulates becomes distorted and is led into every form of deception and lie until far from the self being glorified as a 'god' you are actually in a deep pit of delusion and have become caught in a trap.

In 2 Timothy 2: verse 26, then they will come to their senses and escape from the devil's trap. For they have been held captive by him to do whatever he wants.

In Ephesians 2: verse 2, those who were once spiritually dead because of their disobedience and sin, who followed their carnal nature by God's grace were saved. They were obeying the devil, the commander of the powers in the unseen world, the spirit at work in the hearts of those who refused to obey God. A person who is an atheist doesn't have to worship the devil, but nevertheless that atheistic heart is in trouble and is under demonic influence and spiritual death and bondage by disobeying and living to gratify the carnal nature and feeding the ego inflating its own sense of pride that only leads to self-destruction not some kind of god status.

CRSO

I wrote a song called Flesh and Bone. Here are the words:

Verse 1:

    Flesh and bone
    sit on a throne
    craving your attention
    It's bound in a deathly direction
    Addiction at your door
    Hungry for the next score
    ripping at your hearts core
    these words you will hear for sure.

Chorus:

    I want my own way, don't tell me what to do
    Don't resist me now, I can grow in you
    I can fill you with every desire
    Igniting your soul on fire
    I am eating machine
    feed me

Do what I want
feed me
you're making me strong
feed me
Then I will rise like a god in my eyes
If you feed me

Verse 2:

Flesh and bone,
sit on a throne
deception is its game
It will drive you insane
Indulgence is the key
A darken sorcery
Ripping at your hearts core
These are the words you will hear for sure.

Chorus

Verse 3:

Flesh and bone sit on a throne
Its conscience has gone numb
while having so much fun
It's going at the speed of light,
heading for hell in the dark of night
ripping at your hearts core
These are the words you will hear for sure.

In my heart I pray and hope that those who have a defiant cause against Christianity that they have a Damascus experience.

In Acts 9 Saul (who later became Paul) was a Jew, a strict Pharisee and saw the Christian faith as a threat to the Jewish religion. Saul was zealous in his pursuit of Christians; he persecuted the church and believers. It says in Acts 9 that he uttered threats with every breath and was eager to kill the Lord's followers. He wanted to have them arrested, chained, and brought back to Jerusalem. He was on mission and had already built up a bad reputation. But he was struck down in the midst of his mission by a blinding light (that kept him blind for three days) he heard the voice of Jesus speak to him. The men with him also heard the voice but could see no-one. Jesus said to Saul, 'why are you persecuting me?'

'Saul asked, 'who are you Lord?'

And the voice replied, 'I am Jesus the one you are persecuting. Now, get up and go into the city, and you will be told what to do'.

Saul became God's chosen instrument, taking the gospel message to the Gentiles (non-Jews) and to Kings, as well as to the people of Israel. Saul's sight was regained, he was filled with the Holy Spirit and was baptized.

There is hope for even those who seek to persecute Christians.

CROND

Many who were under this spiritual slavery were delivered. Colossians 1: verse 13 says, 'for he has rescued us from the kingdom of darkness and transferred us into the kingdom of his dear Son, who purchased our freedom and forgave our sins.'

'Know that the Son of God has come to destroy the works of the devil.' 1 John 3: verse 8

In the book of Jude, some ungodly people had wormed their way into the churches, saying that Gods marvellous grace allowed them to live immoral lives. They defied authority and scoffed at supernatural beings. But even Michael (an archangel) one of the mightiest angels, did not dare accuse the devil of blasphemy, but simply said, 'the Lord rebuke you'.

These people scoff at things they do not understand, like unthinking animals, they do whatever their instincts tell them, so they bring about their own destruction. They brag about themselves, flatter others to get what they want, they grumble and complain, living only to satisfy their desires.

CROND

Revelation 21: v 14. 'Blessed are those who wash their robes. They will be permitted to enter through the gates of the city and eat the fruit from the tree of life. Outside the city are the dogs, the sorcerers, the sexually immoral, the murderers, the idol worshippers, and all those who love to live a lie.'

Those who love to live a lie will not have spiritual life, this is why the father of lies Satan seeks a soul like a devouring lion, Satan is a predator, the one who pursues your soul, he is the thief, the destroyer, the one who steals and kills.

But God does not want one soul to perish, you have a choice, there is still time to make the right choice. For Jesus came into the world as a light to those in darkness.

I don't believe in censorship because people must always have the free will to choose what they believe and what they do. Free will, free speech, freedom to choose, even if at times we use our free will to go in a wrong direction.

In Revelation 21: verse 11 it says, 'let the one who is doing harm continue to do harm, let the one who is vile continue to be vile, let the one who is righteous continue to live righteously, let the one who is holy continue to be holy.'

God Cannot Be Mocked

Although we see occult power at work in Exodus 7 verses 9 to 13 It is God's power that is supreme.

God knew that Pharaoh would want some kind of miracle so Aaron was to throw down his staff in front of the Pharaoh and the staff would turn into a serpent. So, when Aaron and Moses went to the Pharaoh and did what the Lord commanded them, Pharaoh called in his own wise men and sorcerers, and these Egyptian magicians did the same thing with their magic. They threw down their staffs that also became serpents. But then Aaron's staff swallowed up the magicians' staffs showing them that their magic was no equal with God's supreme power.

In Acts 16: verse 16

Paul and others were going down to a place of prayer when they met a slave girl who had a spirit that enabled her to tell the future. She earned a lot of money for her masters by telling fortunes. She followed Paul and the others, shouting, 'These men are the servants of the most high God and they have come to tell you how to be saved.'

This went on day after day until Paul got exasperated that he turned and said to the demon within her, 'I command you in the name of Jesus Christ to come out of her'. And instantly it left her. Her masters hope of wealth were now shattered.

In Daniel 5 King Belshazzar was having a great feast and orders were given to bring in the gold and silver cups from his predecessor Nebuchadnezzar which had been taken from the God's temple in Jerusalem. While they drank from them, they praised their idols. This was a sacrilegious act.

Suddenly, the King and others saw the fingers of a human hand, writing on the plaster wall of the King's palace. The King was filled with fear, he shouted for the enchanters, astrologers and fortune-tellers to be brought before him and said to the wise men of Babylon, 'whoever can read this writing and tell me what it means will be dressed in a purple robe of royal honour and will have a gold chain placed around their neck. He will become the third highest ruler in the kingdom.'

But none of the men could read the writing or tell him what it meant.

When the Queen mother heard what happened she spoke to the King and mentioned Daniel had the spirit of the holy gods, a man with insight, understanding and wisdom. That he can solve difficult problems, explain riddles and interpret dreams. Call for Daniel and he will tell you what the writing means.

Daniel was brought before the King.

Who is Daniel? Daniel whose name means (God is my judge) was taken captive to Babylon and served in Nebuchadnezzar's courts. He interpreted Nebuchadnezzar's dreams and was appointed chief over all the wise men of Babylon. He was a man of prayer.

The King called Daniel and asked him to interpret the writing on the wall. Daniel told the King how he had defied the Lord of heaven and so had not honoured God. The words on the wall were Mene, Mene, Tekel, and Parsin. The text was in Aramaic.

Mene means numbered - God had numbered his days of reign.

Tekel means weighed - the King had not measured up.

Parsin means divided - the kingdom had been divided and given to the Medes and Persians. That very night the King was killed and Darius, the Mede, took over the kingdom.

False Idols

In the commandments, God has forbidden other gods before him. You must not bow down or worship any graven image or idol.

The so-called gods and goddesses that many revere and call upon are demons.

Let's start with 1 Corinthians 10 verse 14 , 'so, my dear friends, flee from the worship of idols.' Then onto verse 19 to 20, 'What am I trying to say? Am I saying that food offered to idols has some significance, or that idols are real gods? No, not at all. I am saying that these sacrifices are offered to demons, not to God. And I don't want you to participate with demons.' Why did Paul say this? ancient worshippers believed that the idols were inhabited by their gods, if the idol was destroyed, they built another one and a ritual was performed, a qualified artisan chose pure materials for the image to be created and cleansed in a purification ritual selecting a pure place for the idol to be placed, vivification followed next, the statue or idol was anointed and clothed to invest the statue with sensory powers, and finally enthronement, done at a specific time, the rising of the sun, where offerings and incantations initiated the deity's active reign. Enthronement took place the next day establishing the deity over the temple, land and people, it was to reign over the people as a medium. This ritual was known as 'opening of the mouth' the idol needed to smell incense, eat food and drink water, the idol had to be a dwelling fit for a god. These rituals originated in Egypt and Mesopotamia.

We see in the Bible a denouncement of the 'opening of the mouth' ritual. In Psalm 135 verses 15-17 it says, 'The idols of the nations are merely things of silver and gold, shaped by human hands. They have mouths but cannot speak, and eyes but cannot see. They have ears but cannot hear and mouths but cannot breathe.'

Habbakkuk 2 verse 19 says, what sorrow awaits you who say to wooden idols, 'wake up and save us.' to speechless stones images you say, 'rise up and teach us.' can an idol tell you what to do? They may be overlaid with gold and silver, but they are lifeless inside.

In Leviticus 17 verse 7 there are goat idols or demons.

In Revelation 9 verse 20, 'But the people who did not die in these plagues still refused to repent of their evil deeds and turn to God. They continued to worship demons and idols made of gold, silver, bronze, stone, and wood, - idols that can neither see nor hear nor walk. And they did not repent of their murders or their witchcraft or their sexual immorality or their thefts.'

In 1 Samuel 5 Israel was at war with the Philistines. The Philistines had captured the Ark of God, they carried the Ark into the temple of Dagon and place it beside an idol of Dagon. (Fish -God) father of Baal. But when the citizens of Ashdod went to see it the next morning, Dagon had fallen with his face to the ground in front of the Ark of the Lord. So, they took Dagon and put him back in his place again. The next morning the same thing happened again but this time his head and hands had broken off and were lying in the doorway. Only the trunk of his body was left intact. To this day neither the priests of Dagon nor anyone who enter the temple of Dagon in Ashdod will step on its threshold.

Deuteronomy 4: 19 says, and when you look up into the sky and see the sun, moon and stars, all the forces of heaven, don't be seduced into worshipping them.

For those who believe that their time of birth, the positions of the planets determine to help forecast their future and present situation are being deceived. All these false beliefs have angered God because when you listen to the Father of Lies it will take you away from the true God which endangers your soul. When the last days come the sun will be darkened and the moon will not give its light, the stars will fall from the sky and the heavenly bodies will be shaken.

In 2 Kings chapter 21 we see the rule of King Manasseh who did evil in the eyes of God. He reigned in Jerusalem fifty-five years. The King followed detestable practices of the pagan nations which the Lord had driven from the land ahead of the Israelites. The King rebuilt the pagan shrines, constructed altars to Baal and set up an Asherah pole.

The King also sacrificed his own son in the fire, and practiced sorcery and divination. He consulted with mediums and psychics. The King also made a carved image of Asherah and set it up in the temple. The King murdered many innocent people, Jerusalem was filled from one end to the other with innocent blood. He also led others to do evil. Later, when King Josiah reigned, he pledged to obey the Lord by keeping all his commandments. All pagan articles were removed from the temple and were burned outside Jerusalem, he did away with the idolatrous priests, he removed all the Asherah poles and burned them.

Asherah pole or stylized trees stood as a monument and as a tribute to Asherah (other names, Astarte, Ishtar, Ashtoreth), a mother goddess of sex and fertility to the Canaanites and Phoenicians who gives life to 70 other gods. Sacred trees were thought to connect between netherworld (place of the dead) and the heavens, charged with divine force (serpent power).

He tore down the living quarters of the male and female shrine prostitutes, he destroyed statues and chariots dedicated to the sun and tore down the altars and ground them to dust. He demolished all the buildings at the pagan shrines and executed some of the priests on their own altars. Josiah got rid of the mediums, psychics, the household gods, the idols, and every kind of detestable practice.

In Deuteronomy 18 it says that these practices are detestable customs and detestable to God, which included sacrifices of children, fortune telling, use of sorcery, interpreting omens, engaging in witchcraft, casting spells, to function as mediums or psychics or call forth the spirits of the dead.

Ecclesiastes 1 verse 9 says, history repeats itself. It has all been done before. Nothing under the sun is truly new, it is a repetitive cycle of disobedience throughout the spans of time.

Idolatry is not just the worship of so-called gods and goddesses or graven images, it is anything that becomes more central in your life that is so time consuming upon the altar of your own heart that it has taken the place of God.

Let us look briefly at some areas of modern idolatry, I am not saying that it is wrong to listen to music for example, but rather how much time you spend in these areas, that takes your focus away from giving God your time and worship from your heart. Perhaps think how you can cut down on some of these areas and deepen your relationship with God.

1. Love of self: this could mean constantly being before a mirror, constant selfies on the internet, addictive areas that include the gym, body enhancements and surgeries to improve body perfection, shopping, finding ways to constantly improve outward appearance. Vanity.

2. Other areas are money, wanting more possessions, greed, (which can be any area, including food) fame, always coveting something, being driven by work until family suffer, sex, wealth, success. Our phones, T.V/Media/Music/online gaming.

3. Drugs, Alcohol, Medication for every minor problem, Sport, Gambling, constantly wanting to be the centre of attention. Power seeking through occult activity. Worshipping the created instead of the Creator.

4. Religious pursuits/ministry/leadership/ascetism, following leaders, celebrities, going outside the word of God, false cults, false teaching or additional alternative gospels. The feel-good factor me, me, me.

The dangers of the occult

The occult and its different branches of teaching is prevalent, it has infiltrated the world in numerous ways, it comes through education, life experiences, books, media, meeting with others, films, games and music, teachings and societies. The occult can be subtle and blatant, hidden and exposed. Those who become connected to the occult and its appealing pathways sadly will not come out unscathed. Your so-called knowledge of the world and its paths that promise to enlighten is foolishness to God.

Firstly, occult teaching will take a soul away from true Christian spirituality. It will divert you to numerous teachings that appeal to the senses and the ego, but never to the one who created you. If a soul remains involved in the occult, it will spiritually die and will not know salvation. This is tragic.

If you stay in the occult, (depending on what exposure you have had) these are some, but not all, of the consequences.

1. You will remain in deception and go even deeper.

2. Your heart will be hardened to the real truth.

3. Your conscience is dead to God.

4. Your soul is enslaved and in bondage to darker forces.

5. You may suffer nightmares, sleep paralysis and sleep disorders.

6. Your health may be affected.

7. You may suffer a traumatic experience which will leave you in need of help.

8. Your mental wellbeing will suffer, you may hear voices, feel suicidal, have compulsions, feel cursed. Have mood changes, bouts of depression, and feelings of grandeur.

9. You will no longer have full control.

10. You may experience episodes of feeling mad.

11. Panic, fear, doubt, pride, and other emotions will be out of control.

12. You will lose your peace.

13. You will become defiled.

14. Your connection to the occult will grieve the Holy Spirit.

15. Your connection to occult practices will deepen your sin of idolatry and spiritual adultery.

16. God is a jealous God who cares for you, by your disobedience you will reap what you sow, your behaviour breaks the commandments that God gave to protect you.

17. You will become exposed to greater forms of evil that are beyond your control or never knew existed.

18. You will allow false light to seep into your soul which will manipulate your thinking.

19. You will be tempted to go further and try new things that are occult related.

20. You will mislead others into the same folly.

21. You will allow demonic activity into your soul.

22. You will descend deeper into the pit of lies and deception.

23. You will mix up evil for good and good for evil.

24. You will develop further self-centred behaviour.

25. Your thirst for power will end in your destruction.

26. Spiritual visitations and torment by Spirits.

27. Suicide.

28. Loss of your true identity, soul and direction.

29. If you remain in the occult, you will pass on your sin and its consequences to your children and future generations.

30. If you come out of the occult and are back on the only true path to God, Jesus, you may have to live with some of the consequences.

31. Your will remain spiritually blind.

32. The falsehood you are under will only get worse.

In 1 Thessalonians 5, v 22 we are told to avoid every form or appearance of evil, if you cannot discern what is evil or good, holy or unholy, pure or corrupt, true or false, then the state of your soul is in a very dark place indeed.

The Living Word of God

If you are someone who does not believe in God, then I have to begin with the words of God.

John chapter 1

'In the beginning the word already existed. The word was with God, and the word was God.'

In 2 Peter chapter 1 verses 20 - 21 it confirms the source again.

Above all, you must realise that no prophecy in scripture ever came from the prophet's own understanding, or from human initiative. No, those prophets were moved by the Holy Spirit, and they spoke from God.

A person must be born again to receive the Holy Spirit. Those of you that are involved in occult practices need to know until you are born again you cannot receive the Holy Spirit who guides you into all truth.

In 1 Corinthians 2 verse 14 Paul the disciple says, but people who aren't spiritual cant receive these truths from God's Spirit. And we have received God's Spirit (not the world's spirit) so we can know the wonderful things God has freely given us.

2 Corinthians 4: verse 4 says that Satan, the god of this world has blinded the minds of unbelievers so they cannot see the glorious light of the good news.

In order for you to see you must turn to the only source of truth and light that matters in the eternal picture of things, Jesus. Are you going to be the soul that listens to the truth?

Satan is the father of lies who will do anything to keep you from the truth. God warned Adam and Eve that if they ate from the tree of the knowledge of good and evil, it would bring death.

This was not just an ordinary fruit, it contained knowledge.

In Genesis 3, Eve wasn't actually talking to a real serpent. The description of the serpent is being used as a metaphor, the word serpent in Hebrew is nachash – (pronounced naw-khash) – can mean to hiss, whisper a (magic) spell; enchant, shining one. The serpent's character was of a divine enchanter, it was a blazing cherubim angel, a creature, none other than Lucifer. The serpent starts to sow seeds of doubt and confusion, saying to Eve, 'Did God really say you must not eat the fruit from any of the trees in the garden?' Eve was relaxed and happy holding a conversation with a spiritual being who by its visible appearance seemed to be acceptable.

We can see in Revelation 20: v 2 again Satan is described as the serpent of old. The serpent before the fall was a guardian cherub, a beautiful angel of light, which is descriptive in Isaiah 14 verse 12 (shining star, son of the morning) and Ezekiel 28 verse 12 onwards. Paul tells us in 2 Corinthians 11: v 14 Satan disguises himself as an angel of light to entrap others to follow him, his true corrupted fallen nature being hidden under the guise of false light.

When Eve explained they were not to eat from one particular tree, the serpent then said, 'you won't die, God knows your eyes will be open as soon as you eat it, and you will be like God knowing good and evil.' Eve became convinced, she listened to the Father of Lies, she had been seduced by the enchanter. That lie then passed on to Adam.

2 Timothy 3: verses 16 &17 All scripture is inspired by God and is useful to teach us what is true and to make us realize what is wrong in our lives. It corrects us when we are wrong and teaches us to do what it right. God uses it to prepare and equip his people to do every good work.

Psalm 119: verse 105, 'Your word is a lamp to guide my feet and a light for my path.'

Hebrews 4: verse 12, 'For the word of God is alive and powerful. It is sharper than the sharpest two-edged sword, cutting between soul and Spirit, between joint and marrow. It exposes and innermost thoughts and desires. Nothing in all creation is hidden from God. Everything is naked and exposed before his eyes, and he is the one to whom we are accountable.'

In 2 Timothy2 v 25 it says, gently instruct those who oppose the truth. Perhaps God will change those people's hearts and they will learn the truth. Then they will come to their senses and escape from the devil's trap.

When I read these scriptures, it shows me how vital it is to receive Gods Spirit and God's word, there is a choice to make. God is not an energy or male or female, there is no magic formula that you can tap into whenever you want, you simply need to open up your heart and believe, for if you truly seek him, you will find him. God is Spirit, eternal, the Alpha and Omega, God is triune, Father, Son, Holy Spirit, God does not change, he is omnipotent (all powerful) omnipresent (everywhere) and omniscient (all knowing) God is holy, just, righteous, good, merciful, loving, faithful, patient and long suffering and the full embodiment of God lived in Jesus who is the mediator between man and God, you cannot go to God unless you go through Jesus.

If you want to understand the truth, if you want to understand who God really is, you must be born again through Jesus and then your spirit will understand God's Spirit.

Proverbs 4: 20 -23

'My child, pay attention to what I say, listen carefully to my words, don't lose sight of them. Let them penetrate deep into your heart, for they bring life to those who find them and healing to their whole body.'

God's power changing lives

Let us look at some of the lives changed in the Bible and remember that countless lives are also changed today, why? because not only should God's word to be trusted but there is ample evidence of changed lives all around the globe. People were not just healed, delivered and saved in biblical times; it is the same today.

Matthew 24: v 35 Jesus says, heaven and earth will disappear, but his words will never disappear. In other words, the word of God is eternal and can be relied on more than the physical world.

Hebrews 13: v 8 'Jesus Christ is the same, yesterday, today and forever. Jesus does not change.'

Isaiah 55: verse 11, 'It is the same with my word. I send it out, and it always produces fruit. It will accomplish all I want it to, and it will prosper everywhere I send it.'

Mark 5: verses 7 & 8

'A man possessed by an evil spirit came out to meet Jesus, he lived in the burial caves and could no longer be restrained, even with a chain. No-one was strong enough to subdue him. He wandered day and night among the burial caves and in the hills howling and cutting himself with sharp stones. When he saw Jesus he screamed, 'why are you interfering with me, Jesus, Son of the most high God? In the name of God, I beg you don't torture me'. For Jesus had already said to the spirit, 'come out of the man, you evil spirit'.

Then Jesus demanded, 'what is your name?' The man replied, 'my name is Legion' because there are many of us inside this man'. Now Jesus dealt with the problem by sending the spirits into a herd of pigs which plunged off the steep hillside into the lake and drowned. The man who was possessed was now in his right mind, completely sane. Jesus told the man to go home to his family and tell everyone what the Lord had done for him and how merciful he had been.' I find this story quite amazing. God can do this for anyone, just as he did it for me, the day I got saved, I was clothed in my right mind for the first time in a long time.

Also read Acts 8 and Acts 19 during Acts 19 many who became believers confessed their sinful practices, as a number of them had been practicing sorcery, so they brought their incantation books and burned them at a public bonfire. The value of the books was several million pounds.

In Luke 8, a woman with a bleeding problem who could find no cure had suffered for twelve years, whilst in the crowd, she touched the fringe of his garment and was healed. That same day a 12-year girl had died and in a loud voice Jesus took her hand and said, 'My child, get up'! and at that moment, her life returned and she immediately stood up.

Throughout the Bible many people were healed, delivered and saved, from any type of sickness and any type of demonic bondage, all were healed and that is still happening today around the world.

I can certainly testify to my own healing and deliverance, but let me give you three examples of how God can work using any one of us.

The first story had a great outcome.

In the second story, God is patient, even when the situation looks dismal. Once a seed is sown it is God that makes the seed grow, this can happen at any time. Let me remind you that a whole year passed by before the seed that was sown within my own heart started to come to life.

The third story also had a great outcome and helped another along the way.

Three Divine Appointments

Story One - Joniva's story:

I was driving my car going to the local shop when near the roundabout I saw a man just waiting. I felt a prompting in my spirit by God to go speak with him. I ignored this prompting at first, but it happened again. I got out of my car and approached the man; his appearance was a bit scruffy and he looked a bit unstable on his feet. He looked extremely sad.

"Hi," I said, "I'm Debz. This may sound strange to you, but can I ask you a question? Do you believe in God?"

"Yes, I do" he replied.

I could smell the drink on his breath and boldly told him that I felt God wanted him to give up the drinking and as I said that tears welled up in his eyes. I then invited him to my home for a coffee. Joniva shared he had been drinking for over twenty years and that he once had his own business and knew a lot about computers. His hands could barely hold the cup they were shaking so much. I asked him if he would like to spend some time in prayer with me, which he agreed to. I shared with him about a Christian rehab that I knew about and that I could get him into one. Joniva seemed interested and said he wanted to call the rehab himself. He said that he had never heard of such a place. Days went by and I found out through his family that he was too confused to do it himself. Joniva's family came to see me thanking me for what I had done. But you see I hadn't done a great deal, I just pointed him in the right direction, you see, Jesus wants us to simply care, to take a moment to guide someone in the right direction, it's about obeying the Holy Spirit at the time instead of serving our own agenda, I could have ignored the prompting by God and gone home. And I can hear some Christians right now thinking, Debz shouldn't have invited a man, a complete stranger into her home, that was dangerous. Well, let me say, when you know that the Holy Spirit has directed you to do something, you obey the Holy Spirit.

Joniva was only in his mid-forties but he looked so much older, I believe when I met him, he was quite ill. God had a different plan for his life. In the end Joniva did go to rehab, he detoxed and became a Christian and after a year's support at the rehab he left and set up a computer programming course to help others get employment. I let a few years pass by and found out he is still doing well. Praise God!

Story Two – Christian meets Satanist:

I went to the house with my delivery item and knocked on the front door. To my surprise I was invited in. As I looked around, I could see the walls in the house had been painted black, the furniture and floors were also black. I didn't particularly like the atmosphere, in fact I felt so uncomfortable I wanted to leave pretty sharpish. But the lady then asked me if I would like a cup of tea and so to be polite, I answered yes. During our tea break we had a conversation, and this is how it went.

"What do you do for a living?" The lady asked in her Polish accent. I told her that I had just published my book and explained it was a true supernatural story. She seemed interested.

"This is what I read." She handed me the Satanic bible by Anton Lavey, "Have you read it?"

I shared with her that I had.

"Tell me more," she said "because I am a second-degree black witch, do you know about this?"

I shared with her about my own experiences with Witchcraft and her response was a long Hmmmm!

I then shared briefly my testimony of how Witchcraft entered my life and how I converted to Christianity. She listened intently then asked to buy two copies of my book, one for herself and one for a friend.

I went to the car and picked up two books and decided to also get a Christian CD I had been listening to.

I wasn't going to stop long but ended up staying four hours. I decided to be bold and suggested we play the CD, because I thought she might like it. She listened then said "Now it's my turn." A spiritual tug of war had begun.

On her large 50-inch screen she played a satanic mantra, she told me when she plays the song as it makes her happy. As I listened, I noticed a link to the Church of Satan on the screen and when the song had finished, she showed me quite proudly a gold Satanic pendant with the head of Baphomet on it.

"Do you like it?" she asked.

I then took my jumper off and showed her the tattoo of Baphomet on the top of my shoulder.

"So, it seems you do understand."

I made it perfectly clear that I did understand. In my thoughts I remembered that God's ways are not necessarily our ways, I had prayed often about removing the tattoo but instead it was now relating to a self-confessed Satanist. (Just in case you missed it, earlier in my book I reveal that the tattoo now has extra words that surround it which are, father of lies, defeated, Jesus saved me, false light).

As we talked this lady mentioned how she was subjected to domestic violence. It was like looking at myself. Then her mood changed quite quickly and out of the blue she said, "It's nothing for me to take someone's life."

I nodded, not really sure what I could say to that statement, but I did feel a little threatened. Before I left, I asked if I could pray with her, taking another bold step. The tone in her reply was very challenging, she said, "Let's see what your God can do."

As the lady remained seated, I prayed and sang in tongues and felt the peace of God. It was a brief time, about 2 to 3 minutes.

"STOP!" The lady said firmly.

I stopped. She said "As you were praying it felt like water was pouring down on my head but there is something in the way, like heavy metal."

191

I explained that water is symbolic of the Holy Spirit and the feeling of heaviness that felt like heavy metal represents her soul in bondage to sin and Satanic practices and beliefs, that in order for the heaviness to be lifted, repentance and prayer ministry was required. The prayer stopped.

I was eager to see this lady saved but I did not want to run ahead of God. God always has perfect timing in these things.

I stayed for another cup of tea as I could clearly see that she wanted some company. She had read the back cover of my book and noticed I was a counsellor.

"Would you be my counsellor? I will pay you whatever you want, every week, starting now."

This temptation to have more money was just a dangling carrot. I explained that as I lived over 50 miles away, it wasn't practical. I then said "Read my book and connect with a local Christian where you live, if you would like to pursue things further."

Patience and wisdom were required in this situation. This lady not only had a dark occultic background but there was definitely an issue with violence, not just the violence that she was subjected to, but the violence that she had within her. When she asked me to stopped praying, I knew she was not ready. I left this matter in God's hands in the hope that she would seek help locally.

Before meeting this lady, I had woken that morning and did not want to eat, the Holy Spirit had already put me on a fast for the day in readiness to meet with someone demonically bound. When the spiritual tug of war commenced, I experienced the peace of God, in Romans 16 verse 20 it says, the peace of God will crush Satan under your feet. I felt on a couple of occasions that Satan wanted to cause some havoc, but he was not allowed. Meeting this lady tested my resolve, took me out of my comfort zone and challenged my faith. When I first published my book, I wasn't sure whether I wanted to publish and highlight my short breakdown into Satanism, but now I was absolutely sure I did the right thing. My time spent with this lady showed me that I must not rely on feelings, but on the word of God and just as God showed me patience and mercy, I must do the same when meeting with others, to shine my light, testify, and love those who are difficult to love.

Story Three. A Busker set free

Many Christians do not believe that a Christian can be demonized but I would like to share this story and maybe touch upon the subject a little afterwards.

I was in Norwich with a Christian friend having a look around when we came upon someone in the street busking. We noticed the songs were Christian, so we stayed around and enjoyed the singing. After a few songs the young man sat down on the green nearby to have a break and we decided to join him. After introductions I asked him how long he had been a Christian for, and found out he converted to Christianity 6 months ago. It was then that I felt a strong conviction in the Holy Spirit to pray for him. I asked the young man if that would be OK and he said, "Yes, that would be great."

None of us knew what would happen next.

As we prayed, I felt led to pray in tongues and was given the interpretation. I was commanding Satan to leave. The next thing that happened was the young man rolled around on the ground as if in pain and started being sick. We continued to pray and then he sat upright and said, "What happened? I felt something leave." I asked him, "What were you involved in before becoming a Christian?"

 We found out he had been involved in some kind of underground cult movement. This young man who I shall call Peter was so excited how different he felt he said he had to go and share what had happened with the vicar of his church. So off he went to testify of his deliverance. This led to me being invited to the church. I met the Vicar and his leadership team, and we all praised God for Peter's deliverance and one other person was also helped.

Some Christians believe that it is impossible once a Christian is born again to be troubled by or be in bondage to spirits or demons. I do not believe a Christian can be possessed but I do believe that we can have areas within us that need further deliverance.

What troubles the soul must be addressed and the scriptures applied. I do not see demons behind every problem as some Christians do, we also have a battle with the flesh, live in a fallen world and a great deal of issues can be resolved by growing up, facing the issue, repentance, and obedience, and drawing near to God so that the devil will flee, but there are also problems that only deliverance can resolve and Jesus is still in the deliverance ministry. There is a clear distinction between soul and spirit. In Hebrews 4: verse 12 it speaks of cutting between soul and spirit. Only God can deal with the areas of the soul and spirit.

In 1 Corinthians 14: v 14 it says, when I pray in tongues my spirit is praying. This is where the spiritual gifts operate from, it is where the fruits of the Spirit are developed, it is where our God conscience operates from. The Holy Spirit dwells within us and the Holy Spirit can affect all three areas of mind, body and soul. We are triune beings. In the spirit, the Holy Spirit dwells, this takes place when we are born again. Our self dwells in the soul. God continues to help us work on our soul. Our body becomes a temple with the Holy Spirit within us. The Bible teaches there is a war between flesh and spirit.

I believe sanctification is an ongoing process, Latin – Sanctus- holy. Because, although we are dead to sin (no longer enslaved to sin), we still sin. He who says they do not sin deceives themselves. 1 John 1: v 8 to 10 'Through sin the devil can gain a foothold.' (Gives an opportunity for the enemy to get established) Ephesians 4: v 27 I also believe that God deals with each person uniquely and differently depending on their situation and dealing with sin repressed, hidden or otherwise is an ongoing area in us all. A child of God does not continue in deliberate sin but that doesn't mean to say that we are sinless and further work in us still continues.

Points to Consider.

I have listed a few points for you to consider but I have not included every subject otherwise that would be another book in itself nor have I gone into great depth or covered every area, I hope what I have shared will give you time for reflection.

Secular Systems

Our secular systems are under a heavy burden and sadly many people in need fall through the cracks, we have the most amazing dedicated people within the secular system who give their all to support others and without that support life would be unbearable. The good work that is done throughout the NHS and other areas is invaluable and critical. The system however is overstretched, a sexually abused child for example can be waiting a whole year to receive counselling. The systems we have in place are a much-needed safety net supporting many, but it cannot deal with matters of the spirit and some areas of the soul.

For example, the supernatural or paranormal is not recognized by the Psychiatric profession or by most trained counsellors, unless you come under a Christian Psychiatrist or counsellor who is truly born again. Those trained in the secular system will see supernatural experiences as delusional, fantasy, or suffering from hallucinations. Although some areas of the soul can be met with psychotherapy, counselling or care within the community, again many suffer in silence, alone, or are too terrified to seek help. Others once in the system are heavily medicated for years.

For those of you who are Christian who feel going to a secular counsellor is wrong, I would urge you to think it through. I am a trained Psychodynamic Counsellor and God was very much a part of making that happen. Counsellors are needed just like doctors and nurses. They are a lifeline to many people and a person may not be in a place ready to accept Christ, and in that interim period of searching or having someone listen, it can be literally be a life saver and is always a much-needed resource. It is a place where people are accepted just as they are, a place where they are safe. If you fell down the stairs and broke a leg, and let's say you prayed over your leg and said, "In the name of Jesus, bones be healed." and you were healed, that would be miraculous and not a situation that happens normally. Normally you would rely on the system, you would go to a secular hospital to have an x-ray, have your leg put into plaster, and then wait until your bones heal over a period of time. Would you stop seeing the doctor or going to the hospital because they are secular forms of help? Of course not.

And just like the body, the mind also needs help, many go to a counsellor to understand what is happening, to get some clarity, so they can make a better decision, to resolve an issue, or to understand themselves or why something is happening. Although salvation is always knocking on the door, a person may not be ready for a number of reasons. The counsellor may even be the person who helps them get to where they need to be.

There is nothing wrong with understanding basic psychology, no more than understanding human biology and how wonderfully we are made, there is nothing wrong with going to the doctor, the problem is when we go off on a tangent and follow ungodly practices or follow people that take you down a route that is not biblical. But before becoming a Christian, God can use almost any area to bring us closer to him.

For example, I didn't understand quite a few areas about myself and during my training one tiny aspect I learnt about myself was that some parts of who I was were not me at all, some of my thoughts and reactions that were instilled in me as a child, remained with me for years, projecting on to other people, until through counselling I was able to see where the root of the problem was. God showed me the complexities of human nature and helped me to understand more about myself and how I related to others. The experience and training given became the basis of setting up a Christian project to help marginalised people for five years and my counselling training was put into practice. People were able to open up and felt safe to do so. Love in action was far more productive and teaching of the scriptures followed when they were able to deal

196

with it. In fact, some people were so damaged that it was impossible for them to relate to teaching initially. Did I want them to know Jesus and be saved, of course! But I needed to put myself in their shoes, I needed to create a safe space and gain their trust. I needed to listen and offer love and support. At the right time I was then able to take things further. I am not saying that you have to be a professional to help others, because love is the greatest gift of all, and a willing servant heart is precious and used by God, I am sharing how I was used by God and what happened to me personally. I do think some training is valuable, but it is not essential.

Does Satan exist?

Many believe Satan doesn't exist. Jesus met with Satan in the desert. If Jesus met with Satan and dealt with the demonically bound, you have to reach a conclusion, either Jesus was mad or didn't exist, or he did exist, and he was speaking the truth. If you don't believe, seek Jesus while he can be found and ask Jesus to show you the truth and pray that every form of deception is removed from you.

Made in God's image

Whether you believe it or not, every child born into this world is born in God's image. You are not a mistake. God is not in the business of creating a nobody, that doesn't make any sense. God breathed life into you and me.

We are triune beings consisting of body, soul and spirit. Our body (Greek – Soma) is fearfully and wonderfully made being governed by the senses of smell, taste, touch, hearing and sight. Next the soul (Psyche); our souls are eternal. Our soul is the seat of our feelings, emotions, appetites, intellect, memory, personality, reason and conscience. Souls can be saved or lost. Jesus said to his disciples in Matthew 16: v26 and what do you benefit if you gain the whole world but lose your own soul? Is anything worth more than your soul? Could you imagine the worth of the world? And yet that worth is nothing compared to your soul and God does not want one soul to perish.

And lastly, our Spirit (Pneuma) which either connects or refuses to connect with God, our spirit relates to God, for God is spirit, it is where if you regenerate or are born again that the spiritual gifts will operate and it is where the Holy Spirit dwells. All three areas interrelate to each other, so to exclude any one of these areas isn't helpful.

We were created in his image so that we would share in his divine nature, we would display and reflect and communicate who he is, how great he is and what he is like. We have the breath of God within us - Genesis 2: verse 7 'Our life and worth comes from God's spirit.'

In 1 Thessalonians 5: verse 23 Paul the disciple says, 'may your body, soul and spirit be kept blameless.' In Zechariah 12 verse one; it says the Lord formed the human spirit.

In Romans 8 verse 16 it says, 'for his spirit joins with our spirit to affirm that we are God's children.' This is beautiful, this is what happens when we no longer resist but allow God through his Son Jesus to be born again.

Psalm 139 verses 13 to 16

'You made all the delicate, inner parts of my body and knit me together in my mother's womb.

Thank you for making me so wonderfully complex! Your workmanship is marvellous — how well I know it.

You watched me as I was being formed in utter seclusion, as I was woven together in the dark of the womb.

You saw me before I was born.

Every day of my life was recorded in your book. Every moment was laid out before a single day had passed.'

Satan's aim is to disfigure the image of God, abort it, harm it, kill it, confuse it, cloud it in deception, influence the senses and build a wall of spiritual blindness. The good news is that Jesus came that you may have life and have it abundantly (John 10 v10) In Christ you will overcome. God hears our cries. If God heard my cry, he will hear yours. In Isaiah 30 verse 18 it says this, so, the Lord must wait for you to come to him, so he can show you his love and compassion.

Looking after your temple

There are so many different areas that damage our bodies I cannot include them all here, but I will cover some basics. The first one is alcohol. This substance has to be at the top of list, alcohol damages all organs in the body, it causes no end of suffering to families and leads into countless criminal activities, as well as causing huge amounts of NHS input and cost to the tax-payer.

There are alcohol related injuries or death every year from road traffic accidents including the driver or a pedestrian. Other accidents will include drowning, burns and falls. It can lead to sexual risk taking, leading to unwanted pregnancies, STDs (Sexually Transmitted Diseases), sexual assault and rape. It causes no end of damage in families causing arguments, financial loss, abuse to partner or children, divorce, loss of self -respect. Some people mix medication with drink which is extremely risky and pregnant women who drink through their pregnancy can damage their babies, causing alcohol foetal syndrome which means the baby can have a lower IQ, distinctive facial defects and behavioural problems.

Some of the health problems, but not all are poor nutrition, memory disorders, difficulty walking (including nerve damage) liver disease, high blood pressure, muscle weakness (including the heart) rhythm disturbances, anaemia, decreased immunity to infections, gastrointestinal inflammation. Mood changes and depression and this is just the tip of the physical damage caused by drinking.

For a Christian, we are not to copy the pattern of the world but imitate Christ.

Here are a few scriptures for you to consider regarding alcohol or your behaviour.

Proverbs 20: verse 1 says, 'Wine produces mockers, alcohol leads to brawls, those led astray by drink cannot be wise.'

Proverbs 23: verses 31 to 32 says, 'Don't gaze at the wine, seeing how red it is, how it sparkles in the cup, how smoothly it goes down. For in the end, it bites like a poisonous snake, it stings like a viper.'

1 Peter 1 verses 13 to 15 mentions exercising self-control, to be obedient, and not to slip back into old ways of living, but now be holy.

Ephesians 5: Verse 8 'Live as people of the light, for this light within you produces only what is good and right and true.'

Verse 18 in Ephesians 5 says, 'Don't be drunk with wine, because that will ruin your life. Instead, be filled with the Holy Spirit.'

1 Thessalonians 5: 5 to 8 says to be on our guard, stay alert and be clear headed.

Does your action or the way you behave glorify God?

Drugs damage the body and mind although not as systemic as drinking. We live in a society where smoking weed for many is accepted as the norm, there are a host of other drugs people take or want to legalize. Not to mention the numerous drugs a GP will give out every day. As Christians we should pray and be wise about what we put into our bodies and our first line of action should be to pray. Many prescribed drugs have serious side-effects and some that were FDA approved were taken off the market. For example, a drug called Adifax was removed in 1997 after it affected the valves of the heart.

Many heroin users say that coming off Methadone was more difficult than coming off heroin. Many users go from being addicted to heroin to acquiring a methadone addiction. Many remain on Methadone for years when it should have been a short-term program of twenty days to help ease the pain of withdrawal from opiate addiction. Addicts still commit crimes even though they get prescribed help. Long term use of opiates limits the capacity in a person to expand their horizons in life, as Therodore Dalrymple says, drugs will sap the will or ability to make long term plans. I knew a nurse living in Cambridge who was on methadone. She explained to me that the mind set doesn't really change. She still goes out to the local shops to steal. She felt she had no future, that she was trapped in a world of addiction, all legal and above board, making the pharma companies rich, but very little was being done in helping her form a constructive plan to help free her from addiction.

Today drugs are the quick remedy to a lot of problems instead of working out the problems in another way. Society overall is self-medicating in one form or another. Please don't misunderstand me, I am not opposed to prescribed drugs when needed, but they should only be a temporary measure. When I was supporting my ex-partner doing a cold turkey in my home, it was hard. Going to the DDU (drug dependant unit) doesn't work for everyone. My ex would meet with other drug users that he owed money to, this was counterproductive, sometimes they offered him more drugs on top of the drugs he was getting from the DDU. When my ex had finished doing his withdrawal, he shared how depressed he was, how empty he felt inside. He said, "What's going to fill the hole inside? Who is going to employ me? What's going to happen now, I can't afford a private rehab and all the places in the NHS are full, so now what?"

Although I knew a couple of Christian rehabs, they were quite strict, I knew that my ex was not ready to meet with Jesus or listen to what the Bible had to say, what he needed was time out to rehabilitate and face some of his personal issues, but this was an impossible dream unless you had money. I realized the overstretched system was failing many but there are many people who are pro-active in supporting those who are vulnerable, we all need to care.

Matthew 19: verse 26 'With God all things are possible.'

Tattoos

Does the Bible teach that God forbids Tattoos?

Leviticus 19: verse 28 is often quoted, 'Do not cut your bodies for the dead and do not mark your skin with tattoos I am the Lord.' Now we actually need to look at the whole passage which starts at verse 26 to 31 because God is talking to his covenant people Israel, God was protecting the Israelites as they were surrounded by pagan communities.

He is specifically telling them to stay far away from the religious practices. The prohibited religious practices in these verses include eating bloody meat, fortune telling, certain haircuts related to the priests of false cults, cutting or marking the body for dead relatives, cultic prostitution and consulting psychics. All these practices would lead God's beloved people away from him and toward false gods that were not Gods at all.

In the big city of Ancient Mesopotamia, people would mark their slaves with a brand or carving. It was also a common practice in Babylon to permanently mark temple servants, especially shrine prostitutes, with a religious symbol representing a pagan god (demon). For example, people who worship the pagan goddess, Ishtar, would get a tattoo of a star anywhere on their body. According to the Bible, God scattered the people in Babylon all over the earth (Genesis 11:9). Therefore, these practices continued all over the world including in ancient Indian, Middle Eastern and African civilizations.

The practice of making deep gashes on the face and arms and legs, in time of bereavement, was universal among the heathen, and it was deemed a becoming mark of respect for the dead. The Jews learned this custom in Egypt, and though weaned from it, relapsed later.

'...make any cuttings in your flesh.' (v:28): The reference here is to the practice of making deep gashes in the skin while mourning the death of a relative. This was done to provide life blood for the spirit of the dead person rather than to express sorrow. We see in 1 Kings 18 Elijah verse 28 the prophets of Baal cut themselves with knives and swords until the blood gushed out, a normal custom in Baal worship.

Today's tattoo is a decorative means of self-expression and personal decoration.

Tattoos are a choice and must be given some thought. God clearly cares more about the heart than outward appearance. God also looks at the motives of your heart. Jesus also taught that what defiles a person comes from within. Mark 7: verses 20-23 people today are not tattooing their skin in connection with cultic pagan worship. So, it really is a matter of whether what you do glorifies God.

There are some areas of body modification that are concerning. Some people in the world want to look so different they go to extremes lengths by splitting their tongue in two, having razored teeth, or looking like a creature or animal or some kind demon or basing their change of appearance on a mythical figure or fantasy. Other areas of modification would be breast implants and things that enhance the body, again, is this self-glorification? Or is it really necessary due to a medical need. As I said, God will be looking at the motive of the heart.

What Christians should be wary of is quick judgements. Paul says not to evaluate others from a human point of view. If you are going to judge, judge with discernment, judge correctly.

For example, both my arms, wrists and fingers have tattoos, on seeing me for the first time in the summer just wearing a T-shirt it is obvious my arms tell a story. Most of my tattoos were done when I was not a Christian and I was 15 years old, in borstal. The tattoos were made with lead from a pencil. They will never fade. The other tattoo of Baphomet happened when I was not in my right mind. Wording around this particular tattoo was added later, when I was in my right mind, so that anyone looking at it will know that I had changed.

Do I get looked at and judged? Yes, sadly I do. In fact, at a Christian conference one lady moved away from me because she was afraid. I spoke with her and told her not to allow fear to rule but love.

Today there are far more important things to be concerned about than what a person wears, or what they look like. Remember Jesus said, 'you will know my disciples by the fruit they bear.' Matthew 7: verse 16. 'Look for the fruit in a person.'

Baphomet

Baphomet, the Horned God, or Goat of Mendes as well as other titles.

The image of Baphomet has been a symbol to many throughout history. More commonly known more through Eliphas Levi, a French mystic who left the Roman Catholic priesthood and the masonic lodge, who wrote several books on magic. Levi said that the image represented pure immorality inspired by deities. Anton Lavey adopted the image as a sigil (a symbol or seal of magic and power) for the church of Satan in 1966. It has had different meanings to different groups of people. But in short, the image in occult circles represents the divine torch of revelation, diversity, wisdom and knowledge, religious enlightenment, fertility, a father of universal peace among men, spirit and matter, protector of travellers, invention and trade, male, female, animal, many paths to truth, the union of opposites, sexuality, universal balance, duality and much more.

In Baphomet's lap, you see two serpents criss-crossing up a rod which is the ancient symbol of the staff of Hermes in Greek paganism, and the caduceus of Mercury in Roman paganism. This occult symbol means Baphomet opens the path to Kundalini energy (taught in Hinduism), it is known as 'Serpent Power', a primal force or life force energy, that when released causes the occultist to transcend to higher levels of enlightenment to unite the body, mind, and spirit in well-being.

Lucifer is not your source of life; God breathed life into you and me. Whatever God has said, done, or is doing, Lucifer or Satan will mimic Gods actions and twist them to fulfil his own purpose, to detract others from the real truth and this creature has been doing this for a very long time.

Aleister Crowley said, "This serpent, Satan, is not the enemy of man, but he who made Gods of our race, knowing good and evil, he bade, know thyself and taught initiation. When a person sees themselves as a so called god, they are truly deceived."

This takes us right back to the Garden of Eden when the serpent tempted Eve to eat the fruit that was forbidden. The serpent said to Eve, "God knows that your eyes will be opened as soon as you eat it, and you will be like God, knowing both good and evil."

Being like God does not involve an act of disobedience or listening to Satan.

Isaiah 14:13-14 'For you [Lucifer] have said in your heart:

1.   **I will** ascend into heaven,

2.   **I will** exalt my throne above the stars of God;

3.   **I will** also sit on the mount of the congregation in the sides of the north;

4.   **I will** ascend above the heights of the clouds,

5.   **I will** be like the Most High.'

This passage is often referred to as 'The Five I wills' of Satan. The statements reveal Satan's sinful nature, his rebellion, his disobedience, his self-sufficiency, his pride, his self-exaltation, and his all-encompassing pride and arrogance.

For Satan, it's all about him, and nothing about God.

The same is today, Baphomet is an image of the same old problem, man wanting to be as a god, to be puffed up with pride and filled with rebellion rather than be humble and truly learn.

৪০৫৪

In the Bible in the book of Revelation, Chapter 2, Pergamum was a city full of Greek culture and education. It had a political centre, it was there that all the rulings were made that affected the whole of Asia Minor, the people were inventors, innovator's and built the first world's psychiatric hospital, it was also a well-known centre for the arts.

On the flip side, the people were also known as the temple keepers of Asia, there were four cults; it rivalled Ephesus in its worship of idols. Pergamum is where Satan had his throne. The four cults were Zeus, Dionysius, Asclepius, and Athena.

The city's chief God was Asclepius, the symbol of the serpent, one snake on a rod, a symbol of healing. People came from all over to seek healing.

Patients who were sick went through an underground tunnel, drank a sedative, and spent the night in the dormitories of the Asklepion, while snakes crawled around them and over them all night. Their God would speak to them in their dreams and healing would come.

Nothing has changed, for many pagan beliefs are still in the open today, still in defiance, still not listening, there is nothing new under the sun. God has seen it all from generation to generation and is patient with us and long suffering in the hope that one soul may repent and turn back to the one and only true God who gave them life.

The sound of hooves

When I prayed to God, I asked the Lord, 'How do I explain the sound of hooves without sounding like I was some kind of mad person?' Although it helped that Kevin was there and heard the sound of hooves too, I needed to know how to explain it from a biblical point of view. I felt led to go to Ezekiel chapter one verse 7.

Ezekiel chapter one verse 7: 'Their legs were straight, and their feet had hooves like those of a calf and shone like burnished bronze.'

This led me to study further. In the Bible there are different angels, some are 'spirits' sent to minister to the children of God, they are messengers, from the Greek word 'aggelos'. Hebrews 1 verse 14 says, 'Therefore, angels are only servants, spirits sent to care for people who will inherit salvation and then there are Cherub's or Cherubim that are angels who minister to God not to man.' Cherubim creatures are a winged angelic being and very different to ministering angels. Cherubim were the highest form of angelic beings and their appearance can be that of part creature. Then there are Archangels and Seraphim.

Cherubim are mentioned in different places, we can see for example that Cherubim are mentioned in Genesis 3: v 24 it says, 'The Lord stationed mighty Cherubim to the east of the garden of Eden. And he placed a flaming sword that flashed back and forth to guard the way to the tree of life.'

In Hebrews9 verse 5 'Above the ark were the cherubim of divine glory whose wings stretched out over the arks cover, the place of atonement.'

In 2 Samuel 22: verse 11, 'Mounted on a mighty angelic being he flew, soaring on the wings of the wind.' In the King James translation, it says, 'he (God) rode upon a cherub.' Mentioned again in Psalm 18: v 10

In Ephesians 6 verse 12 it tells us we fight against not flesh and blood enemies, but against evil rulers and authorities of the UNSEEN world, against mighty powers in this dark world, and against evil spirits in the heavenly places. In Colossians 1 verse 16 it says, he made things (God) we can see, and things we cannot see, such as thrones, kingdoms, rulers, and authorities in the unseen world. There is an unseen world.

At 3am I had a visitation from Satan, his powerful presence was felt, it was a presence that dominated the room, it was not visible to my eye, it was unseen, but Satan's presence was tangible and his pursuit of me thundered in my ears, when Kevin spoke the words, "Get behind me Satan in the name of Jesus," that presence retreated. Those words are found in the scriptures when Jesus was talking with Peter in Matthew 16 verse 23. Or simply put, get away from me. This is an example of a dual reference; when Jesus was speaking to Peter and Satan at the same time.

Fear of coming into the light

In John 3; Verses 19-20 it says,

'And the judgment is based on this fact: God's light came into the world, but people loved the darkness more than the light, for their actions were evil. All who do evil hate the light and refuse to go near it for fear their sins will be exposed.'

I can hear you shouting now, "I'm not evil!"

But we have all fallen short of the glory of God. Jesus came into the world not to condemn it but to save it. Jesus is the light of the world and you must go to him with all sincerity of heart and confess your sin. You may not have done anything evil or morally wrong in your eyes, but you need to understand your situation not from your own perspective but God's.

Galatians 5 verses 16 to 26 teaches areas that oppose the Spirit which are sinful; sexual immorality, impurity, lustful pleasures, idolatry, sorcery, hostility, quarrelling, jealousy, outbursts of anger, selfish ambition, dissension, division, envy, drunkenness, wild parties.

Other areas would be pride, lying, violence, murder, theft, and much more, none of us are without sin.

1 Thessalonians 5 verse 23

'Now may the God of peace make you holy in every way, and may our whole spirit and soul and body be kept blameless until our Lord Jesus Christ comes again. God will make this happen, for he who calls you is faithful. '

Pride

Pride is refusing to acknowledge the wrong you have done. It is being obsessed with self, it is thinking you are better than other people, it is wanting success at the expense of others, it is the very opposite to humility. Your attitude is that you can manage on your own that you don't need anyone else, even when your circumstances clearly show you do need help. Pride won't be told what to do, pride is not willing to learn or listen as you already know it all. Pride revels in its own glory and is very self-opinionated. Pride is rebellion, going against what is right and true and ultimately going against God. There is not one positive thing about pride.

My name is Pride. I am a cheater.

I cheat you of your God given destiny, because you demand your own way

I cheat you of contentment, because you believe you deserve better, you want more,

I cheat you of knowledge because you already know it all, and your healing cannot come, because your too full of me to forgive or show mercy

I cheat you of holiness, because you refuse to admit when you are wrong, or confess your sins,

I cheat you of vision; because you'd rather look in the mirror and pursue your own ideas, then surrender.

I cheat you of genuine friendship, nobody's going to know the real you

I cheat you of love, because real love demands sacrifice and a giving heart

How can you know greatness in heaven when you refuse to wash another's feet on earth?

I cheat you of Gods glory, because you seek your own

My name is Pride and I am a cheater.

Stick with me and you can have everything you want.

But in your foolishness, you will have lost everything.

Be a free woman

Don't let anyone put you down because you are a woman especially in the church. As I have said before any scripture can be used out of context. I accept all the teachings in the Bible, but context is everything. In Christ you are free, and it is the Holy Spirit that gives you your spiritual gifting, leads you into all truth, and helps you develop the fruits of the Spirit, you are to shine your light before men, be a vessel for God, whatever you do, do it for the glory of God, you must not allow yourself to be bound by man-made rules or religion. You must look at all scriptures and remember to take into account Jewish culture, and the problems Paul came up against. Those who oppose women that teach or preach are ultimately opposing God. I have suggested some books to read on this matter in the section, 'Books I recommend'. Some of the books I recommend on this subject matter particularly give great clarity in what Paul taught and how Paul the disciple was not against women preaching or teaching as some people suggest.

Only accountable to God

You are accountable to God and to God alone. Do not be bound by the fear of man this is a snare which will entrap you and cause you pain.

Hebrews 4: verse 13 'Nothing in all creation is hidden from God. Everything is naked and exposed before his eyes, and he is the one to whom we are accountable.'

2 Corinthians 5: 10

'For we must all appear before the judgment seat of Christ, so that each one may receive what is due for what he has done in the body, whether good or evil.'

It seems evident to me from scripture that we are accountable to God. A pastor recently said to me that accountability is about speaking into each other's lives. I believe we are not responsible for each other, I am no more responsible for you as you are for me, I am responsible for my own actions and attitudes, however as a family of believers we are to treat each other in the way the scriptures encourage us to and if I as a Christian in the body of Christ was in deliberate sin against Gods word then I do believe it is scriptural for someone to speak into my life gently and expose this or if there is a problem with your brother or sister to go have a word with them in the hope of winning your brother or sister back, there is set in the scriptures a pattern to follow. We have Luke 17 v3 So watch yourselves! "If another believer sins, rebuke that person; then if there is repentance, forgive."

Let us use the words that scripture itself does and give the word 'accountability' to its proper place, that it remains between you and God.

Some words that the scripture uses are love, compassion, think of others more than yourself, be merciful, confess and pray for one another, be patient, be devoted, forgiving, carry each other's burdens and pray for one another.

Catholicism v Christianity

There is a huge divide between what the Catholic church teaches and what the word of God teaches in the Bible.

Christians believe that the scriptures are sufficient and not one word as taught in the scriptures can be added or taken away.

The Bible is complete, authoritative, and true. 'All Scripture is God-breathed and is useful for teaching, rebuking, correcting and training in righteousness' (2 Timothy 3:16).

Having been indoctrinated into the Catholic church for seven years, receiving instruction by nuns, I can tell you that there is a great deal of teaching in the Catholic faith that is not based upon the word of God or God's truth. I will list some of those areas here, but I will encourage you to do your own studies in the matter. You will need to be discerning to know the difference to what is right and what appears to be almost right, many teachings in different denominations can appear to be truthful but have actually veered off onto a different path.

Here are some areas to pray about:

1. You do not have to go through a priest to receive forgiveness, Jesus said in 1 John 1 verse 9, if we confess our sins, he is faithful and just and will purify us from all unrighteousness.

2. In the confessional the priest after a confession may give you a penance. For example, three 'Hail Marys', the Lord's Prayer. Penance is not necessary when you have confessed with a sincere heart. It is done. Nowhere in scripture does Jesus ask for a person to do a penance.

3. The rosary is a string of over fifty beads of Hail Mary's, and other single prayers. Mary although blessed among women to bear God's son, nowhere in scripture are we told to venerate Mary or focus on Jesus through Mary. We can all draw near to the throne of grace with confidence Hebrews 4 verse 16. Christians do not go through Mary or the saints, there is only mediator between God and men, that is Jesus Christ, see 1 Timothy 2: verse 5

4. Catholics believe in purgatory a final stage of purification; there is no such scripture to back this up. Catholics separate sin into two categories, mortal sin and venial sin, which is a lesser smaller sin, and it is these venial sins that are supposedly cleansed from us in a temporary place known as purgatory before entering heaven. Purgatory is not scriptural because Jesus died on the cross once and for all, for all time to cleanse us from all our sin and it is through grace that we are saved, so no man can boast. Jesus taught on heaven and hell, NOT PURGATORY. Read Luke 16: verses 19-31

5. Catholics during mass believe in transubstantiation, that somehow under the appearance of the bread and wine an actual change takes place of the body and blood of Jesus. This is not scriptural. In John 6: verse 63 it is the Spirit

who gives life, the Lord's supper is a memorial, look at
Luke 22: 19 it is not meant to be taken literally.

6.   The Catholic Church believes in the stigmata as a holy gift
       and a connection to suffering with Christ. This is not a gift
       from God. Why would God delight in sending suffering
       to his children, to crucify Jesus again and again? Hebrews
       9 verse 12 says, Jesus died once for all and secured our
       redemption. Bleeding from the eyes, the crown of thorns
       and the stigmata are not from God. Most of those who
       had the stigmata were troubled by evil spirits, went into
       trance like states, had religious fervour to an unhealthy
       degree or were able to experience bio-location, so for
       example Padre Pio was able to be in two separate places
       in different parts of the world. (Soul travel) This is not
       scriptural but stems from the occult. Nowhere in scripture
       is any of this backed up. I remember being given a piece
       of cloth in a card that supposedly belonged to Padre Pio
       to protect me.

7.   The Catholic Church believes that the pope is the Vicar of
       Christ, a Father representation on earth, a successor to
       Peter and his purpose is to govern the universal church,
       the Pope in matters of morals is preserved from the
       possibility of error according to the Catholic faith. This is
       not scriptural because Jesus is our high priest Hebrews 7:
       verses 23-25 In John 14 verse 26 it shows the Holy Spirit is
       our helper and will teach us everything. The pope is just a
       man and is not infallible in his teaching especially when
       outside the word of God.

I have touched upon a few problems within the Catholic Church
and hope this helps others to make sure you have a clear biblical
foundation to what you believe. Do not follow other doctrines, I
believe it was Paul who said in Galatians 1 verses 8-9 let him be
eternally condemned or cursed if another follows a counterfeit
gospel.

Let us pray for those who are misguided and show them the truth.

Torniquet on the Holy Spirit

The more control methods that are in the church the less the Holy Spirit is able to be free. The Holy Spirit is not meant to be bottled up like a consumer perfume. Every born-again Christian has the Holy Spirit dwelling within them, so when control, leadership, man-made rules dominate it blocks the Holy Spirit from working and it's not what God would want. Hindering or grieving the Holy Spirit leads to those within the church just becoming a mouthpiece of automated responses, with a lack of spiritual development and growth. Leaders should not stop those within their congregations from developing, they should encourage everyone.

These are some of the areas and practices but not all that I have seen at work in churches that I believe are very damaging and do not have a biblical foundation or specific scriptures are taken out of context.

1. Stopping others from sharing scripture, a song, a psalm, or sharing a testimony.

2. Making members go down the front of the church to share first with the leadership what is on their heart so that it can be checked BEFORE speaking to the rest of the church. If the leader doesn't like what you have shared or thinks it isn't suitable or correct that person is prevented from speaking.

3. Only designated people on the prayer team can pray for another Christian.

4. Only women can pray for women and men with men.

5. Only a minister can baptize another person

6. A person must become a member, or they will not be considered for more responsible positions in the church.

7. Only those who are elders can distribute communion.

8. Only when a person has attended introduction courses or jumped through the hoops expected can a person be used or accepted.

9. Prevention and sometimes banning of speaking/singing in tongues

10. Time restrained programs preventing the use of spiritual gifts as well as little encouragement of using spiritual gifting.

11. Set prayers on the screen instead of praying from the heart.

12. A very small amount of time allocated to those sick within the church.

13. Lack of teaching on spiritual warfare, hell, sin, and helping the lost.

14. Lack of teaching on how to integrate the lost into the church body.

15. Allowing only leaders to guide the church forward instead of submitting to each other and listening to those within the church as well as the leadership.

16. Women are to be kept in place and only be allowed to do certain things. They are not allowed to teach or preach.

17. Leadership/pastors allowing practices, songs, teachings into the church that are clearly not biblical.

18. Lack of home visiting to those in need.

19. Stating that one has to be a professional counsellor to counsel others.

20. Sending those who are sick or unwell to secular agencies first rather than offering love and prayer first.

I have only touched upon some of the problems that the church in general has practiced for some time. Check everything out by the word of God and be wise.

Leaders! Do not be like the shepherds in Ezekiel 34 who,

1. Looked after themselves but not the flock.

2. Did not take care of the weak.

3. Did not tend to the sick or bind up the injured.

4. Did not look for the lost or those who have wandered away. Many have left the church today who still serve Jesus, did you go visit the one who left the church, did you find out why? What action did you take?

Is your leadership too harsh?

It is my hope that your motive for becoming a pastor, leader or Vicar within the church was to serve and be a blessing, to promote the truth of the gospel and win souls for Jesus but if you have strayed from the path of God, God is waiting with open arms. But remember these words, 'do not cause one of these little ones who trust in me to fall into sin, it would be better for you to be thrown into the sea with a large millstone hung around your neck.' Mark 9: verse 42

Deception and Syncretism

From the beginning of the Christian Church forming there have always been those who have sought to disrupt, accuse, or deceive those within it. I have personally seen numerous teachings and practices come through the church over the many years that I have been a Christian which have sadly not had its roots in Christianity. I am deeply saddened and disturbed by what I see happening today, but not shocked, because it is not new but old and pagan and in last days more and more falling away will happen. In Matthew 13 verse 24 onwards the parable shares about the enemy (the devil) who comes along and plants weeds (those who belong to the evil one) among the wheat (those in Gods Kingdom) As Gods kingdom grows so weeds also grow. Jesus said, let the weeds and the wheat grow together because the time will come when the Son of Man will sort it all out. In the meantime, as a Christian, we are to do our best to warn, guide, teach, others to remain on the narrow path and if need be, expose the evil that is happening, not remain quiet. In Ephesians 5 verses 10 and 11 it says, carefully determine what pleases the Lord. Take no part in the worthless deeds of evil and darkness, instead, expose them. Just like in those days there were those who were false prophets and false teachers, we also have false prophets and teachers today. In 2 Peter 2 these false teachers taught destructive heresies. (Denied Jesus) The way of truth was slandered, and in their greed, they made up clever lies to get hold of money. They were proud, arrogant, had twisted sexual desires, despised authority, scoffed at supernatural beings, (Angels) indulging in evil pleasures in broad daylight. Delighting in deception, they ate with Christians in their fellowship meals, they were within the Church. They lured unstable people into sin.

In the book of Galatians Paul says in chapter 1 verses 6 to 8, I am shocked that you are turning away so soon from God, who called you to himself through the loving mercy of Christ. You are following a different way that pretends to be the Good News but is not the good news at all. You are being fooled by those who deliberately twist the truth concerning Christ. Let Gods curse fall on anyone, including us or even an angel from heaven, who preaches a different kind of good news than the one we preached to you.

In Galatians 2 verse 4 it shows false ones, sneaking in to spy on Christians to take away their freedom and to follow Jewish regulations rather than the gospel.

In Ephesians 4 Paul explains about coming together in a unity of faith and knowledge, using the gifts given to the church, in order to be mature, so that they won't be tossed and blown about by every wind of new teaching. So that they will not be influenced when people try to trick them with lies so clever, they sound like the truth. Verse 14. Although we have many mature Christians sadly the church generally today has a great deal of immaturity as it is so affected by other teachings that are not biblical as well as indulging in practices that are worldly. What has impeded this lack of maturity is the failure of many of its leaders to encourage the use of spiritual gifts in the church.

Proverbs 4: verse 23 says, guard your heart above all else, for it determines the course of your life.

Proverbs 15: verse 10 says, whoever abandons the right path will be severely disciplined, whoever hates correction will die.

Isaiah 5: verse 20 says, what sorrow for those who say that evil is good and good is evil, that dark is light and light is dark, that bitter is sweet and sweet is bitter.

Don't remain an overfed baby

Many Christians have become like babies paralysed on spiritual milk resulting into spiritual inertia rather than action. Like a large overfed baby that is unable to crawl or go forward, the milk vomits from the mouth instead of the milk being digested, then the word of God is not as effective as it should be, it lies in the belly instead of the heart and does not spring to full life but gets bogged down and stuck, when it should be free and unfettered.

Obedience is the catalyst that propels the word into action. Some people digest the milk of the word and still lack understanding, some seek solace of the word to comfort themselves and although that is fine to seek solace from God it should not become self-absorbing. If Gods people are to be mature and effective, the milk of the word needs to become a living action of love. Love in action helps the milk digest when it has entered deep into the heart.

Staying a slothful baby that seeks self-gratification in what God can do for you and you alone cannot be the type of life that God called us into, it is when you give your life away like water that you will truly know a fulfilled life. We must all take up the cross and deny self in order for Jesus to live through us. Of course, in order for Jesus to live through us we need the freedom to develop and use our spiritual gifts as well as develop the fruit.

Spiritual stagnation does not bring glory to God nor does Christian self-indulgence, what's in it for me attitude, what can be done for me, me, me, me. Surely, as servants of Christ, it's what can I do for another? And how best God can use me in his service.

We must stretch our spiritual muscles and use them daily if we are to grow in faith. Sometimes that faith is tested out in the midst of a storm or trial, it is then when the trial remains that our character is put to the test and we see how we can improve or what we need to pray. Faith must always operate through love.

Don't be a slothful baby always getting the milk of the word but never acting upon it. Don't be a greedy child that seeks to want its own way all the time, life is not like that, and at times God will say no! For his ways are not our ways. Feed upon the word and allow the word of God to grow in you, be obedient, surrender, be willing to be moulded and shaped by the potter, even though at times it may be painful.

'Faith is a living action of love and faith without works is dead.' James chapter 2 verse 17.

In 2 Timothy chapter 3, Paul shares about persecution and that evil imposters and evil people will flourish, they will deceive others and they themselves will be deceived.

In 2 Corinthians 11 Pauls shares about deceitful workers who disguise themselves as apostles of Christ. Adding in verse 14 that even Satan disguises himself as an angel of light.

These so-called super apostles preached a different gospel, a different Jesus, a different kind of Spirit.

This is happening today. I can't tell you how heart-breaking it is that Christians choose to ignore the scriptures on this matter as well as the people who can help them, those who have converted from an occult background who are now Christian who have the spiritual gift of discernment are only too aware how subtle the devil is.

Persistent disobedience will result in serious damage to the body of Christ and will entice young converts onto a different path away from the Christian faith altogether. Those who continue in sin need to ask themselves if they were truly born again, especially when blatantly ignoring God's warning and the warnings that have come from their Christian brothers and sisters.

Your persistent disobedience will lead into having a damaged relationship with God. God cannot bless you in areas of rebellion, it may be that you have already developed a seared conscience which means your heart and mind is numb, dead, in an area that no longer knows the difference between right and wrong, and cannot differentiate between what appears to be right and what is truly right. When someone is deceived, it can lead into further and further deception and whilst under that deception it is possible to be in spiritual bondage to demonic activity.

Let us briefly look at areas of deception that have come into people's hearts and the church. I cannot list all the false apostles of Christ or movements or churches as there are far too many, in your own time I encourage you to do your own research, but I will begin with Bethel Church based in California, Redding as a good starter, please stay away from its teaching, practices and music. Let us start with scripture:

In 2 Corinthians chapter 4 verses 1 & 2 it says, 'therefore, since God in his mercy has given us this new way (ministry), we never give up. We reject all shameful deeds and underhanded methods. We don't try to trick anyone or distort the word of God. We tell the truth before God, and all who are honest know this.' (New Living Translation) In the KJV it says in verse 2, 'but have renounced the hidden things of dishonesty, not walking in craftiness, nor handling the word of God deceitfully.'

Nothing is hidden from God, yet people in their dishonesty will hide things, they are crafty, especially those who want you on board to support their ministry even when it goes against Gods teaching and they have distorted God's word. As Christians we worship God in spirit and in truth. John 4: verse 24 'We cannot mix truth with lies; we cannot mix the Spirit of Christ with a false Christ.'

1 Thessalonians 5: verse 22 'Stay away from every kind of evil or the appearance of evil.' (KJV)

Romans 16: verses 17-18 'Watch out for people who cause division and upset people's faith by teaching things contrary to what you have been taught.' Stay away from them. Such people are not serving Christ our Lord, they are serving their own personal interests. By smooth talk and glowing words, they deceive innocent people.

1 Corinthians 10: verse 21 'You cannot drink from the cup of the Lord and from the cup of demons, too. You cannot eat at the Lord's Table and at the table of demons, too.'

Verse 24 'Don't be concerned for your own good but for the good of others.'

I Timothy 4: v 16 'Keep a close watch on how you live and on your teaching. Stay true to what is right for the sake of your own salvation and the salvation of those who hear you. '

A false Holy Spirit at work

Music has a great influence particularly attracting the young; our worship to God can come direct from the heart, be traditional or follow certain bands and singers. But how can worship be in Spirit and in truth when truth is clearly not on the table? For those who create an atmosphere to lure in hearts, affecting the emotions so that worship just becomes an elevated experience above doctrinal truth are in dangerous waters, that experience becomes addictive, in the end it becomes all about you, what YOU need and want, how YOU feel, it becomes a self-centred experience. True worship of God should lead to humility, a spirit of order and self-control, confession of sin, a broken spirit and contrite heart, reverence, holiness and truth, a heart that is thankful giving due praise to our heavenly Father through his Son Jesus, and a heart filled with servitude. Lift up your heart to God by all means and yes, our emotions are positively affected but make sure everything is grounded in Spirit and Truth.

Romans 12: verse 1 'And so dear brothers and sisters, I plead with you to give your bodies to God because of all he has done for you. Let them be a living and holy sacrifice, the kind he will find acceptable. This is truly the way to worship him.'

Pastors must protect their flock from the wolves not come alongside them. In Ephesians 5 verses 15 to 20 we are told to be careful how we live, to be wise, and to make the most of every opportunity in these evil days. To not be thoughtless but to understand what the Lord wants you to do, to not be drunk but to be filled with the Holy

Spirit, singing Psalms and hymns and spiritual songs and making music to the Lord in your heart, giving thanks for everything. When you are filled with the Holy Spirit do you think the Holy Spirit would then bring in practices that are unholy? Or not founded upon God's word? Of course not.

In Jeremiah 6 verse 27 Jeremiah is made a tester of metals to determine the quality of Gods people who have become the worst kind of rebel, hard as bronze and iron, leading others into corruption, but they are not purified and are labelled 'rejected silver'. Later in Jeremiah 7 those in Judah who worshipped were given a message to quit their evil ways, evil thoughts and to start treating each other with justice, to stop exploiting foreigners, orphan and widows, to stop murdering and harming themselves by worshipping idols. Because the temple was there, the people thought they were safe. God said, do you think you can come into the temple and stand before me, behave this way, be safe and chant, 'we are safe' only to go right back to their evil behaviour. God saw all that was evil and what was going on there in the temple that bared his name. God sees everything.

Today syncretism is rife in many churches and cult movements abound you may not behave in the same ways like those in Judah, but spiritual adultery, self-idolatry, mixing up beliefs that go against the word of God, enticing others into the same thing, is sinful and sows' seeds of corruption, spreading deception like a virus. Are you not going into God's house or temple believing you are safe when following false prophets' practices and beliefs, rebelling just like those in Judah? Doing what you like. What has happened to your fear of God? Or has your heart become like iron or bronze?

Matthew 7 verse 15 to 18 says, 'Beware of false prophets who come disguised as harmless sheep but are really vicious wolves. You can identify them by their fruit, that is, by the way that they act. Can you pick grapes from thornbushes, or figs from thistles? A good tree produces good fruit, and a bad tree produces bad fruit. A good tree cannot produce bad fruit, and a bad tree can't produce good fruit.'

These are some of the practices and beliefs that have come into the church that have stemmed from cult movements and some churches. Weigh all these practices against the word of God. Does the word of God back these experiences and practices? This is just the tip of the counterfeit iceberg.

1. Laughing and jerking in the Holy Spirit.
2. Waking up angels.
3. Angel boards and Christian Tarot Cards.
4. Using tuning forks for prophecy.
5. Gold dust.
6. Drunken glory, behaving as if drunk.
7. Toking the Holy Ghost.
8. Being slain in the spirit.
9. Ye are Gods
10. Grave sucking.
11. Angel orbs.
12. Treasure hunting.
13. Fire Tunnels.
14. Tattoo reading.
15. Visualization.
16. Glory clouds.
17. Quantum sounds.
18. Opening portals.
19. Soaking in the spirit.
20. Kenosis. (Jesus laid aside all divinity)
21. Spirit or angel guide.
22. Sozo ministry.
23. To be willing to go off the map.
24. Barking like dogs, howling, and other strange and weird noises.
25. Signs and wonders taking dominance.
26. Word of faith movement.
27. Prosperity gospel.
28. Those who have come under a false spirit otherwise known as Kundalini, will experience some of these symptoms: shaking, trembling, energy rushes, tingling, drunkenness, violent jerking, bodily contortions, uncontrolled laughter, altered states of consciousness. The Kundalini Spirit is the

energy of Lucifer himself, (serpent power) once your soul is open to this area the energy that enters is meant to help a person transcend and experience a higher spiritual consciousness, but it opens a doorway into a counterfeit heaven (astral world) and this deception is called 'an awakening'. It is not your primal energy, (creation, higher self, the divine) that is at work, it is a fallen power and Lucifer is not your source of life or your creator, God is. Remember Lucifer masquerades as an angel of light and will deceive the world.

I am quite sure more areas of deception will come, which is why wearing the armour of God is necessary and keeping to the truth of the word of God essential.

2 John verse 10 'If anyone comes to your meeting and does not teach the truth about Christ, don't invite that person into your home or give any kind of encouragement. Anyone who encourages such people becomes a partner in their evil work. This scripture is to do with false teachers and their teaching who denied that Jesus came in a real body.'

And I believe we should also apply that scripture to false teachers today, a genuine Christian will not cause another person to stumble. Unless they show signs of repentance or are willing to listen, it is best to pray for them until such a time that they ask for help.

I John 4 verse 1 'Dear friends, do not believe everyone who claims to speak by the Spirit. You must test them to see if the spirit they have comes from God. For there are many false prophets in the world.'

2 Timothy 3 verse 13, 'but evil people and imposters will flourish. They will deceive others and will themselves be deceived.'

2 Timothy 1 verse 13 'Hold onto the pattern of wholesome teaching you learned from me, a pattern shaped by faith and love, that you have in Christ Jesus. Through the power of the Holy Spirit who

lives within us, carefully guard the precious truth that has been entrusted to you.'

1 Timothy 4 verses 1 & 2, 'Now the Holy Spirit tells us clearly that in the last times some will turn away from the true faith, they will follow deceptive spirits and teachings that come from demons. These people are hypocrites and liars and their consciences are dead.'

Ephesians 5 verse 11 'Take no part in the worthless deeds of evil and darkness, instead, expose them.'

The Impact of Anger

Anger is one of our many emotions but how you and I handle our emotions is quite another matter. It is good to think through how anger impacts our lives with prayer and discipline. Anger can go inward or outward and come out in ways that are unexpected, for example, maybe something happened at work, you didn't react at work because you don't want to lose your job, you leave work, go home, slam the door, kick the cat, shout at your partner, or go silent and don't want to talk, the problem you left at work has now transferred to others.

Anger is habit forming, some people thrive off anger and have almost become addicted to the drama it brings, without it in their lives they would be lost and bored. Some areas of anger are connected to pride with the refusal to not apologize or forgive someone or hold a grudge, to believing they are always right and will not admit their wrongs. Anger can lead to bitterness which affects others, it can harden the heart and can wallow in self-pity. Anger doesn't let go and will keep you going round and round in the same destructive circle so that you never go forward.

The impact that anger can have upon our emotions and body is huge.

1.   Anger can heighten the pain in some people who are already unwell, as well as cause tension in the muscles. Other impacts on the body are headaches, gritting of teeth, pulling hair out,

226

or loss of hair, stomach ulcers, bad nerves, agitation, mood changes, depression, uncontrolled outbursts, self-harm, harming others. Anger leads to loss of peace, your heart rate, blood pressure and respiration increase, anger affects how we look after ourselves, anger can turn into a rage and lead to murder, hate, or revenge, a heart attack or make someone else's life miserable. It can cause lack of sleep, nightmares, and blow things out of proportion. Anger can lead to prison or get you into trouble especially if a person has a short fuse. It can lead to making wrong decisions. If you are angry, it is far better to wait until you have calmed down and have thought through the situation before doing or saying something.

2. Anger refuses to take some responsibility it can lead to you blaming others and blaming God. In domestic violence situations many partners have unresolved anger issues or quick tempers they take out on their partner.

3. Anger left to stew can lead to drinking away the problem, overuse of medication or drugs, and road rage, sometimes causing harm and even death to others.

4. Anger can simply be an immature response and a defiant refusal to grow up and be a mature person. It is important to acknowledge you have a problem and try to resolve it, find out what triggers your anger, find the root cause and face it head on. Or you will simply remain as you are having a miserable existence as well as affecting your relationships with friends and family. If you cannot resolve the problem yourself then perhaps it is time to see a counsellor and look at anger management.

Let us look at what some of the scriptures say about anger.

Psalm 37: verse 8 'Stop being angry, turn from your rage! Do not lose your temper, it only leads to harm.'

Psalm 4: verse 4 'Don't sin by letting anger control you. Think about it overnight and remain silent.'

Proverbs 14: verse 17 'Short tempered people do foolish things and schemers are hated.' Verse 29 – 'People with understanding control their anger, a hot temper shows great foolishness. '

Proverbs 29: verse 22 'An angry person starts fights; a hot-tempered person commits all kinds of sin. '

Ephesians 4: verse 26 to 27 'And don't sin by letting anger control you. Don't let the sun go down while you are still angry, for anger gives a foothold to the devil.' Verses 31 to 32 'Get rid of all bitterness, rage, anger, harsh words, and slander, as well as all types of evil behaviour. Instead, be kind to each other, tender-hearted, forgiving one another, just as God through Christ has forgiven you.'

Romans 12: verse 19 'Dear friends never take revenge. Leave that to the righteous anger of God. For the scriptures say, I will take revenge. I will pay them back, says the Lord.' In verse 21 it says, 'Don't let evil conquer you, but conquer evil by doing good.'

James 1 verse 19-20 'Understand this my dear brothers and sisters: You must be quick to listen, slow to speak, and slow to get angry. Human anger does not produce the righteousness God desires.'

Hebrews 12: verse 15 'Look after each other so that none of you fails to receive the grace of God. Watch out that no poisonous root of bitterness grows up to trouble you, corrupting many.'

What you do with your anger is what counts.

Abusive Partners - Woman Know Your Worth.

Because I care deeply for other women who are trapped in abusive relationships, I just wanted to say this, Woman, know your worth.

If the partner you are with refuses to do something about their anger or the way they treat you, then it is far better to live alone or separate than live a life of misery.

It is not only you that suffers, but your children also. By staying with an abusive partner you send a message out to your children that it is OK to be abused. You must find the courage to leave and stop the cycle of abuse.

You may feel confused and afraid, thinking that to get out of your situation is impossible, but it is not. I know you are worn down, manipulated, have low self-esteem, feel that perhaps if you behave better your partner may change.

It is very rare, that an abusive partner will change.

You have a right to be happy and safe and so do your children. Surely it is better to be alive and be with your children than risk losing your life and the children losing their mother.

You may feel overwhelmed; in your head you may have a million questions, what about money? Can I cope on my own? I will have to leave my home, change schools, start again?

Yes, but you will be free from violence and abuse. Your children will thrive instead of living in fear and confusion. You will have a new life and realise that you deserve to be treated with love and kindness. You will overcome your fears and will become a new you. You will be free from control. You will start to live in fullness not half measures.

Create a safety plan, trust just one or two people who can support you. Bit by bit put aside small amounts of money in a safe place or give that money to someone you trust. Open up a new bank account. Explain your safety plan to the school.

Think about how you are going to get to your 'safe place'. Get your mail forwarded to an P.O.Box address or other location.

Contact the National Domestic Violence Helpline, Women's Aid or Women's Shelter or any other similar organization that deals with domestic violence to get advice and support.

Use a different mobile phone to the one you have in your possession, if it takes you being secretive to get out alive, do it.

If your partner is doing any of these things it is a red flag.

1.   Constantly puts you down, criticises or humiliates you?
2.   Uses emotional blackmail.
3.   Controls your money, where you go, who you see, what you wear.
4.   Doesn't like it when you have your own opinion,
5.   Threatens you.
6.   Is physically abusive, slaps you, shoves you, pins you against a wall.
7.   Tries to isolate you from friends and family, gets jealous and accuses you of having an affair.
8.   Downplays the abuse.
9.   Checks your phone, social media, uses GPS locators or follows you.
10. Stops you from wanting to improve yourself, going to work or college or some other course.
11. Pressures you to have sex.
12. Keeps reminding you of your past mistakes.
13. Makes you feel guilty even when you haven't done anything wrong.
14. Has moments of being really nice to you but then goes back to being abusive.
15. Tells you he is going to change but never does.
16. If you are a Christian, does your partner use scriptures against you to suit his own agenda? For example, you are to forgive me; God does not believe in divorce. You are to obey me. I am the head of the house so you will do what I say. You should know your place and be submissive. God expects you to stay with me for life. What will other Christians think if you decided to leave me?

Read 1 Corinthians 13. Love is kind, not bullying, it is patient, it doesn't demand its own way.

Love is not jealous, proud or rude. It doesn't keep a record of wrongs.

God abhors violence; God does not want you to remain in an abusive relationship.

Remaining in an abusive relationship will cause depression, self-harm, a sense of utter weakness and low self-worth, a total lack of confidence, a sense of shame and guilt even though you have nothing to be ashamed or guilty of, disrupted sleep, deep anxiety, fear, loss of peace, confusion, nightmares, dread, suicide, the inability to trust anyone, covering up and lying. The effects on your children are extremely detrimental.

Seek support and even though you may not feel strong, you have survived until now, you are strong, do the right thing for yourself and your children, protect them, look up to the one who perfects your faith and go forward.

To all women, you are truly amazing, you carry life within you and help bring into the world beautiful babies.

You give your heart; you are a multi-tasker, coping with several responsibilities.

I know you have tried to do your best; you have given your all, but now your confidence has been smashed, you no longer feel appreciated, the trust in the relationship has broken. You fear your partner, you dread the next accusation or punch, your voice is no longer heard, the kids are scared, you feel lost.

I know you are concerned because you are the vicar's wife or the fact you may be married to a leader. What will the congregation say? Gossip will be spread, what will others think? Your life, peace, safety and sanity are more important than the opinion of others.

Jesus has got you, he is holding your hand; he will never lose you. Jesus will give you strength and be the light you need in the darkness,

Get your life back. Move out, move on, move forward. Never back.

Fear, Anxiety and Depression

It is interesting to me when I meet with other Christians who think depression is demonic and a Christian should be totally fearless. I understand to a point, sometimes both these areas can be used by the enemy, but we do need some perspective, we are human beings with several emotions. It is quite natural if a ten-ton truck is coming your way if you are in its path to suddenly experience fear, in fact the fight or flight response in us is normal, we will experience fear if we are threatened.

Throughout scriptures we have people in the Bible who knew about depression and fear. It doesn't mean God didn't use them or cannot use you, it does mean we are to apply the scriptures and work out our salvation and sometimes that can take a while. We also need to help ourselves.

All our emotions are part of who we are, and it is more a case of what we do with them that matters. It is our human traits that we need Gods help on. Sometimes the area of fear or depression can be overwhelming or crippling in some people and for a time either ministry or medical help, or both, may be required.

Some of the effects of anxiety and depression can be paralysing as well as other symptoms like chest pains, chills, dry mouth, over or under eating, sweating, heart racing, being restless, tense, trembling, feeling weak and tired, trouble concentrating, lack of sleep or too much sleep, putting things off, a sense of impending doom or panic, isolation, self-harm, the problem magnified larger than it is, not taking care of ourselves properly. Many people have a phobia, fear of rejection, fear of heights, fear of the dark, fear of living to the full, agoraphobia, in fact there are countless phobias. When fear or any other emotion takes over it enslaves and causes suffering.

I have heard a few teachings from Christians who say, 'Don't hang around negative people they will only drag you down.' Your walk is in Christ and is not dependant on what another person feels about you or on how you feel about them.

Where is it in the Bible that Jesus said, do not hang around with your Christians brothers and sisters who are negative, because it could make you negative.

It says in Luke 6 v 32 'What credit is it to you, if you love those who love you back, even sinners do that.' The whole passage is in context of loving your enemies. If we are called to do that, surely, we can love someone whether Christian or not who is depressed or negative. If God had mercy on you, should we not have mercy on another? 'Blessed are the merciful for they shall be shown mercy.' Matthew 5: v 7. Did Jesus run from the Leper? From the sick? From the demonised? No, nor should we, we should not avoid those who are depressed, negative, mentally ill, or sick. The battle is not just against the flesh it is also spiritual.

Jesus came into this world as a light. For those of us born again we carry the light of Jesus in our hearts. Surely whatever the condition of our brother or sister, or anyone we come into contact with, should we not be loving and shine our light?

Let us look at a few bible characters who were afraid.

In Exodus chapter 3 we see God wanted Moses to lead God's people but throughout chapter 3 Moses protested on more than one occasion. In chapter 4 God showed Moses his power and encouragement but Moses felt inadequate and more concerned about himself, saying, 'I am not very good with words, I get tongue-tied, my words get tangled.' Moses continued to plead to God to send someone else. In the end God allowed Aaron to accompany Moses and Aaron was God's mouthpiece.

In Matthew chapter 26 verse 69 onwards Peter denied Jesus three times, previous to this denial Peter was adamant that he would rather die than deny Jesus. Peter was afraid and look how God used Peter in the end.

Another example of Peter was when he went out to meet with Jesus and walked on the water, but when Peter saw the strong wind and the waves, he was terrified and began to sink. The disciples were terrified when they first saw Jesus' walking on the water and believed it was a ghost.

Job said, 'The thing I feared the most has come upon me.' Job 3: v 25

Gideon in the book of Judges chapter 6 was afraid he might die after seeing angel of the Lord and in verse 27 Gideon was also afraid of the other members of his father's household and the people of the town.

Elijah in 1 Kings 19 verse 3 was afraid and fled for his life.

There are many more examples.

I have put together some coping strategies for you on page 229 and hope they are of help to you.

Using The Arts.

God gave us all a wonderful ability to be creative, we can use our creativity is so many ways, sculpting, painting, drawing, singing, dancing, designing, cooking, making things, drama, poetry, gardening, performance art, writing and crafts and I am sure there are many more avenues.

God also gave us emotions and those emotions need to be released in a positive way, use the creative arts to discover yourself in a safe way and in a safe place.

Jesus, was a carpenter from the Greek (Tekton) meaning artisan or handyman who would have used his skill in different ways and would have followed in the footsteps as a trainee under Joseph until the timing of his ministry went public.

In the bible new songs were sung, people danced, beautiful garments were adorned and made, Psalms were written, Solomon sent for craftsmen to help build the temple. God is the source of creativity.

When you embark on a new journey you will face new challenges which is great because not only can it be a test of your faith or patience, it can also mature you giving you a new understanding or perspective of who you are.

I want to encourage you to release what you feel and free those caged emotions. Using art in whatever capacity means you can release yourself without being judged by anyone else, helping you to resolve issues within yourself. Painting can help for example when you cannot find the words you want to speak. You will discover new hidden talents in yourself and while meeting others, be a real blessing to those around you. Releasing your emotions shows that you are taking a step and taking responsibility for yourself and it is one way to keep your emotions in check. When your emotions are out of control it is counter productive and can be destructive.

Using the arts gives you freedom to know your potential, surprise yourself, and release areas in a safe manner. As a Christian God can bless your heart with new songs of worship and other creative areas, not just to honour God but to bless others.

Whether you are a Christian or not, repressing emotions or refusing to face up to things is never the answer. If you cannot find an avenue through the arts, perhaps consider counselling. Feeling sorry for yourself is self-torture. Talk, debate, pray, worship, dance, write a poem, do a video, share your testimony, write a book, paint a picture, open your heart up to the Holy Spirit, warfare, meet others, help another, care for an animal, ask how your neighbour is, visit the sick, help a charity, even the smallest of tasks is something, be proactive and allow yourself to become a blessing in every way. Even the things you make or paint can be such a blessing to someone else, God put creativity in YOU! So, be the best you that you can be. Cast your anxiety upon Jesus because he cares for you and develop who you are. God wants the best for you, so don't give up.

If you think you don't have a creative bone in your body, that is not true, you just haven't discovered it yet.

God bless,

Deborah.

Coping Strategies

1. Stand under a hot shower or soak in a bath with your favourite soaps. Treat your hair to a special conditioner. Pamper yourself.

2. Talk to one trusted friend or family member as often as needed.

3. Join a support group online.

4. Watch a comedy or favourite film or read a book.

5. Don't skip meals, eat small and often.

6. When it is safe, have a massage.

7. When you DON'T FEEL LIKE IT fight that feeling and do something anyway, you will be surprised at the positive result.

8. Release stress by punching into a pillow, better still have a pillow fight with someone, allow your stress to come out in a safe way, talk, scream, dance, exercise, go for a walk, pick up the phone, talk yourself down, distract yourself. Think of all the positives in your life and appreciate your circumstances, that you have family, you are alive, you don't have covid, you have clothes on your back, food in your cupboard, a roof over your head, remind yourself how fortunate you are.

9. Keep a journal and write down exactly how you feel. You will be able to see how your journey over one year has changed.

10. Remind yourself of your strengths and good points.

11. Volunteer to help another person or charity.

12. Take someone's dog for a walk.

13. Eat healthy and avoid recreational drugs or alcohol, the occasional drink is fine but dependency on substances is counterproductive.

14. If you blow it, accept responsibility for your actions, try to avoid the blame game. Life is not black and white so if you

mess up it's not the end of the world, there is always tomorrow. Self-condemnation is a pointless exercise.

15. If you have a garden grow some flowers or veg, this is very rewarding.

16. Try to keep to a routine.

17. If you can't sleep do something positive with your time until you are sleepy.

18. Find time for art, music, poetry, writing. Even if you have not done this before, have a go, you might surprise yourself.

19. When negative thoughts come through, recognise them, and write down the solutions or opposites. For example, if you have the thought 'I am useless. Write down, I am not useless even if my feelings say this, because yesterday I did this and that, write down what you have achieved no matter how small. Think of the good stuff.

20. Have small realistic goals for each day.

21. Don't be afraid to ask for help when you need it, pride or fear are the two dominating factors that prevent this. Most of what we FEEL OR FEAR doesn't happen.

22. Fear always magnifies a feeling or situation and distorts reality. Try to find the root cause of your fear, where did this fear originate from? What is the worst thing that could happen if I did face my fear? Get a friend to support you if needed. Chat with others who have similar issues to you and see what they did to confront their own fears. Some fears are irrational or overwhelming and you may need professional help. Recognize the physical warnings, i.e., heart racing, dizzy, breathless, tense, etc and counteract it with breathing techniques, talk yourself down, ride the wave, it will pass. Do some research on fear, anxiety, depression.

23. If you are open to spiritual ministry in the Christian faith, find someone who will pray with you, find scriptures on peace and how to trust God in the midst of your storm.

24. If you are feeling desperate and alone ring the Samaritans or some other agency/friend to talk to someone.

25. Although routine is important some people feel trapped by their situation, think about what you can do if this is you to change that, maybe a new type of job would be good, a new hobby, new friends etc.

26. Find new hobbies, unless you try them you won't know if you like them or not.

27. Try to avoid feeling too sorry for yourself and becoming too introspective, balance is the key to most things.

28. Avoid caffeine and too much sugar.

29. In argumentative situations, walk away and chat when all is calm.

30. Learn to be kind to yourself and establish boundaries.

31. Learn about how to be self-assertive.

32. Don't succumb to pressure, learn how to say no.

33. Count to 10 and be patient with yourself.

Examine Your Own Heart

In order to reflect and pray about your own personal situation I have devised this basic questionnaire, please start with being honest. Take time out to choose a quiet moment alone, or have someone with you if that helps. Do not feel pressured to rush through the questions.

Allow for the possibility that there may be areas you may have repressed that may come to the surface later. All the questions relate to now and in the past.

Some questions may not be relevant to you. If at any time you become overwhelmed, stop, and start again another time. This questionnaire is to help evaluate different areas for prayer or ministry and to examine your heart before God.

I believe that there are areas of the flesh that you can work on or repent of, and there are areas that the enemy has a foothold in. I am aware that not all problems relate to the demonic, discernment, wisdom, prayer, and if necessary, fasting might be needed. You cannot blame Satan for all your problems, a person must take responsibility for their choices.

Before you start, begin with a simple prayer.

Lord Jesus, help me to understand your ways, in order for me to be free I surrender every area of my life to you. I ask that all areas including hidden sins that I may not be aware of are revealed and that everything within me comes into the light of Christ.

I ask for courage and strength as I place myself under the protection of Jesus Christ.

I pray for the Holy Spirit to show me God's truth, I pray in Jesus' name that every form of deception is broken, and every disobedient thought is taken captive to Jesus Christ. Whatever has exalted itself against you that remains in me, I pray now, tear it down and destroy it, I repent of sin in my life and any ungodly practice or belief or any form of idolatry, and ask for your forgiveness and cleansing, in Jesus' name, Amen.

You do not have to say this prayer if you are not ready and need time to think things over or discuss your situation with someone. You can also arrange to see someone in a local church near you. Whatever you decide to do, if you do decide to become a Christian at some point, please email and let me know, so I can rejoice with you.

Regarding all questions, if you need to add anything else, feel free to make notes on a separate piece of paper. In my questions I have not covered everything, but the questionnaire does show you how you should begin to tackle some of the areas that may be affecting you. Seek Christian help and look at scriptures in the Bible to help you.

If you have any questions or need to contact me, my email is: debzj@hotmail.co.uk

Please write N/A not applicable if the questions do not apply to you. If you are not ready to answer some of the questions write beside the question Later.

Occult Section:

Have you been involved in, practiced or have beliefs in the areas listed below?

1. Witchcraft yes/no

2. Satanism yes/no

3. Black Magic yes/no

4. New Age yes/no

5. Secret order/ cult movement/ pagan beliefs/ or those that are anti-Christian? yes/no

6. Mysticism/alternate states of consciousness/trance or ecstasy experience/meditation/chants and Mantra's yes/no

7. Have you attended a séance/visited a medium? Yes/No

8. Do you believe you have a spirit guide or angel guide? Yes/No

9. Astral/soul travel. Yes/No

10. Levitation. Yes/No

11. Any form of divination or fortune telling, i.e., Tarot cards, crystal ball, palm reading or other. Yes/No

12. Have you ever practiced the Ouija board? Yes/No

13. Do you feel governed by Astrology, your zodiac signs? Yes/No

14. Are you superstitious? Yes/No

15. Do you believe in UFO'S? Yes/No

16. Have you at any time experienced apparitions or ghostly forms? Yes/No

17. Have you encountered any other supernatural disturbance of any kind? Yes/No

18. Do you have items in your possession that you feel protected by? Yes/No

19. Do you feel in charge of any kind of power or control? Yes/No

20. Do you believe you have a supernatural gift of some kind? Yes/No

21. Have you shared a blood pact with anyone? Yes/No

22. Is there any other bonding/pact or promise you have made Yes/No?

23. Do you feel oppressed or possessed in some way? Yes/No

24. Do you have occult material in your home? Yes/No

25. Do you have any other item that you cannot let go of? Yes/No

26. Do you believe you are cursed or that curses work, or have you have cursed someone? Yes/No

27. Do you have any family members who have had similar experiences connected with the above questions? Yes/No

28. Have your problems continued over a period of (a) years (b) months (c) weeks (d) Recent? Tick, which one applies to you.

29. Do you have pagan images/ statues/ in your home? Yes/No

30. Do you believe in reincarnation? Yes/No

31. Do you believe you have a soul? Yes/No

32. Have you suffered with sleep paralysis? Yes/No

33. Do you believe you are physic? Yes/No

34. Have you been involved/influenced by Bethel and Toronto? Yes/No

35. Have you been involved in Spiritualism? Or Necromancy, automatic writing, Yes/No

36. Have you been part of Freemasonry or any other society? Yes/No

If there is anything else that you can think of, write it down.

Emotional Section

Have you at any time experienced a breakdown, emotionally or mentally? Yes/No

Do you or have you suffered with panic attacks or anxiety that is disabling. Yes/No

Do you have any phobias or major fears? Yes/No

37. Do you experience uncontrolled mood swings, or outbursts? Yes/No

38. have you hallucinated? Yes/No

39. Have you ever heard a voice inside or outside your head? Yes/No?

40. Do you feel compelled or driven by something? Yes/No

41. Is your sleep disturbed by nightmares? Yes/No?

42. Is your sleep disturbed in some other way? Yes/No

43. Do you strive for perfection in a particular area? Yes/No

44. Have you ever contemplated suicide? Yes/No

45. Have you attempted suicide? Yes/No

46. Do you feel you have masochistic or sadistic tendencies? Yes/No

47. Are you now in bereavement? Yes/No

48. Is there a member of your family that is having similar problems to you? Yes/No

49. Have you seen a counsellor or psychiatrist in the past or present? Yes/No

50. If diagnosed with a mental health condition write down the name.

51. Do you feel you have lost the centre of who you are? Yes/No

52. Do you feel detached from what is going on around you? Yes/No

53. Are you depressed? Yes/No. If yes rate the depression from 1-10

54. Are you angry? Yes/No

55. Do you want to take revenge? Yes/No

56. Are you filled with guilt? Yes/No

57. Are you filled with regret? Yes/No

58. Do you have to be in complete control? Yes/No

59. Do you find making decisions difficult? Yes/No

60. Do you need to forgive yourself? Yes/No

61. Do you need to forgive someone else? Yes/No

62. How do you feel about death?

63. How do you feel about your life right now?

If there is anything else, please write it down.

Physical Section

64. Are you currently taking medication prescribed by your Doctor? Yes/No. If you are on medication, could you, please write them down.

65. Are you taking illegal substances? Yes/No

66. Do you have a hormone imbalance? Yes/No

67. Do you have any allergies? Yes/No

68. Are you a registered addict? Yes/No

69. Are you a secret drinker? Yes/No

70. Are there any hereditary medical problems? Yes/No

71. Are you a twin? Yes/No. Is your twin alive? Yes/No

72. Do you have a habitual sexual problem or are addicted to pornography? Yes/No

73. Have you suffered any kind of physical assault? Yes/No

74. Have you suffered rape? Yes/No

75. Other forms of sexual abuse? Yes/No

76. Domestic Violence? Yes/No

77. Any form of bullying? Yes/No

78. Do you have any kind of obsession in regard to your own body? Yes/No

79. Are you in physical pain? Yes/No. If yes rate between 1-10

80. Do you have any disabilities or illness? Yes/No. Please write them down

81. Do you need support in communicating with others? Yes/No

82. Are you receiving any other help from others at this present time? Yes/No

83. Is there anything else that you may share later that you find difficult to share now? Yes/No.

84. Are you in withdrawal? Yes/No Have you relapsed? Yes/No

85. More than one relapse? Yes/No

86. Are you confused about your sexual orientation? Yes/No

87. Do you suffer with PMT/PMS? Yes/No

88. Do you have a compulsive behaviour problem? Yes/No

89. Are you willing for me to contact your doctor if necessary? Yes/No

90. If the answer to 26 is no, please explain why.

91. Have you had an abortion? Yes/No

92. Are there physical illnesses that run in the family? Yes/No

93. Have you ever self-harmed? Yes/No

94. If you have had any form of body modification or tattoos do you now regret it? Yes/No

Your personal view

What is your understanding of Church? Please tick

    a) Boring
    b) Hypocritical
    c) Out of touch with the times
    d) Too controlling
    e) Mixed feelings
    f) Judgemental
    g) Overwhelming
    h) Scary
    i) Confusing.

Please write down your own thoughts.

If you believe in God, how do YOU see him? Please write down.

If you believe in something else, please write down.

95. Have you been abused by a minister of the Church? Yes/No

96. Was the problem resolved? Yes/No

97. How do you feel about mainstream church? Please write down.

98. Have you received prayer ministry before? Yes/No

99. How do you feel about taking communion?

100. Do you read the Bible? Yes/No

101. Have you felt rejected or hurt by the church in any other way? Yes/No

102. Was it resolved? Yes/No

103. If you went to church but have now left, did anyone contact you to find out why? Yes/No

104. Do you have any other faith or belief? Yes/No

105. Is there pressure on you from your friends or family regarding your beliefs? Yes/No (b) Are you confused about your beliefs? Yes/No

106. Write down your dreams, aspirations and goals in life. Where do you feel your talents are best used?

107. Are you open to someone praying with you? Yes/No

108. Or do you just want to talk and have someone listen to you? Yes/No

Write anything else down that is on your heart on a separate piece of paper and come back to the questionnaire a second time to make sure you have covered everything. Think about how you can align your answers to the word of God and take action to remedy what you can.

Sixty guidance tips

1. Get rid of any books, objects, jewellery that are pagan or anti-Christian.

2. Seek moral support from a Christian friend/confidante.

3. Study the word of God and let it renew your mind.

4. Pray even when it is difficult.

5. Put on worship songs or write one yourself.

6. Thank God for what he has done for you.

7. If you slip up its ok, there is no self-condemnation for those in Christ Jesus. But repent each time until victory comes.

8. Seek counsel when you need it and get others to pray for you.

9. Let your family and friends know you have become a Christian, don't be ashamed of the gospel.

10. If you are not working, try volunteering or doing some good work somewhere. But be Covid safe.

11. Healing can sometimes take time, not all healing is spontaneous especially when it comes to our emotions.

12. Seek counselling if you need it.

13. If a particular emotion is dominating find all the scriptures relating to the problem and read them out.

14. Get a Bible if you don't have one.

15. Think about a retreat of some kind and be kind to yourself.

16. Mourn with those who mourn, be compassionate.

17. Be honest with your feelings and if you don't know the answer to something just say so.

18. Remember the Lord looks at the heart not appearance.

19. God has shown mercy to you, show mercy to others

20. Stop evaluating others from a human point of view, 2 Corinthians 5: verse 16 see others through the eyes of Jesus.

21. Don't promise to help another and then let them down.

22. Don't conform to the pattern of the world and the way the world thinks, for example, there is a saying, 'Once an addict always an addict'. Always go to the word of God.

23. Do not follow people, leaders, celebrities, titles, follow Jesus.

24. If you know someone who has a different belief system, find out as much as you can, you will know how to pray more effectively for that person.

25. Pray when you rise each morning and just before going to sleep.

26. Carry a tract of your testimony with you. You never know who you might bump into. Share your testimony whenever you are able.

27. 'Don't waste what is holy on the unholy, be wise.' Matthew 7 verse 6.

28. If you share with another person and the reaction is not good one, don't be concerned, God is still working, it may take a little time.

29. You witness, God saves. You plant the seeds, God waters.

30. Don't allow yourself to become a religious Christian following man-made rules and rituals.

31. Overcome evil with good.

32. Learn about spiritual warfare.

33. Test the word of God against everything.

34. Never give up, persevere. God will never leave you or forsake you.

35. Take one step at a time and set realistic goals.

36. Submit all your plans to God.

37. Stretch your faith especially in hard times, your faith will get stronger especially in the storms of life.

38. When you don't know the answer or don't know what to do, humble yourself under Gods almighty hands, cast your anxiety upon him, because he cares for you.

39. Pray and ask God to show you how to recognise Satan's tactics and nip it in the bud.

40. Allow the Holy Spirit to guide you into all truth.

41. Let God know that you are willing to be used and be open to receiving spiritual gifts.

42. Sometimes Gods discipline is painful and uncomfortable, God is the potter, you are the clay. Pray for strength.

43. When the enemy comes out to attack you, remember Greater is he (Jesus) that is in you, then he (Satan) that is in the world.

44. Remember the fruits of the Spirit and pray about developing the fruits.

45. Testify online when you are ready.

46. God is faithful even when we are not.

47. Pray daily and repent of sin, don't develop a hard heart.

48. Do an online free Bible course. Emmaus Bible School UK offer free courses.

49. Count your blessings and be thankful.

50. If after prayer certain areas remain, trust God's timing, trust God regardless, sometimes God says no or may use specific areas to discipline you or teach you to lean on him. Whatever the reason for a delay or prayers not being answered, remember we do not see the bigger picture and we need to trust God even in difficult circumstances. God cannot be manipulated.

51. Do not listen to those who say that it's because you don't have enough faith that you are not healed. This statement may at times pertain to the odd individual or situation but for the majority it does not apply. Many Christian people that have great faith have been taken home to Jesus and have not been healed. Every person who became a Christian has a measure of faith. Nor do you have a divine right to wealth and prosperity, God made the rich and the poor and whatever our situation, Paul says to be content. In Romans 8 verses 20 to 23 it says, against its will, all creation was subjected to God's curse. But with eager hope, the creation looks forward to the day when it will join God's children in glorious freedom from death and decay. For we know that all creation has been groaning as in the pains of childbirth right up to the present

time. And we believers also groan, even though we have the Holy Spirit within us as a foretaste of future glory, for we long for our bodies to be released from sin and suffering.

52. Keep completely away from churches that clearly do not follow the Bible and the word of God but do their own thing. False teaching and false prophets abound. If you see a practice or belief that you are not sure of, test it against God's word.

53. Be wary of those who spout on about faith but have no love. Faith unless expressed through love counts for nothing.

54. Jesus said, 'you will know my disciples by the fruit they bear'. Look for the fruit. Galatians 5 verse 22, 23. Paul in Philippians 1 verses 9-11 says this, 'I pray that your love will overflow more and more, and that you will keep on growing in knowledge and understanding, for I want you to understand what really matters, so that you may live pure and blameless lives until the day of Christ's return. May you always be filled with the FRUIT of your salvation, the righteous character produced in your life by Jesus Christ, for this will bring much glory and praise to God.'

55. If you hear Christians teaching that you can lose your salvation, please address this by going to the word of God which quite clearly says in several scriptures the opposite. God's word never contradicts itself or returns to God void. Hebrews 6 in particular is often taken completely out of context. Don't just take someone's word (including the pastor or leader) at face value, study the word yourself. God's call and gift can never be withdrawn. Romans 11: v 29

56. Get Baptized

57. Forgiving others and forgiving yourself. Sometimes this may take time, that's ok.

58. Don't be afraid to share with family but do it gently.

59. Timing is sometimes crucial so have patience and persevere.

60. Keep a spiritual journal.

Books I recommend

Some books that I have read have been a blessing to me. I have heard some people say that you just need the Bible and no other books, but God works through his children in all sorts of creative ways, writing a book is just one of them. Whatever book you read does not have to be a distraction from the Bible, surely, we are to be a blessing to each other? Many books use the scriptures and point out areas that we may not have even considered, I personally have been very blessed by many writers who undoubtedly know the Bible very well. Obviously test the word of God at all times.

Here are just a couple of books I really enjoyed.

- 'Romancing Opiates (Pharmacological Lies and the Addiction Bureaucracy)' by Theodore Dalrymple. Theodore a prison doctor and psychiatrist sees heroin as a moral and spiritual problem.

- 'Pills for the Soul? (How medication falls short of Christ's healing of the emotions)', Dieter K Mulitze Ph.D

- 'Fresh Encounter', Henry & Richard Blackaby/ Claude King

- '10 Lies the Church Tells Women' by J Lee. Grady

- 'Why not Women?' by Loren Cunningham, David Joel Hamilton

- 'Women of the Bible. A visual guide to their lives, loves and legacy.' Smith, Sanna, Philips.

- 'A Crash Course on the New Age Movement', Elliot Miller.

- 'Spiritual Depression (its Causes and Cures)', Dr. Martyn Lloyd-Jones.

- 'Authority in heaven Authority on earth', Tom Marshall.

- 'Shelter in God', Dr. David Jeremiah

- 'Gods Promises', Charles H Spurgeon

  'How to let God solve your Problems', Charles Stanley

- 'Hell Under Fire', Christopher W. Morgan/Robert A Peterson.
- 'Beyond Broken (Finding Power in the Pain)', John Andrews
- 'Unshockable Love', John Burke
- 'The Unseen Realm', Michael S. Heiser
- 'Kundalini Spirit', Andrew Strom.
- 'The Bleeding Mind', Ian Wilson
- 'Beware the New Prophets', Bill Randles

About the author Deborah J Hawkins

Work History: Auxiliary Nurse and Home Help.

Ex Project Founder of The Focus Foundation that was active for five years (supporting the marginalized).

Psychodynamic Counsellor.

Single mother of six beautiful children and a Nana to seven grandchildren (so far).

My favourite colours are Purple, Burgundy, Black and Royal Blue.

One of my favourite rock bands: Skillet.

One of my favourite singers: Lauren Daigle

Love watching films and nature documentaries.

I enjoy Mango, Raspberries, Blueberries and Dairy-free Raspberry & White Chocolate Truffles.

Favourite naughty dish: Fried potato cooked in olive oil with garlic, onions, salt and pepper.

Favourite healthy dish: Fish with any kind of vegetable.

Favourite naughty treat: London Cheesecake (puff pastry and coconut).

Love cars, motorbikes, motorbikes and motorbikes, but it's been that long, I have no idea if I can actually get on one (Sad face).

I love animals, nature, drama, performance art, music, theatre, reading, art, creativity, worship, writing songs and poetry, I have a good sense of humour, love God's amazing creation.

I like gothic architecture and alternative clothing including velvet as I can be a bit of a hippy (Bring back velvet dresses).

I love flowers and plants.

I live with two cats, Ruby and Fester. If I had land, I would have pygmy goats.

My Dream Man: Jason Momoa

My Dream Home: A country cottage.

Love open discussion and encouraging others.

Pet hates: Snobbery, ageism, smoking and swearing, judging others by the way that they look (including tattoos), greed, cruelty to animals, lying, violence, bullying.

Likes: Honesty, courage, creativity, those willing to listen or learn, people who are passionate, compassionate, and willing to help others. Those who are down to earth. Those who never give up.

Reality Check

When the body and mind has gone through different traumas, the recovery can vary from person to person. I am living with the consequences of some of my actions and the actions of others. Living with several physical conditions makes my everyday living challenging. The cause of my suffering is complex as different factors have to be taken into account.

I live in a fallen world. God's creation will not be fully right until the new heaven and new earth have come. Remember what Paul says in the scriptures in Romans 8 verse 20 to 23. All creation groans. I did not choose the family I was born into, nor did I know of the consequences of sin that had passed on in my family from generation to generation, spiritual roots that entered through the cracks of disobedience. Genetics, environmental factors, the choices I have made all play a part. I will always have hope in the living God, one who is merciful, gracious, and compassionate and if some of my prayers are not answered in the way that I expected, I know that the hope in me will not be disappointed, for God is faithful and just and I must trust God in all circumstances. It is not just about the life that I am living right now; it is also about the eternal picture. I am aware of a miraculous God who can intervene in the blink of an eye and answer prayers sometimes directly and sometimes in ways I never thought were possible, for God's mercies are new every morning. The choices I made in life have consequences for better or worse, and sometimes those consequences remain.

As a Christian, having such a serious relapse brought with it extremely serious consequences. Directing anger and blaming God for my situation was foolish, to blaspheme God and the Holy Spirit was soul destroying, I had cut myself off from the main body of Christ, I allowed anger to turn into rage, to fester in my soul giving the devil a foothold, and once a stronghold had firmly rooted itself, all hell broke loose, my mind shut down, and everything was lost.

It reminds me of some scriptures in the Bible that when certain things happen there must be discipline and consequences that God allows in order to save a soul. By that I don't mean that you can lose your salvation, because a person's salvation is sealed and assured.

Let me remind you that in the midst of a sinful gothic, punk, satanic broken-down lifestyle, a woman, a complete stranger, approached me in the street and said, 'I have a message for you, I don't know who you are, but I believe God wants me to say this. Jesus loves you; you are his child and you don't belong to anyone else.'

In 1 Timothy 1: verses 18-20 Hymenaeus and Alexander violated their consciences, shipwrecked their faith and were thrown out, handed over to Satan so they might learn not to blaspheme God. These men were Christians who had strayed off the path and listened to false teaching and then passed on that false teaching which it says in the new living translation Bible, spread like a cancer. This undoubtedly affects many other believers. God does not take lightly the spreading of heretical false doctrine. Being handed over to Satan meant their life was no longer in the church, perhaps, excommunicated. They were now in Satan's territory, the world.

In 1 Corinthians 11: it shows that those who took communion in an unworthy manner, who did not examine their hearts, ended up weak, sick, and some even died. When God's judgement comes upon a Christian, that Christian is being disciplined so that they will not be condemned with the world.

When God does not intervene, there is a reason. When God disciplines us, it is for our own good and is mainly to bring us back to God if we stray or go on a wrong path.

The relapse I had took me on a dark journey for a time, I was always his child, God is always faithful, I repented and slowly over a period of five years my recovery took place. Gods' ways are not our ways. In Proverbs 15 verse 10 it says, 'whoever abandons the right path will be severely disciplined, whoever hates correction will die.' God brought me back from a bad place and showed great mercy, but I am quite sure that I will be disciplined, because God disciplines those he loves.

When I hear Christians teach that if you blaspheme the Holy Spirit there is no forgiveness that teaching must be understood in its correct context otherwise many prodigal children could not return to God. In 1John 1: verse 9 it quite clearly says that if you confess your sin, you are forgiven and cleansed. If a person claims they have not sinned, we are calling God a liar and showing that his word has no place in our hearts. It would mean many who blasphemed God could not be forgiven and that is not the case. When I personally screamed at God to take the Holy Spirit from me, that was not the same as calling what Jesus Christ did demonic and that his powers were from Satan.

The religious pharisees refused to accept Jesus as the Messiah and accused him that the power he was using was of the devil. These Jews called what was holy, evil. Their blasphemy could not be forgiven because they could not repent. The Pharisees had witnessed proof that Jesus worked miracles by the Holy Spirit, the contention started in the synagogue on the Sabbath day healing a man's hand, then Jesus healed a demon possessed man who was blind and couldn't speak, it was then he was accused of getting his power from the prince of demons, Satan. Their hatred of Jesus was so great that repentance was not possible. Jesus called these Pharisees broods of snakes! Their hearts and minds had become full of evil by the serpent, Satan. 'An evil person produces evil things from the treasury of an evil heart.' Matthew chapter 12.

I would rather take all the discipline God wants to give than fall away from his grace, for in all the areas I may have suffered, there is no greater suffering than to relapse, fall away, return to the ways of the world, filled with anger and pride and reject the purest love that God has given us, his Son Jesus Christ.

Many areas within my life have been healed, time itself is a healer and God's love has patiently put me back together, the love, smiles and warmth from my children lift my spirit every day and I am truly blessed. I am aware that I have been left with a sensitivity regarding men. I do not like to be in the presence of violent men, arrogant and aggressive mannerisms put me off instantly, when I see a man shouting and bullying a woman or his children I cringe inside.

I remember an occasion when I was living in Cambridge, I saw a man in the street screaming at this woman, he had pushed her up against the wall and was hitting her. I pulled my car over and went straight over to the man and told him to leave her alone, forcing my body between them. It came out of blue, normally, I prefer not to get involved in other people's business, but that day, I decided enough was enough and spared no thought for the fact that I could have been hurt. I managed to keep them apart and told the woman that she must not accept physical or emotional abuse and to do something about it.

I can't stand to be shouted at, if a person can't talk to me at a normal voice level, I refuse to continue the conversation, I hate arguing, I much prefer to have a discussion, or a healthy debate, or work things out patiently. I don't shy away from helping others when it is needed, I will always be an open door for God to use me but never a door mat for people to walk on.

I live with some physical challenges every day, but thankfully nothing life threatening, I am truly amazed that I have completed this edition. I have Fibromyalgia which has numerous symptoms. It has been a real challenge to write as cognitively it can be frustrating and very difficult, especially editing. This particular symptom is called Fibro Fog. Another symptom I have is chronic fatigue and sometimes my life is like wading through a pot of treacle. Arthritis is in most of my bones, so sitting on a computer chair for too long is also an issue. I pray before I write and ask for God's strength to complete each section of writing. I commit my plans each day into Gods hands.

I am so grateful to still be here, normal, happy, at peace, counting my blessings.

Be Encouraged

Isaiah 31: verse 18, 'so the Lord must wait for you to come to him so he can show you his love and compassion. For the Lord is a faithful God. Blessed are those who wait for his help.'

'We are to resist the devil, come close to God, and the devil will flee.' James 4 verse 7.

'Jesus came to destroy the devil's work.' 1 John 3: 8.

'In Christ we have all authority over all the power of the enemy, to trample on snakes and scorpions.' Luke 10 verse 19.

'Greater is he (Jesus) in me than he that is in the world (Satan).' 1 John 4, v 4.

2 Thessalonians 3 verse 3, 'But the Lord is faithful he will strengthen you and guard you from all evil.'

Hebrews 2 verse 14 and 15, 'Because Gods children are human beings made of flesh and blood, the Son also became flesh and blood. For only as a human being could he die and only by dying could he break the power of the devil, who had the power of death. Only in this way could he set free all who have lived their lives as slaves to the fear of dying.'

'Jesus is the resurrection and the life, if you remain in him, you will live even after dying.' John 11 verse 26.

John 10 verse 27 to 30, 'My sheep listen to my voice, I know them, and they follow me. I give them eternal life, and they will never perish. No one can snatch them away from me, for my father has given them to me, and he is more powerful than anyone else. No one can snatch them from the father's hand. The Father and I are one.'

'Jesus said, 'come to me all who are weary and carry heavy burdens, and I will give you rest. Take my yoke upon you. Let me teach you because I am humble and gentle at heart, and you will find rest for your souls. For my yoke is easy to bear and the burden I give you is light.' Matthew 11 verses 28 to 30.

Keep your eyes on Jesus for he is the one who perfects your faith.

Romans 16 verse 20, 'The God of peace will soon crush Satan under your feet.'

Hebrews 13: 5, 'I will never fail you; I will never abandon you.'

Hebrews 13: 6, 'The Lord is my helper, so I will have no fear, what can mere people do to me?'

Proverbs 3: verses 5 & 6

'Trust in the Lord with all your heart, do not depend on your own understanding, seek his will in all you do and he will show you which path to take.'

Proverbs 3: verses 21 & 22

'My child, don't lose sight of common sense and discernment, hang on to them, for they will refresh your soul.'

John 5: verse 24, 'I tell you the truth, those who listen to my message and believe in God who sent me have eternal life. They will never be condemned for their sins, but they have already passed from death to life. '

Romans 11: verse 29, 'For God's gifts and his call can never be withdrawn.'

1 Thessalonians 5 verse 22, 'Now may the God of peace make you holy in every way and may your whole spirit and soul and body be kept blameless until our Lord Jesus comes again. God will make this happen, for he who calls you is faithful.'

My thanks to God

I am grateful to God for so much but here are just a few areas that I would like to mention.

1. Thankyou God for the greatest miracle that man will ever know, the salvation of souls. I cannot put into words the depth of gratitude I have towards God for saving my soul, it is truly an amazing. When my cry to Jesus was heard and my own soul was saved, sanity returned, my soul was no longer in darkness or lost, voices in my head disappeared, Schizophrenic symptoms caused initially by the use of L.S.D. gone, torment gone, in danger of going to hell, gone! Spiritual blindness gone, my sins forgiven and cleansed, eternal life given, true peace released as the head of Satan was crushed, demonic strongholds broken, because of Jesus I am free to be a child of light, destined for heaven. Saved by the only true morning star.

2. Thankyou God for miracle number two, I had Systemic Lupus for over ten years, it is in full remission and having been retested I still do not have it. I constantly went forward for prayer and asked God to remove this life-threatening illness from me. I am extremely thankful for that.

3. Thankyou God that you heard my plea for you to preserve my life and also my children's, twice I was left for dead by strangulation, and one other occasion when my ex was going to stab me in the chest with a crucifix, the last threat by my ex was on his return to Cambridge that he would kill me and my children.

4. Thankyou God for all the times that you stepped in to give me crucial financial help, your timing is always perfect.

5. Thankyou God that all my children were found and returned to me, I have six beautiful children and seven beautiful grandchildren. (So far)

6. Thankyou God that at the right time I was able to receive help to be delivered from demonic oppression.

7. Thankyou God for your mercy, compassion, love, power, peace, healing and deliverance.

8. Thankyou God for your provision for The Focus Foundation in helping others and the provision that came from Barclays Bank.

9. Thankyou God for all your provision that paid for all my counselling training.

10. Thank you for all the times you have protected me, given me guidance, shown your patience, sent your peace, used me for others, and lifted my soul from a difficult place, for always being faithful, for never leaving me, for your amazing scriptures and for sending your Son Jesus.

11. Thankyou God for the Bible, prophetic words given, holy spirit inspired moments, new songs of worship written, and the spiritual gifts I have received as your child.

12. Thankyou God that you have been my place of refuge, and my source of strength, thank you for every new morning.

13. Thankyou God that even when I was abducted as a child the abductee did not fulfil his evil intent.

14. Thank you for giving me the strength to write this book.

15. Thank you for all the people you sent across my path who testified of your faithfulness, who shared a message, who shared the gospel.

I continually surrender myself to you Lord Jesus so that I may grow deeper in your love and walk in obedience. Thank you that your mercy triumphs over judgement, that you see the bigger picture, Amen!

'Trust the Lord with all your heart, lean not on your own understanding, seek his will in all you do, and he will show you which path to take.' Proverbs 3: verses 5 & 6

To my brothers and sisters in Christ

If we are to bring the hurting, the unsaved, the relapsed Christian to Christ, to fellowship with others, we need to build a bridge built on compassion, structured in faith and designed in hope, walking in a unity of purpose. That purpose is to heal the sick, save the lost, and bring God's truth and love to those who desperately need it. Let us not limit God by our own mortality, praise him because of it, for within our earthen vessels the Holy Spirit dwells. In humility let us seek God with all our heart, mind, soul and strength, and in so doing reap the heavenly promises that lay in store for us all. May the peace of Jesus be with you all in this difficult time, shine your light, expose evil, fight the fight, keep your eyes on the one who perfects your faith, don't give up, pray, be humble, and trust God even when everything is falling apart.

For the soul that sits on the fence

After reading my book I hope that you will find the time to ponder on what I have shared. Jesus is the way, the truth and the life and no-one, absolutely no-one can get to the Father unless through his Son.

Your precious soul is in God's hands. He made you. It says in the scriptures what does it profit a man if he gains the whole world and loses his soul? Your soul is worth more than the whole world.

2 Peter 3 verse 9 The Lord is not slow in keeping his promise, as some understand slowness. Instead, he is patient with you, not wanting anyone to perish, but everyone to come to repentance.

Luke 19: v 10 For the Son of Man (Jesus) came to seek and to save the lost.

Our sin separates us from God, if you go to Jesus, he is waiting with open arms to receive you, nothing you have said or done is a shock to him, he knows already what your life has been like. No-one feels worthy to approach Jesus in the first instance but through his grace and love there is forgiveness and restoration of your soul, Jesus laid down his life for you on the cross. Don't hesitate one moment longer. Give your heart and thoughts to Jesus, talk to him, he will hear you. I pray you will take that step, do not be afraid, do not listen to that negative voice in your head, Jesus is waiting to have compassion on you, to save and deliver you.

I have written from my heart a prayer, you do not have to use this prayer, it is just a guide, the important thing is for you to be genuine. You can contact a Christian if you want support via your local church if that helps, or you may contact me and I would love to support you in your decision to become a Christian.

Pray

Lord Jesus,

Your word in Acts 2: verse 21 says that whoever calls upon the name of the Lord will be saved, so I call upon your name, Lord Jesus and I come before you with every sin that I know of and that which is hidden, I ask that you forgive me of all my wrong doing and all the sin that has caused me to be separated from you. I pray for the Holy Spirit to come upon me and wash me clean, I no longer want to look the other way, or ignore you. I ask Lord Jesus that you as my Saviour will come into my life and into my heart so that I may enter into your heavenly kingdom. I pray that you will open my mind to the scriptures and give me understanding. I renounce every form of evil, I reject Satan and all his lies, and pray my heart and mind to be open to the word of God. Help me, I pray, to overcome and resist temptation. I pray that every form of deception and lie that I have been exposed to will be broken and that your truth will remain in me as I seek your heart on all matters. Protect me from evil as I entrust my life into your hands. Help me to keep my eyes fixed on you, for you are the one who will perfect my faith. Take all fear from me, and break every form of pride, for you are the potter and I am the clay.

In Jesus name, I pray, Amen.

Remember, work out your salvation step by step, taking one day at a time, there is no self-condemnation for those in Jesus, so do not put yourself down, if you sin, repent, if you hear yourself saying, I am no good, I can't do it, I'm not going to make it, what if? I am not disciplined enough, I am not worthy, I am too afraid, and what if I fail, and so on. What does Jesus say about you? Jesus thought you were worth it when he laid down his life for you. Read and meditate upon the word of God and discover Gods beautiful promises and guidance for your life. Take captive every thought and make it obedient to Christ. 2 Corinthians 10: verse 5

God willing, I hope to continue writing and have three more books in the pipeline.

Book One – Little Foxes. This book will be about all the areas that have come into the church and the Christian mindset that ruin the vine, dealing with bad theology and other areas that are damaging Christian growth.

Book Two – The Bubble Babies. This book will be truly exciting. A fantasy story for older children with adventure, humour, a huge array of creatures, challenges, tense moments, and lessons to be learned and much more.

Book Three – Focus Fellowship.

This book will share how to set up Focus Groups to encourage freedom in developing maturity as a Christian, to help others reach their potential, encourage others to develop their spiritual giftings and remain pure in heart for Jesus, not tolerating any form of syncretism and not having a one pastoral system. It includes having a heart for those who are lost or different and how to integrate those who need to be heard, saved and delivered, bridging the gap between the world and church. It would be great to use in your homes.

In purchasing 'Pursued by the Soul Destroyer' you have contributed to poverty and basic needs in the UK and Africa, a cause that I would like to help with.

My heart goes out to all the doctors and nurses and those who have helped in numerous ways during the pandemic. You are truly awesome and amazing and I, for one, appreciate all your hard work, dedication and bravery. Thank you so much for all you do.

I am acutely aware of the pain that this pandemic has caused to many. For those who have lost a loved one, I have mourned with those who mourn. I pray that you will find great comfort, strength and peace in these difficult times that we are living in and be surrounded with all the love you need.

My email address: debzj@hotmail.co.uk

God bless, Deborah.